DATE DUE

~~AP 29 '09~~			
~~MY 28 '98~~			
~~2 7 '08~~			
NO 2 3 '10			

DEMCO 38-296

Arguments about Aborigines

The emergence of anthropology in Britain coincided with the publication of Darwin's book on the origin of species. In the context of inescapable questions about the natural history of our own species, Australian Aborigines were assigned the role of exemplars *par excellence* of beginnings and early human forms. In the last quarter of the nineteenth century, European scholars bent on discovering the origins of social institutions began a rush on the Australian material that lasted well into the present century. The Aborigines have consequently featured as a crucial case-study for generations of social theorists, including Tylor, Frazer, Durkheim and Freud.

Arguments about Aborigines reviews a range of controversies (some still alive) that played an important role in the formative period of British social anthropology. The chapters cover family life, male/female relationships, conception beliefs, the mother-in-law taboo, various aspects of religion and ritual, political organization, and land rights: all subjects that have been matters of lively international interest and long-running research. Along the way, the study traces changes in Aboriginal circumstances and practices and notes the ways in which these changes affected the scholarly debate.

This elegant book will serve as a valuable introduction to Aboriginal ethnography for students and scholars as well as general readers. It is also a shrewd and stimulating history of some of the great debates of anthropology seen through the prism of Aboriginal studies, to which they so often referred.

Arguments about Aborigines

Australia and the evolution of
social anthropology

L.R. HIATT

*Visiting Fellow, Australian National University and Australian Institute of
Aboriginal and Torres Strait Islander Studies*

CAMBRIDGE
UNIVERSITY PRESS

e of the University of Cambridge
on Street, Cambridge CB2 1RP
York, NY 10011–4211, USA
ו, Melbourne 3166, Australia

© Cambridge University Press 1996

First published 1996

Printed in Great Britain at the University Press, Cambridge

A catalogue record for this book is available from the British Library

Library of Congress cataloguing in publication data

Hiatt, L.R. (Lester Richard)
Arguments about Aborigines: Australia and the evolution of social anthropology /
L.R. Hiatt.
p. cm.
Includes bibliographical references.
ISBN 0 521 46008 5 (hc)
1. Australian Aborigines – History.   2. Australian Aborigines –
Antiquities.   3. Australian Aborigines – Public opinion.   4. Public
opinion – Great Britain.   5. Anthropology – Great Britain – History.
6. Anthropology – Great Britain – Philosophy.   I. Title.
GN666.H533 1996
306′.089′9915–dc20   95–20518 CIP

ISBN 0 521 46008 5 hardback
ISBN 0 521 56619 3 paperback

CE

To my teachers

JOHN BARNES *and* MERVYN MEGGITT

Contents

Illustrations

Plates

Figures

Preface

The essays in this book arose from a course of undergraduate lectures I gave as Visiting Professor of Australian Studies at Harvard University in 1990–1. My students for the most part had only a superficial knowledge of Aboriginal culture, and quite a few enrolled because they were planning a holiday in Australia or had recently been there. For better or worse, I decided to introduce them to the subject not with a catalogue of settled facts but through a history of disputation. In developing the lectures for publication, I have retained both the dialectical mode and the assumption of an audience lacking close familiarity with the issues. In accordance with the friendly mission on which my country had sent me, I gave prominence at Harvard to contributions in Aboriginal Studies made by American scholars, beginning with the United States Exploring Expedition of 1838–42. Although I have removed that particular emphasis from the present work, I have not omitted the contributions nor, I hope, diminished their importance.

The arguments reviewed fall within subject areas that would conventionally be considered essential for an understanding of traditional Aboriginal social life: land, kinship, marriage, politics, gender, religion, initiation, avoidance and conception beliefs. Beyond that, selection from the corpus of available controversies was largely an outcome of my own previous involvement in them. As far as possible I have tried to place ethnographical questions within a wider context, usually theoretical and historical but occasionally political and contemporary as well. In some instances debates arose at a factual level in the context of attempts to use Aborigines as evidence for particular theories; in other cases, disagreements occurred when ethnographers tried to account for agreed facts by recourse to different analytical approaches. Whatever the provenance, the common objective of the essays is to proceed from the earliest recorded observations of some problematic aspect of Aboriginal culture to the fullest account of its form and meaning available from anthropological argumentation.

The emergence of anthropology as a distinct discipline in the middle of the last century coincided with the publication of Charles Darwin's book on the origin of species. In the context of inescapable questions about the natural history of our own species, Australian Aborigines were assigned the role of exemplars *par excellence* of beginnings and early forms. Their main qualification for this honour was an astonishingly low level of parasitism on other species: they neither cultivated plants nor domesticated animals for the purposes of eating them. Furthermore, their material possessions were few, they wore no clothes, there were no visible places of worship, and they had no leaders. In the last quarter of the nineteenth century European scholars bent on discovering the origins of social institutions began a rush on the Australian material that lasted well into the present century. From the ore were fashioned some of the most celebrated and influential works in the history of anthropology.

All the arguments in the present collection have their own origins in the evolutionist tradition. Their early development, under the twin auspices of Darwinism and Empire, took place largely within the institutional framework of British social anthropology. To set the stage, I have therefore written a prologue describing a train of events that led to the formation of the Anthropological Institute of Great Britain and Ireland in 1871. Our ancestry is not quite as bad as I had been led to believe. The founding fathers (there were no mothers) certainly regarded themselves as members of a culture at the pinnacle of human progress. Some even believed that the black races constituted an inferior biological species. But others, just as influential, held steadfastly to the doctrines of the unity of man and the equality of all men before the law. Anthropology in Britain was born when the two parties came reluctantly together in a marriage of convenience.

The book is meant to be read from the front to the back. However, the chapters are more or less autonomous, and I have indicated connections in the end-notes for readers who wish to proceed in some other order. Although the arguments in their original form were all very long, I have tried to condense them so that each can be read, like the essays of Montaigne, within an hour.

Fig. 1 Tribes and places. The map shows tribes and places mentioned in the text. The rendering of tribal names has often changed over the years, and nowadays the following spellings are regarded as phonetically more accurate (old spellings in brackets): Arrernte (Aranda, Arunta); Diyari (Dieri); Gunditjmara (Gournditch-mara); Kariyarra (Kariera); Loritja (Luritja); Murrinhpatha (Murinbata); Ngarrindjeri (Narrinyeri); Wunambal (Unambal); Arabanna (Urabunna); Warlpiri (Walbiri); Wik-Mungkana (Wik Monkan).

Acknowledgments

I am grateful to John Barnes, Adam Kuper, Ken Maddock, Francesca Merlan, Alan Rumsey, and Roger Sandall who read the full manuscript of this book and made numerous valuable comments. I am also grateful to Jim Fingleton, Alfred Hiatt, Ian Keen, John Mulvaney, Mary Patterson, Nicolas Peterson, Gary Robinson, Sally White, Peter Worsley and Richard Wright, who read particular sections. Helen Proudfoot gave me the benefit of her knowledge of early Australian paintings. I owe a debt of gratitude to the Committee on Australian Studies at Harvard University, especially in the persons of Bernard Bailyn, Hal Bolitho, and Janet Hatch; to Irven DeVore and Stanley Tambiah who took such good care of me in the Anthropology Department during my tenure of the Visiting Chair of Australian Studies in 1990–1; and to Ursula Hiatt who enabled me to turn my mind to the task of developing the Harvard lectures into an exposition suitable for publication. Rhys Jones suggested the general idea of the book to me some years ago, and Jessica Kuper guided it with a firm but friendly hand towards its final form.

1

Prologue

In the autumn of 1768, just after the *Endeavour* had set out from Plymouth on its voyage of discovery, a London ordnance clerk named Granville Sharp sent a manuscript to the eminent jurist William Black- stone,[1] seeking his opinion on certain arguments relating to the liberty of the person. The response was not encouraging. Nonetheless Sharp published his manuscript the following year, setting in motion a train of events that led to the abolition of slavery in the British colonies. A slightly later and not nearly so much celebrated consequence was the formation of the institutional framework of the discipline of anthro- pology in Great Britain and Ireland.[2]

Sharp was the youngest son of a Northumberland archdeacon whose fertility outran his ability to pay for higher education.[3] After an apprenticeship in linen-drapery that came to nothing, he settled for a job in the civil service. In 1765, while visiting the medical surgery of his brother William, he noticed a badly injured negro awaiting attention and asked what had happened to him. The man, Jonathon Strong, was a slave from Barbados whose master had maimed and then abandoned him. The Sharp brothers restored him to health, clothed him, and found a position for him with an apothecary. Two years later his erstwhile owner, a lawyer named David Lisle, saw him in the streets and, perceiving that he was marvellously rehabilitated, resolved to retrieve him. Shortly afterwards, at the lawyer's bidding, two men from the office of the Lord Mayor of London intercepted the errant slave and took him into custody.

When the apothecary sought to intercede on Strong's behalf, Lisle deterred him with a threat of legal action for infringing his property rights. Granville Sharp, though still a young man, was not so easily intimidated. On hearing the news, he presented himself to the master of the prison and charged him, at his own peril, not to deliver up the slave to anyone who might claim him. He then persuaded the Lord Mayor to summon before him all concerned. While this was being arranged, Lisle sold his interest in Strong to a Jamaican planter named Kerr, on the understanding that no money would be paid until the goods were in transit. At the meeting in the Lord Mayor's office, the principals to the transaction were represented by the notary who drew up the bill of sale and the captain of a ship about to sail for Jamaica. After listening to their claims, the Lord Mayor stated that as Strong had not been charged with any offence he was at liberty to go wherever he wished. The captain forthwith seized the slave by the arm and told the Lord Mayor he took him 'as the property of Mr Kerr'. Prompted by the city coroner, who whispered in his ear, Granville Sharp turned upon the captain and said loudly: 'Sir, I charge you for an assault.' The captain released his grip, and they all bowed to the Lord Mayor and left. Strong and Sharp returned home unmolested.

Several days later Sharp received a writ charging him with having robbed David Lisle of a negro slave. With the backing of his brother James, a wealthy ironmonger, he consulted a solicitor in the Lord Mayor's office and retained an eminent counsel. In due course his legal advisors told him the case could not be defended. The basis for their opinion was a statement issued jointly in 1729 by the Solicitor-General and the King's Attorney, and confirmed subsequently by the Lord Chief Justice in court, that a slave from the West Indies did not become free merely by setting foot upon the soil of Great Britain or Ireland. His master's property right in him persisted and could be legally exercised by compelling him to return to the plantations.

Sharp was advised to settle out of court as best he could and leave the slave to his fate. Instead, driven by a conviction that the law of England could not be so bad, he searched the libraries and constructed his own defence. As he expected, no process survived in English common or statute law whereby one person could unwillingly be made the slave of another. Furthermore, the Habeas Corpus Act (1679) empowered the courts to bring before them any person whose liberty was restrained so that the legality of his or her detention might be investigated and determined. The question was whether a person enslaved in accordance with the laws of another country continued to be a slave in England unless emancipated by the owner. Here Sharp advanced an original and compelling argument. A statute proclaimed in the reign of Henry VIII expressly confirmed that all aliens living in England were bound by English law. As they were subject to its authority, they were surely entitled to its protection. On entering England, a slave became a subject of the sovereign and thus entitled to the same freedoms as all other subjects. Because it could be said that in a sense he was now the property of the sovereign, it followed that he need not continue to be the property of anyone else.

Sharp circulated his manuscript among some twenty lawyers. In the event, Lisle withdrew the charge and paid treble costs. No doubt the law was uncertain, but if Sharp turned out to be right there would be heavy damages to pay as well. If Strong was a free man from the time he entered England, then clearly the various assaults and restraints inflicted upon him were illegal and subject to penalty. At the conclusion of his memorandum Sharp left his accuser in no doubt as to his intentions. If he acknowledged his error in writing, he would not press a case against him on behalf of Strong. But were he and his advisors to reject these friendly conditions,

> they may be assured that I shall think myself in duty bound, as a man, a Christian and subject of England, to defend the said Negro, and this my opinion, in the King's Courts to the utmost of my abilities; for my opinion is not founded on my own presumption, but on the plainest literal expression of statutes formed and ordained by the wisdom and authority of Kings, Lords, and Commons.[4]

On 3 July 1770 Joseph Banks recorded in his diary that a spring tide had floated the *Endeavour* off a beach on the east coast of Australia after repairs to her hull had been completed. An 'alligator' swam for some time by her side.[5] On the same day back in London his mother made an urgent visit to Granville Sharp. During the night her servants, hearing shouts of distress from the garden next door, found two men dragging a negro towards a boat lying in the Thames. They knew him to be Tom Lewis, a West Indian slave who had run away from Mr Stapylton, Mrs Banks's neighbour. When the kidnappers assured them they had authority to retrieve and ship him back for sale in Jamaica, the servants returned with the news to their mistress. Mrs Banks, having heard of Sharp by reputation, now sought his advice.

Sharp immediately obtained a warrant to intercept the ship, but it had been cleared for sailing and the captain refused to comply. As soon as possible, one of Mrs Banks's servants was despatched to Portsmouth with a writ of habeas corpus. A few days later he returned to London accompanied by Lewis, on whose behalf Mrs Banks then brought an action against her neighbour and his accomplices. The case was heard by Lord Chief Justice Mansfield early in 1771. Stapylton defended himself on the basis of property rights but, on being asked by the judge for documentary evidence of ownership, was unable to produce any. The jury subsequently agreed that he could not therefore claim Lewis as his property. However, when Mrs Banks's counsel pressed for a judgment on the defendants for an assault, Mansfield declined to pronounce one. Mrs Banks had saved the negro, and she should be satisfied with that.

The outcome was patently scandalous. What lay behind it was the presence in England of between 14,000 and 15,000 slaves, whose masters had brought them with them on holidays or upon retirement. Their market value was approximately £700,000. Previous judgments, including opinions stated in court by Mansfield himself, had given owners confidence that their property was legally secure. The Lord Chief Justice was on the horns of a dilemma: acknowledge the arguments of a layman or continue in complicity with West Indian merchants. To his ultimate credit he chose the former. In 1772 Granville Sharp retained counsel on behalf of James Somerset, a runaway slave whose master was attempting to ship him back to Jamaica. After lengthy legal argument, several adjournments, and much prevarication, Mansfield told a packed court that 'no foreigner can in England claim a right over a man: such a claim is not known to the laws of England'.[6] The job of the court was to find the law, not to make it. If the merchants considered the finding injurious to trade and commerce, they should look for help among the legislators.

Late in 1772 the West Indian lobby pressed for the introduction of a bill in the Commons exempting them from Mansfield's determination, but the motion was thrown out. Public opposition to slavery was mounting, aroused in particular by principled objections from the Evangelical Movement and the Quakers. From the time of its formation a century earlier the Society of Friends had exhorted members to mitigate the evils of slavery. In 1774 it issued a decree threatening any member involved in the slave trade with expulsion and, two years later, a similar sanction directed at slave owners. In 1783 English Quakers established a standing committee for the relief and liberation of slaves, to be sought through personal influence and the publication of books and articles. Granville Sharp, though not a Quaker, accepted an invitation to join it. When the committee petitioned Lord North (then Secretary of State), he described their objectives as humane but impractical.

About this time Sharp was visited by a negro who drew his attention to impending litigation arising from the jettisoning of cargo from an English slave-ship bound for Jamaica. Early in 1781 the *Zong* set out from Africa with 440 slaves and a crew of fourteen. Sickness broke out, some sixty slaves died, and many others seemed in danger of suffering the same fate. The captain informed his officers that the loss of slaves in transit as a result of illness was not covered by insurance. However, if those about to die were sacrificed in order to save the rest, the owners would be compensated. Accordingly, on the pretext of a shortage of water, 130 ailing slaves were thrown overboard. In due course the owners claimed the market value of their lost property and, when the insurers refused to pay, took them to court. Lord Chief Justice Mansfield expressed the opinion that there was 'no doubt, though it shocks one very much, that the case of slaves was the same as if horses had been thrown overboard'.[7] The jury found in favour of the owners.

Sharp petitioned the Lords of the Admiralty and publicised what would otherwise have passed unnoticed as a minor dispute between underwriter and client. No action was ever taken against the captain and his officers, but the name of their ship was at least imprinted on the public conscience as a stigma of its own culpability. In 1787 the Quaker committee increased in size and appointed Sharp as its chairman. After a conference with him the following year, Prime Minister Pitt moved a resolution binding the House to discuss the slave trade in the next session. Not all his colleagues regarded it as an act of political wisdom. Lord Sydney, whose name had just been given to a convict colony in the antipodes, was against tampering with a traffic so necessary to the health of the nation. Nevertheless Pitt's friend William Wilberforce, who lived among Evangelicals at Clapham, took up the case against it and in 1791 sought leave to introduce a bill which would abolish it. The motion was defeated 163 to 88. As one speaker during the debate put it, 'though men may be generous with their own property, they should not be so with the property of others'.[8]

Every year for the next decade Wilberforce moved his motion with no more success than the first time. The French Revolution, Napoleon, and war with France had turned men's minds elsewhere, and it was not until 1807, two years after the Battle of Trafalgar, that the British slave trade was finally abolished by Act of Parliament. The stage was now set for emancipation. The Quaker committee became the Anti-Slavery Society, eminent non-Quakers enlarged it, and the Duke of Gloucester became its President. In 1824 Wilberforce, his health declining, handed the parliamentary baton to Thomas Buxton, a recently-elected prison reformer and son of a Quaker mother. Two years later Buxton was able to exhort fellow-members with the backing of 32,000 signatures. By 1831 the Anti-Slavery Society had branches in all large towns, as well as 1300 affiliated societies throughout the world. In the meantime, as moral pressure rose, profits from West Indian sugar fell.[9] In 1833, against a counterpoint of slave rebellions and floggings in the Caribbean, Parliament found the will to make slavery illegal in British colonies.

With the main objective of the abolition movement achieved, Buxton sought to harness its resources and goodwill for the benefit of indigenous peoples throughout the British Empire. In 1837, at his urging, Parliament appointed a Select Committee on Aboriginal Tribes to advise on the protection of their rights, the spread of civilization among them, and the voluntary and peaceful reception of the Christian religion. In the opening section of its report, the Committee made three main points: (1) Intercourse with Europeans had been uniformly calamitous for native peoples, unless attended by the exertions of missionaries. (2) Whites had regularly entered the domains of native inhabitants without invitation and then treated them as trespassers on their own land. (3) Setting aside considerations of justice and decency, a more friendly policy towards the natives would contribute to the civil and commercial interests of Great Britain.

The report then reviewed the situation of indigenous people in each of the British colonies. With regard to the Aborigines of New Holland, it seemed that enlightened principles had been abandoned everywhere with the possible exception of the new colony of South Australia. The committee recommended an increase in expenditure on missionaries, who should be chosen and directed by missionary societies in England. There was also a need for official Protectors, who should learn the vernacular languages and gain familiarity with the traditional cultures. Protectors should devise codes of customary law adapted to modern circumstances, although the use of native police was inadvisable. They should also claim on behalf of their charges as much land as was needed for their support. So long as Aborigines found agriculture distasteful, they should be allowed to subsist by hunting and gathering.

In order to continue the good work of the Select Committee, some of its members formed an organization called the Aborigines' Protection Society, with Buxton as president. In 1839 the Society was able to inform members that Mr G.A. Robinson had been appointed as the First Protector of the Natives of New South Wales. Following his appointment, Mr Robinson had told a public meeting in Sydney of severe cruelties inflicted on Aborigines by sealers, whalers and stockmen; even 'the most vehement opponent of the cause of the Aborigines, the editor of the *Sydney Herald*, admitted that "the narrative was a statement of plain facts of which no man entertained a doubt"'.[10] At the same meeting the Rev. Threlkeld, a missionary and honorary member of the Aborigines' Protection Society, spoke of atrocities and said that 'he could make out a list of five hundred blacks slaughtered by whites within a short time'.[11] In a subsequent publication the Society presented a full account of court proceedings in Sydney following the massacre of twenty-eight Aborigines at Myall Creek in 1838.[12]

The prime mover in the formation of the Aborigines' Protection Society, and its most active member, was a Quaker and medical practitioner named Thomas Hodgkin.[13] In 1839 Hodgkin received a letter from his colleague and fellow-Quaker Dr James Prichard of Bristol, apologizing for his inability to attend the anniversary meeting in May.[14] While warmly endorsing the humanitarian objectives of the Society, Prichard took the opportunity to emphasize its potential value for science as well. He himself had been investigating the natural history of mankind for many years and was keenly aware of the necessity to obtain physical, psychological, and linguistic information from tribal peoples before it was lost forever. Shortly afterwards Prichard developed the same theme in a paper on the extinction of human races which he presented at a meeting of the British Association for the Advancement of Science. As a result, a committee (including Prichard, Hodgkin, and also Charles Darwin) was appointed for the purpose of drawing up a list of questions to guide individuals in contact with uncivilized communities on how to obtain data of value to scholars. In due course the Association published a document entitled 'Queries Respecting the Human Race, to be Addressed to Travellers and Others', which the Aborigines' Protection Society helped to distribute.[15]

Nevertheless, it was soon evident that the priorities of the Society lay in political humanism rather than dispassionate inquiry. In 1842 Dr Richard King, who had been on an expedition to the Arctic and knew a lot about Eskimos, decided to form a break-away group for those members who felt their scientific interests were being swamped by philanthropy. With Hodgkin's approval, he issued a prospectus for an 'Ethnological Society of London', which would investigate the physical and moral characteristics of the varieties of mankind, both past and present, publish scientific findings, acquire a library of the best books on ethnology, and provide financial aid for travellers. In due course informal meetings took place in Hodgkin's rooms, and the society was formally inaugurated towards the end of 1843. Prichard became a member the following year, and president a few years later. He and King represented the Ethnological Society at British Association meetings, where Ethnology became a subsection in Section D (Zoology-Botany). Although Hodgkin maintained a strong presence in both the Aborigines' Protection Society and the Ethnological Society, the institutionalization of charity and learning, having diverged at that point, proceeded thereafter on separate and not always mutually sympathetic courses. Many years later an eminent British scientist, discoursing on the cleavage, spoke of it as a rift between 'the missionary party' and 'the student party'.[16]

In his Anniversary Address to the Ethnological Society in 1847 Prichard defined ethnology as the history of human races, and its task to elucidate their origins and relations.[17] In 1848 the Society began publishing papers and communications presented at its meetings. Most were accounts of populations still surviving in remote parts of the world, along with investigations of peoples and cultures now extinct. Although, like the founders, a majority of the contributors had been trained in medicine, philology served the objectives of the Society more actively than comparative anatomy. Over shorter spans of time and space, it seemed, languages were better guides to connections than bones. Not all articles were theoretically focussed; a good many owed as much to the older literary tradition of travellers as to the newer models of science. Typically, authors had been to the places they wrote about. They described the people who lived there objectively, but with respect and occasionally admiration.

After four volumes of the journal, the last dated 1856, publication ceased. Two years later, the year in which Charles Darwin and Alfred Wallace presented their theory of evolution to the Royal Society, only seven members turned up for the annual general meeting. The resources of the Society, financial and intellectual, were drying up. In 1860, whether for this or some other reason, the president moved 'that Ladies be admitted as visitors'.[18] Although in the event a slightly less radical amendment was passed, reserving a right of exclusion, not all members were pleased. During the following year the secretary, Dr James Hunt, complained of ill health and an inability to perform his duties properly. Two years later he resigned in order to form a rival organization, which he called the 'Anthropological Society of London'. In doing so he publicly declared his wish to emulate the Anthropological Society of Paris and its dynamic secretary, Dr Paul Broca.[19] Furthermore, in a published statement addressed to his French counterpart, he explained that the Ethnological Society had been ruined by a president who wished to emulate the fashionable and popular Royal Geographical Society by admitting women. 'You will doubtless smile', he went on, 'at the strange idea of admitting females to a discussion of all Ethnological subjects. However, the supporters of the "fair sex" won the day, and females have been regularly admitted to the meetings of the Ethnological Society during the past three years.'[20]

In the same statement Hunt set out an alternative conception of Ethnology, apparently beyond the reach of his meretricious adversaries, as 'a grave, erudite, and purely scientific study, requiring the most free and serious discussion, especially on anatomical and physiological topics...'[21] The contents of the first volume of memoirs published by the Anthropological Society made clear why some of these grave matters could not be freely discussed (or perhaps discussed at all) in the presence of ladies. At a meeting of the Society on 1 November 1864, Captain Richard Burton read a paper entitled 'Notes on Certain Matters connected with the Dahoman'. After a brief account of Dahomey history and language, the speaker announced that he now intended to 'notice certain peculiarities in the Dahoman race, which, in the usual phrase, are "unfit for the drawing room table"'.[22] They included the topics of prostitution, circumcision, clitoridectomy and castration. On 17 January of the following year, Mr W.T. Pritchard presented a paper 'On Some Anthropological Matters connected with the South Sea Islanders (the Samoans)', these being childbirth, menstrual taboos and ritual defloration.[23] On the same occasion a communication from Mr Edward Sellon was read on phallic worship in India.[24] To conclude an unusually heavy evening, Fellows discussed the pathology of a syphilitic monkey whose remains had been forwarded to the Society from a zoo near Manchester.[25]

Female attendance was not the only issue on which the two Societies were divided. In November 1863 Dr Hunt addressed his colleagues on 'The Negro's Place in Nature'. As they hardly needed to be reminded, the father of English Ethnology, the late Dr Prichard, maintained that all the present varieties of mankind had descended from a single negro stock and constituted a single species.[26] But while it was true that negroes were capable of inter-breeding with Europeans, it had not yet been established that the offspring were indefinitely prolific. After reviewing the best evidence available, particularly from Dr Broca and contemporary American experts, Dr Hunt was forced to conclude that the justification for classifying negroes and Europeans as separate species was at least as good as for distinguishing asses from zebras. If intelligence criteria were taken into account as well, the difference between whites and blacks was greater than between chimpanzees and gorillas. While doubtless he would be accused of helping the slave trade for saying this, no one deplored the horrors of that unregulated industry more than he did. The fact of the matter was that, by preventing Africa from exporting its worthless and surplus population, British legislation had harmed the negro race more than helped it. The highest type of negro now in existence was to be found in the Confederate States of America.

Not surprisingly, the paper produced a lively debate. Mr Burke, a speaker from the floor, expressed the view that there was no difference in principle between a white man's refusal to allow his daughter to marry a black man and a nobleman's refusal to allow his daughter to marry a peasant. Racial discrimination was therefore of the same order as class discrimination.

> Mr. McHenry: No; it is not.
> Mr. Burke: I differ from you in opinion very widely.
> Mr. McHenry: And I do from you. I am afraid you are an abolitionist, sir.
> Mr. Burke: The gentleman is at liberty to have his own opinions, and, of course, he will allow me to have mine. I contend that the difference is one of degree only.

Mr. McHenry: I pity you; you do not know better.

Mr. Burke: I must call on the Chairman to prevent these unseemly interruptions. The gentleman can speak after I have done. If I have a servant in my house, I find that servant has a different order of feelings, and is a different kind of being, in some respects, from the members of my own family. Does it follow that I am to make a particular distinction of species, and cut off that poor creature from us simply because she is a grade lower than we are? I for one maintain there are gradations... I do not for a moment hold that the Negro is equal to the White, no more than that the peasant is equal to the gentleman. I do not mean to say, that out of the peasant may not spring a gentleman.

Mr. McHenry: Out of a black man there cannot spring a white man.[27]

By profession James Hunt specialised in the treatment of stammering, having inherited a technique devised by his father.[28] In 1854, while a Cambridge undergraduate, he came under the influence of Robert Knox, a Scots anatomist, atheist and anti-Prichardian, who maintained that the races of mankind were immutable species.[29] Hunt joined the Ethnological Society during the same year. Later, when he proposed Knox for membership, the nomination was allegedly blackballed by the Quakers. Over and above his strong views on race and gender, Hunt was driven by a vision of anthropology as a total Science of Man, encompassing ethnology and much else. At a time when the intellectual world was in the throes of re-thinking Man's place in Nature, the ethnologists were sunk in a torpor induced by the 'sedative works of Prichard'.[30] Instead of keeping abreast of developments in evolutionary biology, particularly in regard to relationships between human races and anthropoid apes, they were still plodding along with philology and travellers' tales. It was imperative that anthropology be given a section of its own in the British Association, instead of sharing a section with geography as ethnology now did. A College of Anthropology was needed to provide professional training. Some day it would be taught in every university worthy of the name. In the meantime the Anthropological Society of London would publish the most advanced ideas in the subject, draw attention to their practical applications in public affairs, and provide a forum for discussing the burning social issues of the day.

By 1865 the new organization had over 500 members. Hunt was its president and, from his own resources, published a journal called *The Anthropological Review*. Under the stimulus of competition, female membership, and public interest in the evolutionist debate, the Ethnological Society also grew (though not so fast) and began publishing its journal again. To cursory outside observation the aims of the two Societies seemed much the same, so that when bitter rivalry erupted in public (as on the question of representation at the British Association) explanations were sought at the level of personal antipathies. While these may have aggravated the difficulties, Hunt himself was in no doubt that the critical division was doctrinal: the Quaker hard-core in the Ethnological Society adhered steadfastly to a rationalised biblical concept of human origins as 'monogenetic', while the intellectual avant-garde of the Anthropological Society insisted that they were 'polygenetic'. Accordingly, when leading Darwinists joined the Ethnological Society and argued that *The Origin of Species* pointed to a single origin and a single species in the case of man, Hunt became an anti-Darwinian. In reviewing the history of the Anthropological Society towards the end of the decade, he noted that 'If the Society, as a body, have shown unanimity of sentiment on any one point, it has been, I believe, against the Darwinian theory of man's origin, as propounded by Professor Huxley.' [31]

Nevertheless, when Huxley became president of the Ethnological Society in 1868 he immediately began working for an amalgamation. The antagonism between the two bodies had become a chronic source of embarrassment to the British Association, and the importance of welding together the best elements to form a genuine scientific discipline was now manifest. Fortunately there were men of goodwill in both Societies, some of them (including Richard King) with dual membership. Hunt, moreover, was facing disaffection on a number of matters, including editorial control of *The Anthropological Review*. In the event he responded cordially to Huxley's overtures and drew up a list of reasonable conditions. But what should the new organization be called? Conscious of strong opposition within each Society to the name of the other, Hunt suggested as a compromise 'The Society for the Promotion of the Science of Man'. The ethnologists authorized Huxley to go ahead on that basis, and when the anthropologists rejected the rubric as absurd Hunt felt obliged to offer his resignation as president. The gesture was declined, but the following year ill-health forced him to step down and within a few months he was dead.

In his last speech Hunt urged his colleagues to unite in the cause of science: 'There must ever remain great diversity of opinion in a Society like our own, but we can all unite, even with those with whom we differ, in the object common to us all - the diffusion of truth, be it acceptable or unacceptable to the world at large.'[32] In May 1870 members of the Anthropological Society opened their doors for the first time to women, inviting 'the fairer portions of mankind' to join them in hearing a paper on the soothing subject of 'Race in Music'. By the end of the year the ethnologists had conceded the name in return for the first presidency, and early in 1871 the two Societies merged to form the Anthropological Institute of Great Britain and Ireland. In 1907 his Majesty the King was graciously pleased to command that henceforth the name should be prefaced by 'Royal'. The president presented the order in the form of a motion, and there was no dissent.[33]

2

Real estates and phantom hordes

During the 1850s, while Darwin continued his labours on the origin of species, a young classical scholar and jurist named Henry Maine was undermining the central presumptions in European thought on the origin of private property.[1] Nowhere more succinctly were these enshrined than in the great legal textbook of the eighteenth century, William Blackstone's *Commentaries on the Laws of England*. The received doctrine was founded upon revelation and reason. Starting from the axiom that by gift of the Creator the world was the property of all mankind, it proclaimed that the fruits and creatures of the earth were initially available to whomsoever took the trouble to harvest or hunt them. In regard to the land itself, the first rights of possession were no more than the acknowledgment of transient occupation and use. If a man occupied a certain spot for rest or shade, natural law dictated that it would be unjust to drive him off. But as soon as he vacated it, another might rightfully use it.

Once men began to construct fixed habitations for comfort and safety, transient usufructuary rights became unsatisfactory. The builder's labour was deemed to entitle him to uninterrupted enjoyment of his abode. Furthermore, after agriculture was invented, the idea of permanent rights in soil came into being. Who would till if another might help himself to the harvest? Social compacts thus became necessary for the protection of property. As society grew, every man acquired for his own use such spots of ground as seemed most agreeable, provided he found them unoccupied by anyone else. Eventually the right to use the land by virtue of occupancy was converted into a concept of individual ownership of the substance of the land itself.[2]

When a population had expanded to its territorial limits, its members might despatch expeditions to find land elsewhere. Of the process of colonization by a mother-country, Blackstone had this to say:

> So long as it was confined to the stocking and cultivation of desert uninhabited countries, it kept strictly within the limits of the law of

nature. But how far the seizing of countries already peopled, and driving out or massacring the innocent and defenceless natives, merely because they differed from their invaders in language, in religion, in customs, in government, or in colour; how far such conduct was consonant to nature, to reason, or to Christianity, deserved well to be considered by those who have rendered their names immortal by thus civilizing mankind.[3]

Earlier in his discourse, when specifying the contemporary jurisdiction of English laws, Blackstone held his scruples in reserve. Whether a desert and uncultivated country had been merely occupied, or a cultivated country gained by conquest or treaty, dominion was founded upon the law of nature.[4] In the former case, English law came into effect from the moment of colonization. In the latter, the laws of the indigenous population remained in effect unless they were contrary to the law of God (as in an infidel country) or until they were explicitly changed by the Crown.

Born half a century later in an era of burgeoning natural science, Maine was unable to take seriously a theory of natural law based on alleged primaeval events for which there was no empirical evidence whatsoever. More to the point, the speculations derived largely from attempts made by jurists in the mature period of the Roman Empire to rationalize individual ownership. In order to do so, they developed a set of fictions which effectively liberated modern society from the burden of its archaic heritage. Ancient law, Maine insisted, knew next to nothing of individuals. Property was held and transmitted not by private citizens but by corporations of blood relatives linked by descent in the male line and putatively descended from a common male ancestor. Corporate identity was perpetual; corporate property was undivided, unmalleable, and sometimes absolutely inalienable. The fallacy in philosophical constructions of a state of nature, and of a natural law regulating it, consisted in projecting into the distant past conceptions of rights and agreements whose political and economic origins were in fact quite recent. Neither ethnology nor classical scholarship supported the view that human social life began on the basis of contracts between individuals. What they suggested, rather, was that society had evolved *towards* contract and private property from an earlier condition in which the rights of individuals were defined and protected on the basis of their status as members of corporate descent groups.[5]

With regard to the acquisition of foreign lands, Maine argued that the sections of modern international law dealing with dominion were directly derived from Roman property law. One of the 'natural modes of acquisition' authorized by imperial codes was occupancy of *res nullius*, things belonging to no one. These fell into two categories:

(a) things that had never had an owner, e.g. jewels disinterred for the first time; (b) things currently without an owner, e.g. abandoned moveables, deserted lands, the property of an enemy. With regard to the last item, it was reasoned that warfare returned the combatants to a state of nature in which the institution of private property fell into abeyance; the acquisition of the property of a defeated enemy by occupancy was therefore an institution of natural law. Modern writers on natural law, Maine noted, had found the logic of this argument perverse and distasteful. Yet, he observed, although the Roman jurists were undoubtedly attempting to dignify practices with roots deep in antiquity, at least they were not denying that the acquisition of property by the victors entailed loss of property by the vanquished. The genius of modern international law was to find among the more benign principles of occupancy a rule entitling a monarch to claim sovereignty over a newly discovered land *and* its inhabitants once his servants 'had fulfilled the conditions required by Roman jurisprudence for the acquisition of property in a valuable object which could be covered by the hand'.[6]

When Blackstone published the last volume of his *Commentaries* in 1769, he had completed protecting his own most valuable intellectual property from the depredations of unscrupulous booksellers, who for years had been pirating his lecture notes. In June of the same year, acting on behalf of the Royal Society, Lieutenant James Cook observed the passage of Venus across the disk of the sun from a vantage point in Tahiti. In the course of his journey back to England, he sailed along the east coast of Australia and made the first detailed map of its bays and capes. Upon reaching its northernmost point, he climbed a hill on an offshore island in search of a passage to Batavia. Having satisfied himself that the way was clear, and knowing that Dutch navigators had already claimed the honour of discovering the west side of the continent, he hoisted the English flag and took possession of the whole eastern coast in the name of His Majesty King George the Third. His men fired three volleys, and the crew on the ship fired three volleys in return. Later, when recording the symbolic event in his journal, Cook called the place of its occurrence 'Possession Island'.

Before leaving England Cook had been handed two sets of instructions, both marked secret. The first concerned observations of planet Venus, the second of southern regions of planet Earth. Specifically, Cook was told to look for a large continent believed to exist to the east of New Zealand. If he found it, he was to make detailed maps, collect specimens of animals, vegetables and minerals, and befriend its human inhabitants. The instructions continued as follows:

15

Pl. 1   Captain Cook taking possession of the Australian continent on behalf of the British Crown AD 1770 under the name of New South Wales. It would appear that the artist, J.A. Gilfillan, erroneously depicted the ceremony at Botany Bay rather than on Possession Island. When the picture was adapted by a later artist for inclusion in a volume to celebrate the centenary of settlement in 1888, the Aborigines in the foreground protecting their eardrums against the volley were omitted. (Australia: The First 100 Years, ed. Hon. Andrew Garran)

You are also with the Consent of the Natives to take possession of Convenient Situations in the Country in the Name of the King of Great Britain; or, if you find the Country uninhabited take Possession for His Majesty by setting up Proper Marks and Inscriptions, as first discoverers and possessors.[7]

Cook proceeded south from Tahiti to latitude 40 degrees, then turned west. There was no continent to be discovered. After circumnavigating New Zealand, he continued westward until he reached the coast of New Holland near Van Diemen's Land, then turned north. At various points along the coast of New South Wales (as he later named it), he saw human inhabitants as well as smoke from their fires. Armed warriors threatened his presence in Botany Bay and, although gifts were offered, 'it was to no purpose, all they seem'd to want was for us to be gone'.[8] A more friendly reception was enjoyed at the Endeavour River (where the ship was beached for repairs), leading Cook to surmise that in general the population was not warlike. Although his men obtained a list of nouns from people living near what later became a town named in his honour, we can be sure that he neither sought nor obtained their consent to the appropriation of situations in their country convenient to the King of England.

Sixteen years later, in October 1786, King George appointed his trusty and well-beloved servant Captain Arthur Phillip to be the first governor of his recently acquired property in the antipodes. In a commission issued on his behalf by Lord Sydney, Secretary of State for the Home Department, the King defined his possession as the lands and off-shore islands from 10 37'S (Cape York) to 43 39'S (South Cape, Tasmania) and from the east coast to 135 E (about the middle of the continent).[9] Seven months later Phillip set out from England with some 750 inmates of His Majesty's prisons deemed suitable as colonists and, after anchoring in Botany Bay and then finding a better harbour a few miles to the north, established a settlement in Sydney Cove. On 26 January 1788, the newcomers celebrated their arrival by running up the Union Jack, firing several volleys, and drinking the King's health.[10] On 7 February, Judge-Advocate Collins read Governor Phillip's commission to a public gathering, as well as letters-patent from the King establishing courts of law. This act, accompanied by martial music and a parade of marines, formally inaugurated British government in New South Wales and transplanted the laws of England to its soils.[11]

There can hardly be any doubt that the rituals of acquisition, occupation and control were intended for the notice of rival imperial powers. As to the natives, Phillip's instructions were simply to conciliate their affections and live in harmony with them. How this objective was to be achieved while simultaneously appropriating their homelands was not discussed. From the beginning of settlement, the question of property in land among the Aborigines was largely academic. Collins, in an account of the colony published in 1804, surprised his readers with the information that the natives not only held property in spears, shields and clubs but 'strange as it may appear, they have also their real estates'.[12] The estates, moreover, were owned by individuals. Bennelong, for example, claimed that he had inherited Goat Island in Sydney Harbour from his father and seemed much attached to it. Collins recorded that various others possessed this same kind of hereditary property, adding 'which they retained undisturbed'.[13] As he himself had played an historic role in its disturbance, we may presume the statement was intended to be ethnographic.

Not surprisingly, once the beachhead at Sydney had been secured and invasion of the interior began, settlers and frontiersmen felt more comfortable with the view that the people they were dispossessing entirely lacked notions of real estate. There was no shortage of spokesmen to articulate it for them. On this issue, however, the ethnographic tradition founded by Collins remained firm. In 1839 Rev. John Dunmore Lang, Principal of Sydney College, wrote to Thomas Hodgkin of the Aborigines' Protection Society, assuring him not only that the Aborigines of Australia had traditional concepts of land ownership but that in practice differences between them and Europeans were more imaginary than real. The indigenous population was divided into tribes (i.e. speakers of different languages), each of which owned a district as well as the animals and plants found within its boundaries. Just as pastoralists now depended on their properties to provide grass for their cattle and sheep, so Aborigines had previously depended on these same areas to nourish their kangaroos. Before the appropriation of their territories under English law, each tribe defended its boundaries against trespassers from other tribes. Within the tribal area, individual members owned particular portions. Proprietors had the right to burn grass for ease of hunting and to invite others to feast on the kill.

Lang's letter was published by the Aborigines' Protection Society and endorsed two years later by George Grey in his journals of exploration in Western Australia.[14] On the matter of individual ownership Grey went even further, insisting that land was the property not of a tribe, or several families, but of a single male. In 1845 his fellow-explorer, Edward John Eyre, verified Lang's account on the basis of his observations of tribes in South Australia. Here particular districts with a radius of 10 to 20 miles were considered to be the property and hunting grounds of the tribes frequenting them. Each man owned a segment of the tribal territory, which he apportioned to his sons before his death.[15] In Eyre's judgment, the manner in which these lands had been appropriated for the benefit of white settlers was thoroughly iniquitous:

Pl. 2 Natives driven to the police court by the police for trespassing. The event depicted here by the artist W.A. Cawthorne took place in 1845 near Moorunde, where Eyre had recently been Protector of Aborigines. The 'trespassers on their own land' were apparently discharged.

Without laying claim to this country by right of conquest, without pleading even the mockery of cession, or the cheatery of sale, we have unhesitatingly entered upon, occupied, and disposed of its lands, spreading forth a new population over its surface, and driving before us the original inhabitants. To sanction this aggression, we have not, in the abstract, the slightest shadow of either right or justice - we have not even the extenuation of endeavouring to compensate those we have injured, or the merit of attempting to mitigate the sufferings our presence inflicts.[16]

Although both Grey and Eyre subsequently rose to high positions as administrators (the former as Governor of South Australia and then New Zealand, the latter as Governor of Jamaica), their views on Aboriginal land rights carried little weight with land-hungry white settlers. As Alfred Howitt put it several decades later, the tide of settlement continued to advance 'along an ever-widening line, breaking the native tribes with its first waves and overwhelming their wrecks with its floods'.[17] Howitt was Grey's and Eyre's intellectual heir - explorer, ethnographer and Aboriginal protector. In 1872 he entered into a scholarly collaboration with a missionary named Lorimer Fison, arising from inquiries circulated by the pioneer American anthropologist Lewis Henry Morgan. The nature of the enterprise that bound the three of them together is described in the next chapter.

In 1883 Howitt and Fison published an essay in the *Journal of the Anthropological Institute* that, although tangential to their main research, proved to be of seminal importance in the conceptualization of Aboriginal territoriality.[18] In order to comprehend the social structure of an Australian tribe, they argued, it was necessary to distinguish between groups defined on the basis of locality and groups concerned with the regulation of marriage. For convenience, they suggested that the two types should be treated respectively under the headings of 'local organization' and 'social organization'. In regard to the former, (i) each tribe was made up of a number of clans; (ii) each clan was located in a separate part of the tribal territory; (iii) the clan was a corporate group with perpetual succession through males; (iv) the clan held hunting rights over the tribal subdivision it occupied; (v) marriage within the clan was forbidden; (vi) female members of the clan went in marriage to men of other clans, whose sisters in turn came to it as wives.

Howitt's and Fison's treatment of Aboriginal territorial organization parted company with early colonial ethnography on two vital points. First, rights were said to be vested in neither the individual nor the tribe but in a group of intermediate size whose membership was determined by patrilineal descent. The authors based their assertion on an accumulated body of the best empirical data available, but it may be noted that they were also familiar with Maine's writings on the primacy of corporate entities in ancient property law.[19] Second, the statement assigned hunting rights to the patrilineal clan but stopped short of acknowledging ownership of the soil. Here the authors were probably influenced by the view of their American colleague that, in evolutionary perspective, the concept of corporate real estate emerged only after the advent of agriculture.[20]

Two years later Howitt and Fison elaborated their account of Aboriginal local organization by introducing the term 'horde'.[21] In their 1883 article they had stated that, whereas local organization was uniformly patrilineal, social organization was patrilineal in some tribes but matrilineal in others. In accordance with Morgan's view that human society had slowly evolved from mother-right to father-right, with admixtures of both in between, the authors proposed that the term 'horde' be used for local groups where marriage organization was matrilineal, while the term 'clan' be reserved for local groups where marriage organization was patrilineal. Although the term 'horde' had been introduced into the literature on the Aborigines twenty years earlier by John McLennan in a world survey of marriage customs, [22] Howitt and Fison made no reference to previous usages; indeed, when repeating the definition some years later, Howitt advised that significations given to the term by other writers were not meant to be included.[23]

The distinction proposed by Howitt and Fison between 'clan' and 'horde' failed to catch on. This is hardly surprising since, when we compare the description of the clan given in their 1883 article with the definition of the horde offered in their 1885 article, we see that the two terms designated the same entity, the difference in application depending on the line of descent used to define membership in other entities of the same system. Furthermore, through clumsy and ambiguous phraseology in subsequent publications, the authors seemed to be saying that clans were patrilineal while hordes were matrilineal. [24] That this was not their intention is patently clear in the 1885 definition and accompanying elaborations.[25] The horde was a geographical section of an Aboriginal community occupying specified hunting grounds. Children belonged to the horde of their father. The horde was exogamous, and residence after marriage was normally viri-local (i.e. wives lived with their husbands' hordes, not their own). Hunting rights were held in common by all members of the horde. A son's inheritance from his father was not land in the sense of real estate but a 'mere continuance in the locality where he was born'.[26]

For some time afterwards, writers on Aboriginal society avoided both 'clan' and 'horde', preferring the less problematic expression 'local group'. Their re-appearance in a modified form followed research in Western Australia by a visiting Cambridge anthropologist named A.R. Brown, who later modified his own patrilineal inheritance with the matronymic Radcliffe. In 1913, in the first of a series of articles dealing with Aboriginal social organization, Radcliffe-Brown referred to local groups making up the Kariera tribe as clans, meaning by that term a body of persons related to each other through either male or female descent. The Kariera local clans were patrilineal and were distinguished from each other by possession of a separate territory.[27] In a second article, published in 1918 and dealing with a wider spectrum of tribes, Radcliffe-Brown continued to use 'clan' in the same generic sense but introduced the term 'horde' to mean a patrilineal local group. It was, in other words, a species of clan, distinguished by its patrilineality, residential localization, and possession of territory. It was synonymous with 'local clan' and could if desired be designated more fully as a 'clan-horde'. [28]

At some stage Radcliffe-Brown must have realized that his revised formulation left the membership status of married women ambiguous. As they did not belong to their husband's clan by descent, in what sense could they be members of his clan-horde? In a revision first published in 1930, he retracted the synonymity of 'horde' and 'local clan' in order to distinguish the horde as a group based on common residence from the local clan as a group based on patrilineal descent.[29] A horde normally comprised all the male members of the clan, the unmarried female members, and the wives of the male members. Whereas a clan changed its composition through the birth and death of its members, a horde changed its composition in accordance with a residence rule following marriage (i.e. females left it to join their husbands elsewhere, females from elsewhere came into it as the wives of male members). Although a woman changed hordes on marriage, she remained a member of her father's local clan for a lifetime.

In that case, who owned the land: the clan or the horde? In the opening pages of his 1930 article, published the following year as part of a monograph entitled *The Social Organization of Australian Tribes*, Radcliffe-Brown declared that throughout Australia the primary land-owning or land-holding group was the horde. Its members possessed in common proprietary rights over the land and its products - mineral, vegetable, and animal. Five years later, in *The Iowa Law Review*, he elaborated the same proposition by speaking of the horde as a 'corporation' with an 'estate', using the terms in broadly the sense in which they are employed in Western law:

> The corporate estate of a Kariera horde includes in the first place its rights over its territory. The continuity of the horde is maintained by the continuity of possession of the territory, which remains constant, not subject to division or increase, for the Australian aborigines have no conception of the possibility of territorial conquest by armed force. The relation of a horde to its territory does not correspond exactly to what we regard as 'ownership' in modern law. It has some of the qualities of corporate ownership, but also partakes of the nature of the relation of a modern state to its territory, which we may speak of as the exercise of 'dominion'.[30]

Although Radcliffe-Brown did not say so explicitly, the implication of his formulation was plainly that a woman, inasmuch as she was a member of her husband's horde, shared rights of ownership in its land. Whether she retained or relinquished ownership rights in the land of her natal horde was left unclear. In his 1913 article he had alluded to a 'sort of right' retained by a woman over the country of her birth, but in subsequent writings he neither elaborated nor repeated the assertion.

In the same year that Radcliffe-Brown published his essay in *The*

Iowa Law Review, a graduate of Sydney University named Phyllis Kaberry completed her field research in the Kimberley region of north-west Australia. It was the first doctoral study of Aborigines by a female anthropologist. On the matter of the jural status of women in relation to land, Kaberry stated flatly that Radcliffe-Brown's general-izations were not valid for the Kimberleys. Although a wife moved about freely in her husband's territory, she did not regard it as her own. Land ownership depended not on residence but on descent, and a woman continued to be a fully fledged joint owner of her father's horde territory even after she left it to join her husband. Ultimately her bones were laid to rest there. Accordingly, for the purposes of her description, Kaberry defined the horde to refer specifically to 'the patrilineal group of men and women who own a stretch of territory, though some of them may be living elsewhere'.[31]

While Kaberry's account of women's land-owning rights ultimately came to be acknowledged as true throughout Australia, her use of 'horde' rather than 'clan' for the land-owning group was not followed. Increasingly, anthropologists preferred the latter term for the land-owning unit, reserving the former for the residential unit. Eventually Radcliffe-Brown himself accepted the usage. In his last statement on Aboriginal local organization, published posthumously in 1956, he wrote: 'The clan is corporate in the sense that its adult members can and do engage in collective action, and that as a clan they have collective ownership and control of a certain territory.... A woman belongs to her father's clan but to her husband's horde.'[32]

Meanwhile another problem had arisen, this time empirical rather than conceptual. Specifically, it was concerned not with the ownership of land but with its use, and with the size and composition of nomadic groups (which we can designate loosely as 'bands' to avoid the problematic connotations of 'horde'). Following the publication of Radcliffe-Brown's monograph in 1931, a number of investigators working in widely separated parts of Australia had been unable to find evidence of patrilineal hordes, either in the present day or within living memory. For instance, Ralph Piddington wrote that in the Kimberleys 'small parties composed of less than a dozen individuals from any horde may go on hunting expeditions lasting several months, over the territory of any other horde, without asking the permission of the owners, who would not object'.[33] Likewise, William Stanner reported that in the country south-west of Darwin bands were 'aggregates of contiguous local totemic clans' and that people moved freely between their own and neighbouring clan territories.[34] Lauriston Sharp ob-served that in Cape York Peninsula people hunted and gathered in each other's clan territories without seeking permission; that bands regularly included men of many different clans; and that individuals frequently moved from one band to another.[35] And from Arnhem Land, Lloyd Warner reported that: 'Friendly peoples wander over the food areas of others and, if their area happens to be poor in food production, possibly spend more of their lives on the territory of other clans than on their own. Exclusive use of the group's territory by the group is not part of the Murngin idea of land "ownership".'[36]

Despite these apparent exceptions, when A.P. Elkin published *The Australian Aborigines* in 1938 he presented an account of local organization very much along the lines laid down by Radcliffe-Brown at the beginning of the decade. By 1950, however, he was having second thoughts. 'The local organization in many tribes', he wrote, 'is not the clearcut patrilineal patrilocal exogamous group occupying a definite territory which some textbooks imply.'[37] In 1953 he was unable to agree that 'everywhere in Australia the fundamental basis of social organization is a system of patrilineal local groups or clans of small size'. [38] His reservations were cautiously phrased and terse. Radcliffe-Brown responded equally tersely by defending his original sources and dismissing Elkin's remarks as too insubstantial to warrant any serious revision .[39]

The need for a systematic re-evaluation of Radcliffe-Brown's territorial model became plainly evident the following year when Mervyn Meggitt submitted the results of his research among the Walbiri peoples of Central Australia.[40] The Walbiri were divided into four major territorial divisions, which Meggitt designated as 'communities'. They ranged in size from 200 to 400 people and comprised from six to twelve patrilineal clans (or, as Meggitt called them, 'patrilines'). The adult male members of a clan formed a cult-lodge associated with a number of localized sacred sites, or 'spirit-centres'. It was not the case, however, that each clan formed the patrilineal core of a horde confined within the boundaries of a clan territory. Members of each community were free to range over the entire community area, the boundaries of which were known and respected by neighbours. The size of nomadic groups varied according to seasonal conditions and available food resources. Composition was flexible and labile; camps usually consisted of people related to each other by blood or marriage, but common descent in the male line was merely one of numerous considerations determining residential associations.

Meggitt's description of land use thus confirmed the observations of those of his predecessors who had been unable to find the horde during the decade before World War 2. Even more radical was his departure from Radcliffe-Brown on the question of land ownership. Among the Walbiri, title to land was vested in the community, not the patriclan. Sacred designs linking particular lodges with particular sites 'formed part of a community's title deeds to its territory':[41]

Neither the patriline nor its associated lodge 'owns' a defined tract of land on which its members reside or hunt to the exclusion of other people; but, when all the ritual relationships between lodges and dreaming-sites are summed, they constitute in part the community's title to its country and to the resources of that region.[42]

The community constituted the maximal political entity; it protected its members from external attack and exercised custodial responsibility for sacred sites within its boundaries. Political criteria were thus deemed by Meggitt to confer 'legitimate title'[43] to domain (what Radcliffe-Brown would have termed 'dominion'), whereas religious criteria were deemed to constitute something less than ownership of sacred sites within it. As many marriages took place between communities, and wives normally lived in their husband's domain, the position of women in relation to land was left unclear.

In 1962 I published the results of my own inquiries into local organization among the Gidjingali of northern Arnhem Land, carried out a few years earlier. With regard to land use and residential associations, my findings were similar to Meggitt's. Concerning ownership, however, I had no hesitation in ascribing primary proprietorial rights in land to patriclans. The estates that made up a community's domain each belonged either to a single named patrilineal descent group, or to several such groups that had amalgamated to form a single land-owning unit. Sacred designs representing sites on an estate belonged to the relevant clan (or amalgamated clans), and not to the community as a whole. More generally, following a review of the data currently available, I concluded that Radcliffe-Brown's concept of the horde was a false inference about the characteristics of resource-exploiting bands drawn from true statements about ritual links between clans and sacred sites. Far from being the basic on-the-ground unit of Aboriginal territorial organization, the horde was a phantom creation of theoretical reconstruction in the aftermath of colonial invasion.[44]

The conclusion generated a certain amount of argument. In 1965 Stanner, despite his own inability to find the horde in the Northern Territory, defended Radcliffe-Brown's formulation as adaptable enough to accommodate the anomalies. The ensuing debate could be fairly described as a contest between sympathetic and unsympathetic readings of the relevant texts.[45] In 1972 the American anthropologist Joseph Birdsell insisted that the patrilineal horde was a reality prior to the arrival of Europeans and that the aberrations summarized in my review were dislocations caused by colonization.[46] As Radcliffe-Brown had done his fieldwork in areas occupied by Europeans for at least fifty years, it was hard to understand in what sense his reconstructions of indigenous local organization were more reliable than those of later investigators working in more recently colonized areas. All systematic observations of Aboriginal social life had been made on the safe side of the frontier. After half a century of professional fieldwork, the indirect and inferential evidence for the prior existence of the patrilineal horde seemed weak, while the same kind of evidence for looser, larger and more flexible arrangements seemed strong.

While anthropologists in Sydney and Canberra were arguing among themselves about the nature of indigenous local organization, Aborigines in a remote corner of the Northern Territory were beginning to argue with the Australian Government about the right of a mining company to dig up their soil. Early in 1963 the Commonwealth had excised 140 acres from the Arnhem Land Aboriginal Reserve for the purposes of bauxite mining on Gove Peninsula, not far from Yirrkala Methodist Mission. In July 1963 senior Aboriginal men from the affected area glued a petition to a bark painting and sent it to the House of Representatives in Canberra. Their prayer, written in both English and their own language, stated that places sacred to the native inhabitants and vital to their livelihood were now under threat. No prior notice of the excision had been given to the traditional owners. The petitioners appealed to the Parliament to appoint a committee to hear the views of the Yirrkala people before allowing the mining to go ahead.[47]

A Select Committee submitted its report two months later. Among the more influential opinions recorded was the view of the Crown Solicitor in Darwin that: 'When Australia was settled, the Aborigines of Australia were considered at that time not to have title to the land. The whole of our system of land tenure is built on that assumption...'[48]

Nevertheless the Select Committee recommended that hunting rights over the mining area be preserved for the Aborigines, that sacred places be protected and not destroyed, and that Aborigines should be given a voice in matters affecting their relationships with residents of the proposed mining town of Nhulunbuy.

Over the next five years test-drilling, sampling, surveying and construction work continued. In 1968 the Commonwealth issued a mineral lease to a company called Nabalco for a term of forty-two years. Shortly afterwards three Yirrkala Aborigines sued both parties in the Supreme Court of the Northern Territory, alleging an unlawful invasion of their interests in land and of the interests of the clans they represented. The central argument advanced on their behalf was that from 1788 they and their predecessors were subjects of the Crown and that, at common law, native rights to land persisted unless terminated

Pl. 3   Yirrkala bark petition

by the sovereign with the consent of the native owners. In the present case the rights had not been extinguished; only the plaintiff clans held such rights to the subject land and had done so from time immemorial; and the right to use and enjoy the said land, in accordance with customary law, was a right of property.

The case was heard by Mr Justice Blackburn.[49] Counsel for the plaintiffs, Mr Woodward QC, sought to establish the nature of traditional land tenure at Yirrkala through two kinds of witness, viz. members of the plaintiff clans, and two anthropologists, Professors Stanner and Berndt. In assessing the evidence, the judge began with matters that were not in dispute: (a) Of fundamental importance in the system of life established by ancestors of the Yirrkala people was the principle of the clan. (b) The clan was a patrilineal descent group. (c) Sexual relationships within the clan were forbidden; upon marriage, a woman remained a member of her natal clan but her children belonged to her husband's clan. (d) Each clan was regarded as a spiritual entity with a spiritual relationship to particular places or areas, and with a duty to care for them by ritual observances. (e) Certain sacred objects, called *rangga*, were tangible symbols of this relationship and of the continuity of the clan through time. (f) The clan had little significance in the economic sense.

The judge then turned to matters in dispute. These, however, were not disputes between opposed counsel so much as conflicts of evidence between the expert witnesses and the Aborigines. For reasons best known to themselves, Stanner and Berndt advanced a model of land occupancy and use based on Radcliffe-Brown's concept of the horde.[50] They maintained that (1) most of the male members of a band normally belonged to a single clan; (2) each band lived most of the time on the territory owned by its male members; (3) the band was an economic arm of the clan. The Aboriginal evidence on all three points was to the contrary. The judge summarized it as follows:

(1) What impresses me most on this question, however, is that not one of the ten aboriginal witnesses who were from eight different clans, said anything which indicated that the band normally had a core from one clan, or that they thought of the band in terms of their own clan, and all of them indicated that within the band it was normal to have a mixture of people of different clans.

(2) Turning to the aboriginal evidence, none of the witnesses said that in the days before the Mission he lived chiefly in his clan territory and to a less extent in the territory of other clans.

(3) I consider that the suggested links between the bands and the clans are not proved....The people of each clan were deeply conscious of their clan kinship and of the *spiritual* significance of particular land to their clan. On the other hand, beyond the fact that a father and his children

were necessarily of the same clan, it was of no importance whether or not the members of a band, a food-gathering and communal living unit, had any clan relationships to each other, or conducted their food-gathering and communal living upon territory linked to any particular clan.[51]

On the question whether the relationship between the plaintiffs and the subject land could be properly described as proprietary, the judge decided in the negative. In reaching his decision he dismissed as inconsequential certain arguments advanced by the defendants, particularly those depending on the the facts that boundaries between clan territories were often vague and that nothing equivalent to registers of title existed. But he was likewise unimpressed by the arguments brought forward on behalf of the plaintiffs, viz. that they expressed ownership by using possessives in their languages equivalent to 'my country', 'our country', etc.; that such usages were acknowledged and respected by others; that myths described the bestowal of land on clans by their spirit ancestors; and that each clan had an exclusive economic relationship with its land through its associated band. The judge was unable to give much weight to the linguistic evidence - possessives in English have a variety of meanings, some of which may be indicative of proprietary relationships, some of which may not (e.g. 'my father', 'my club', 'my occupation', etc.). Mythology seemed to give merely a general account of creation, and in any case it was a field into which he hesitated to venture (having apparently put from his mind the sacred *rangga* revealed to him during the hearings). Lastly, the asserted relationship between clan and band had been shown not to exist.

In the judge's view, the relationship of the clan to the land failed to meet two vital criteria of a property relationship: the right to alienate, and the right to exclusive use and enjoyment. The fact that the spiritual bond between Aborigines and their territories was so profound as to make alienation unthinkable was thus deemed to render their estates as not owned in any commonly understood legal sense of the word. The Aboriginal ethic of generosity that regarded exclusive use and enjoyment as indecent made comparisons even harder. There was so little resemblance between the values of the plaintiffs and those governing property relations in European law that the attempt to accommodate the former under the rubric of the latter had to be judged as hopeless.

Finally, on the central question of extinction of native title, the judge appealed to Blackstone's distinction between settled colonies and conquered or ceded colonies. Whatever Blackstone intended by the words 'desert and uncultivated', they had always been taken to include territory occupied by uncivilized inhabitants in a primitive state of society. Admittedly there was room for argument as to which category any particular colony belonged to, but once a legal decision was made the consequences should not be lightly disturbed. In 1889 the Privy Council had ruled on appeal that New South Wales belonged to Blackstone's first category; furthermore, that at the time of its peaceful annexation the colony was practically unoccupied, without settled inhabitants or land law. English law therefore immediately came into effect in regard to all land transactions. As there was no trace of a doctrine of communal native title in English common law, and as it had never formed part of the law of Australia, the need for extinction did not arise.

Given the hierarchical system of authority in which he laboured, it was natural that Judge Blackburn felt bound by the wisdom of his Lordships on the Judicial Committee. Nevertheless, having invoked Blackstone, he might at least have attempted to state his position as fully and fairly as possible. Blackstone undeniably contrasted 'desert and uncultivated' countries with 'already cultivated' countries, leaving open the possibility that lack of prior cultivation might in itself be sufficient to distinguish a colony as having been merely occupied or settled. In the same passage, however, he made it clear that the critical difference depended upon the presence or absence of human inhabitants:

> But there is a difference between these two species of colonies, with respect to the laws by which they are bound. For it has been held, that if an uninhabited country be discovered and planted by English subjects, all the English laws then in being, which are the birthright of every subject, are immediately there in force.[52]

The implication should be tolerably clear: if an inhabited country became a colony, it normally did so in consequence of either conquest or cession. Blackstone specifically stated that the English colonies in America had been acquired by right of conquest in driving out the natives, or by treaties with them. Presumably he would have said the same about Australia, except that treaties were not deemed necessary. And in that case, the laws of the inhabitants remained in force unless contrary to the laws of God or until changed by the sovereign. After listening to evidence on Aboriginal land tenure in the Gove case, the judge (unlike his learned predecessors in 1889) had no doubt that he was dealing with a true system of law. In order to escape the principle vouchsafed by his own ancestral authority (not to speak of the humanistic sentiments expressed under a different heading in the same source), he argued both that the American Indians (and by inference the Australian Aborigines) were not the victims of conquest and that, in any event, the question was not what had happened in history but what had happened in courts of law. To re-open either the historical issue or the previous legal decision in response to the plaintiffs' prayers in the Gove case would be an exercise in futility.

Mr Justice Blackburn delivered his judgment in 1971. Two years later, following the formation of a Labor Government in Federal Parliament, the sovereign's representative in Canberra commissioned the plaintiffs' counsel (now a judge himself) to investigate traditional Aboriginal rights and interests in land with a view to advising him how they might most appropriately be recognized. The focus of the inquiry was the Northern Territory, at that time directly under the administration of the Commonwealth. In his report, Mr Justice Woodward defined traditional owners in relation to an area of land as:

> a local descent group of Aborigines who have common spiritual affilia-
> tions to a site or sites within that area of land, which affiliations place the
> group under a primary spiritual responsibility for that site or sites and
> for that land, and who are entitled by Aboriginal tradition to forage as of
> right over that land.[53]

He recommended that Aborigines in the Northern Territory (a) be granted title to their Reserves (i.e. some twenty areas of land previously set aside for their benefit and protection); (b) be given the opportunity to lodge claims for title to unalienated Crown land (i.e. land apart from town land in which no one other than the Crown had an estate or interest); and (c) where appropriate, to be assisted with funds to purchase pastoral properties. The first two recommendations became the foundation stones of the Aboriginal Land Rights (Northern Territory) Act 1976. Thus within a few years defeat under the judicature had been transmuted into victory through the legislature, not merely for the plaintiffs in the Gove case but for their compatriots throughout the Northern Territory.

In the years that followed the proclamation of the Act, numerous claims for unalienated land were heard by Land Commissioners. As with the Yirrkala testimony, none of the Aboriginal evidence on band composition and land use upheld the concept of the patrilineal horde. Surprisingly, some of it even raised doubts as to whether the patriline-ality was always the pre-eminent qualification for ownership. My own research in the 1950s had revealed strong custodial rights held by men in relation to the sacred symbols ('title deeds') of their mothers' clan-estates, but I regarded these as subsidiary to the ownership rights of the patriclans themselves.[54] In some land hearings, claimants articulated a similar view and excluded matrifiliates from the lists of traditional owners; in others, they accorded them parity with patrifiliates and included them. In a variation on the same theme, it was argued in the

Ayers Rock claim that individuals at birth inherited rights in the land-owning groups of both parents; that during their lifetimes they came to exercise them predominantly in one group or the other; and that membership of the chosen group was transmitted to the offspring. The principle of descent was not 'patri-lineal' but 'ambi-lineal'.[55]

During the sixties and seventies, independently of the land-claim hearings, a new generation of field anthropologists was likewise finding exceptions to patrilineality as the essence of land ownership. In a thesis submitted in 1979, Annette Hamilton wrote that in the Western Desert region of north-west South Australia: 'Rights to cult complex and associated sites ... do not derive from "patrilineal descent", nor even patrifiliation; rights do not accrue by being born to a particular father, but by being born at a particular place.'[56]

Further north, among the Western Desert Pintupi, Fred Myers found that ownership in its deepest sense depended on neither patrilineality nor place of birth but place of conception. Men conceived in the vicinity of any particular sacred site were regarded as incarnations of its spiritual creator and, as such, exercised rights in the ceremonies, songs and sculptures associated with it. Whether they were related to each other through patrilineal descent was a matter of indifference. While it was true that men transmitted ritual knowledge to their sons regardless of the latters' places of conception, the same applied to their sisters' sons. As ownership depended on revelation of religious knowledge, site-owning cult groups consisted mainly of men brought together by common conception-place in combination with blood links through both males and females.[57]

An even more radical departure from twentieth-century orthodoxy, resonating with early colonial accounts of Aboriginal land ownership, was John von Sturmer's assertion that in western Cape York certain sites belonged not to corporate descent groups (however recruited) but to individual males. Focal sites, as he called them, were in traditional economic terms premium real estate, such as favoured camp locations at the mouth of a river, offering ready access to food and water resources, and strategically placed in relation to trade routes. They were usually invested with mythical and ceremonial importance; also, they were often under the control of a powerful individual who spent most of his time there. 'Big men' or 'bosses' inherited their status from their fathers and passed it on to their eldest sons. Holding on to it in the meantime depended upon political acumen and strength of character. Although bosses did not normally exclude others from their land, they told visitors where they should camp. To all intents and purposes the sites were their personal property.[58]

In 1982 three men from an island north-east of Cape York instituted proceedings in the High Court of Australia against the State of Queensland, seeking declarations to the effect that the latter's sovereignty over their homelands was subject to native rights of ownership. The island, named Mer,[59] had been annexed by Queensland in 1879. Its inhabitants, known as the Meriam, were Melanesians whose ancestors had probably come from Papua New Guinea. Traditionally they had lived as subsistence cultivators, growing yams intensively in gardens mostly owned by individuals and passed from father to son.

Fittingly, as it turned out, Mer was not far from where Cook had taken possession of the east coast of Australia; for although the plaintiffs were not Aborigines, nor claimed in any way to be representing their interests, the High Court took the opportunity to examine the matter of native title as it affected the indigenous inhabitants of the mainland. Justice Brennan expressly rejected the strategy of inquiring whether the Meriam were 'higher in the scale of social organization' than the Aborigines;[60] his colleague Justice Toohey said that, although there were significant cultural differences, the principles relevant to a determination of interests in ancestral lands were the same.[61] In short, the distinction between horticulturalists and hunter-gatherers, or between cultivation of the soil and non-cultivation, was of no consequence. The court showed a comparable (and perhaps connected) lack of interest in the structure of indigenous land-owning corporations and the nature of their relationship to their estates. It was merely noted that the Meriam did not have spiritual relationships of the kind that emerged in the Gove case. The judgments steered clear of anthropological texts, and even elementary technical terms such as 'clan' and 'tribe' were used sparingly and without definition. As far as possible argumentation was confined to questions of law.

On the critical question whether English laws applied immediately upon occupation of New South Wales, the High Court rejected both the factual and the legal basis of the Privy Council's decision of 1889. In discussing Blackstone's distinction between occupied and conquered or ceded colonies, several of the judges introduced the legal expression *terra nullius*, which neither Blackstone nor Blackburn had used but which had gained wide and emotive currency in Australia following the latter's judgment in the Gove case. Meaning 'land of no one', it obviously applied to Blackstone's category of lands that, before colonization, were desert, uninhabited and uncultivated. But later writers on international law expanded the concept to include lands occupied by peoples deemed to be barbarous and without genuine systems of law. As on this theory they could not be said to own their own lands, the latter were open for occupation and settlement; the question of conquest or cession did not arise. Noting Justice Blackburn's positive evaluation of Aboriginal legal systems, the High Court ruled that the doctrine of *terra nullius* was based on false premisses. As it also denigrated the peoples to whom it had been applied, it was morally unacceptable in contemporary Australian society. The contrived distinction between colonies that were *terra nullius* and those that were not should therefore be discarded in law.

This left the question whether sovereignty in itself vested an ultimate title in the Crown that automatically extinguished all pre-existing native titles (regardless of its effect on rights of other kinds). In a minority judgment, Justice Dawson appealed to numerous court decisions implying that pre-existing land rights were worthless. Most of his colleagues, however, agreed with Justice Brennan that where an indigenous proprietary interest in land held by an individual or a community was capable of recognition by the common law, 'there is no reason why that title should not be recognized as a burden on the Crown's radical title when the Crown acquires sovereignty over that territory.'[62] Courts in the seventeenth century had determined that inhabitants of both Ireland and Wales still in possession of land following the conquests needed no new grant from the sovereign to confirm their title under common law. In accordance with that precedent, native title survived unless it was extinguished by specific grants to colonists or by appropriation of parcels of land by the Crown itself for specific purposes.

The Mabo decision (named after the Meriam plaintiff who initiated the action) was handed down by the High Court in 1992. As Maine noted when discussing how the law changes, novel principles override older ones 'on the strength of an intrinsic ethical superiority'.[63] While no one doubted that the High Court had been high-minded, some wondered how well the national interest had been served. Should not the courts eschew 'activism', leave innovation to the legislature, and confine themselves to interpreting and applying the law as it stands? [64] There was also the question, raised by a former Chief Justice, 'whether on the whole it will prove more beneficial for the Aboriginal people that they should be provided with what may be an uncertain basis for making legal claims which are likely to result in protracted controversy and litigation, rather than leaving it to the political process to do justice to them.'[65]

Throughout 1993 the political process took the form of a national debate, culminating a few days before Christmas in the passage through both Houses of Federal Parliament of a Native Title Bill. Never before in the history of Aboriginal affairs had the collective mind of the white majority been exercised so vigorously and at such length on the matter of its rights and responsibilities in relation to the indigenous minority. Indeed, one purpose of the legislation was to allay anxieties among the citizenry that Mabo could cause them personal injury. While it affirmed the principle of native rights in relation to land, the Act proceeded on the basis that such rights had already been extinguished by valid grants of private interests i.e. grants of freehold or leasehold (in the latter case, at least to the extent that the lease provided a right of exclusive occupancy). The Attorney-General stated that, for the most part, native title persisted only in remote areas of Australia, where it was based upon complex spiritual associations and special responsibilities.[66]

The new statute established a body (the National Native Title Tribunal) presided over by a judge or former judge to deal with uncontested claims to native title and compensation, and to attempt to mediate settlements of opposed claims. Where mediation failed, opposed claims would be referred to the Federal Court. Native title was defined as a group's communal, group or individual rights to land (or waters) under its indigenous laws as now recognized by the common law of Australia. In the virtual absence of explicit guidelines, the basis on which the Tribunal and the Court will distinguish between valid and invalid criteria when considering claims is presently a matter for speculation. The extent to which their determinations rely upon anthropological findings and arguments of the past will be an interesting question for anthropologists of the future.

3

Group marriage

At the first meeting of the Anthropological Institute of Great Britain and Ireland in February 1871 the President, Sir John Lubbock, presented to Fellows a lengthy review of a book just published by the Smithsonian Institution in Washington. Its author was Mr. L.H. Morgan, its subject kinship nomenclature. Although Sir John disagreed on certain theoretical points, there could be no doubt about the significance of the material. Mr Morgan's book was one of the most valuable contributions to ethnological science that had appeared for many years

Lewis Henry Morgan had grown up in western New York State, in the expropriated country of the Iroquois Indians.[1] As a young man he campaigned against their threatened deportation to Kansas and at the same time began recording their history and culture. In 1851 he published a book entitled *The League of the Iroquois*, which gave some prominence to traditional political institutions and decision-making procedures. It also contained a small but significant section on degrees of consanguinity.

The Iroquois were a confederation of five tribes formed *c.*1400 AD by the legendary Hiawatha: Mohawk, Onondaga, Seneca, Oneida and Cayuga. Through their civil and military organization, they dominated neighbouring peoples in the pre-colonial era and successfully resisted and negotiated European encroachment for nearly two centuries afterwards. The basis for this highly effective alliance, according to Morgan, was an elaborate concept of consanguinity. Each tribe was made up of a number of totemic clans common to all or most of the others (Wolf, Bear, Turtle, etc.), and members of the same clan regarded themselves as blood relatives by descent from a common ancestor. The confederation was thus held together by chains of brotherhood that were at least as strong as the ties that held together the different clans of the same tribe.

The integrative effect of cross-cutting clan affiliations was facilitated by a system of kinship terminology whose leading object, in Morgan's words, was to merge the collateral with the lineal.[2] This needs some explanation. In Figure 1A, the lineal relatives comprise Ego, his father and mother, and his son and daughter; the collateral relatives are all the rest. One striking difference between the English and Iroquois systems is that in the latter Ego uses the same term for his father's brother as for his father; and the same term for his mother's sister as for his mother. Instead of calling their offspring cousins, he calls them brothers and sisters. He applies the terms son and daughter to the offspring of any male he calls brother; and the terms nephew and niece to the offspring of any female he calls sister. We can see that in the English system Ego distinguishes his lineal relatives sharply from his collaterals, whereas in the Iroquois system he classifies at least some of them together (e.g. F and FB, S and BS). The consequences are

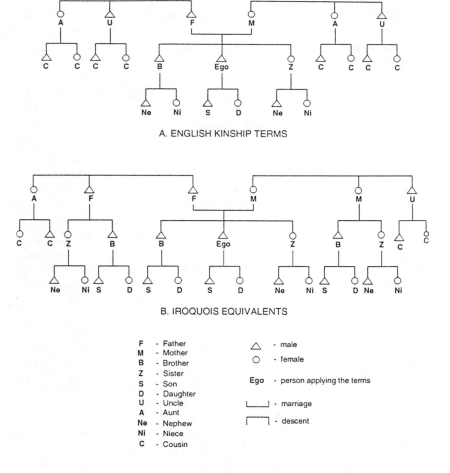

Fig. 2   Comparison of English and Iroquois kinship terms.

profound. If we were to extend the diagram upwards, it would become apparent that the term for brother is applied to individuals whose relationships to Ego are quite remote (e.g. his FFFFBSSSS).

Morgan presumed that the Iroquois system was unique, something they had worked out for themselves. In 1858, however, during a business trip to Michigan, he discovered identical principles of classification six hundred miles away among the Ojibwa of Lake Superior. In a fever of excitement, he sent off questionnaires on kinship to missionaries and government agents throughout the western territories. Although not everyone responded in the same spirit of enthusiasm (an indifference echoed by countless anthropology students in the years that followed), he received enough information to convince him that the basic features of Iroquois kinship were common to all the tribes of North America.

Shortly afterwards Morgan obtained details of the Tamil kinship system from a missionary home on leave from southern India. To his astonishment, the principles of classification were substantially the same as those governing all known systems of North America. The discovery confirmed Morgan's belief that the American Indians had migrated from Asia; more significantly, it started him thinking about the possibility of an ancestral social condition from which all existing systems of consanguinity had evolved. In 1859, the year of publication of Darwin's *The Origin of Species*, he gave a hint of his new theory in a paper presented to the American Association for the Advancement of Science: 'With a thread as delicate as a system of relationships, we may yet re-ascend the several lines of outflow of generations, and reach and identify that parent nation, from which we are, we believe, all alike descended.'[3]

The ascent required a firm and extensive data base. Morgan accordingly appealed for help to the Smithsonian Institution, where friends intimated on his behalf that unless the hypothesis was developed and published without delay British scholars might claim it first. In 1860 the Secretary of State instructed American diplomats to distribute Morgan's questionnaires to appropriate persons and institutions throughout the world. By 1865, despite the death of his two daughters during his absence on a field trip, Morgan had collated the results in a manuscript of some 1500 pages, which he submitted to the Smithsonian. The director, an eminent physicist, found it unintelligible. Two years later, on receiving a revised version, he told Morgan that 'the first impression of one who has been engaged in physical research is that, in proportion to the conclusions arrived at, the quantity of your material is very large'.[4] Although in the event this turned out to be true of authorship in the social sciences generally, Morgan was provoked into summarizing his thesis in a forty-page document entitled 'A

Conjectural Solution of the Origin of the Classificatory System of Relationship', which he read to the American Academy of Arts and Sciences early in 1868.

An additional motivating force for the effort of compression was the publication in 1865 of *Primitive Marriage* by John Ferguson McLennan. Like Morgan, the author was a lawyer, but he lived in Scotland and his interest in the subject derived from inquiries into the early history of Greece and Rome. In his book McLennan postulated a number of causal chains generated by an alleged prevalence in antiquity of female infanticide. One consequence of the resulting shortage of women was, he suggested, the practice of polyandry whereby several men, usually brothers, shared the same wife. As physical fatherhood was inevitably uncertain in such circumstances, consanguinity could be established only through the mother. In support of his argument McLennan quoted the information contained in Morgan's questionnaire, that among the Iroquois no distinction was made in kinship terminology between the father and the paternal uncle.

Morgan's conjectural solution of the origin of classificatory kinship was rather more radical. The Iroquois system makes sense, he argued, if we assume that it originated in circumstances where men who were related to each other as brothers commonly cohabited with women who were related to each other as sisters, so long as the partners were not related to each other as brother and sister. Within the limits of what may be referred to as 'group marriage', sexual intercourse was promiscuous. The resulting offspring, who were reared together in a communal family, referred to each other as 'brother' and 'sister'; and they referred to all the male adults as 'father' and all the female adults as 'mother'. In the course of social evolution, group marriage eventually gave way to marriage between pairs; but, although sexual mores were thus transformed, the old terminology persisted as a survival from a past era in which it faithfully reflected the actual conditions of reproduction.

As we follow the thread of evidence into antiquity, shadows of even more unpleasant scenes begin to appear. Morgan's respondents had indicated that in some systems the merging of collateral with lineal relatives is complete. For instance, in the Hawaian system there are only two terms in each generation: all males and females of my parents' generation are my 'fathers' and 'mothers'; all of my own generation are my 'brothers' and 'sisters'; all of my children's generation are my 'sons' and 'daughters'. This is so even though contemporary marriage is monogamous. Morgan conjectured that the terminology must be a fossil from a period, antecedent to the one reflected in Iroquois terminology, when sexual congress was permitted between brothers and sisters (but not between parents and offspring).

The earliest form of the family would thus have been based on group marriage between siblings. Beyond this, in the lowest conceivable state of savagery, no formal barriers existed at all between consanguine kin. Reproduction was the outcome of total promiscuity.

In 1871 Morgan's arguments, together with tables setting out kinship systems representative of most of the world's major culture areas, were published by the Smithsonian under the title of *Systems of Consanguinity and Affinity of the Human Family*. This was the book reviewed by Lubbock at the Institute. During the previous year Morgan had set out on an extended tour of England and Europe, in the course of which he met Sir John and also dined several times with McLennan, then living in London and a Fellow of the Ethnological Society.[5] Though Morgan parted with McLennan on the most cordial terms, and even tried to get him a job at Cornell University, the friendship was short lived. In 1876 McLennan published a lengthy critique of Morgan's book, which he compared unfavourably with his own, and explained the extended nature of his commentary as arising from a sense of public duty: 'issuing from the Press of the Smithsonian Institution, and its preparation appearing to have been aided by the United States Government, Mr Morgan's work has been generally quoted as a work of authority, and it seemed worth while to take the trouble necessary to show its utterly unscientific character'.[6]

Although McLennan's attempt to accommodate Morgan's data within the framework of his own thesis is no longer of interest, except perhaps as an exercise in tenacity, his main polemical points are still worth noting. First, group marriage is a postulate advanced by Morgan to account for certain features of kinship nomenclature. The only evidence for its previous existence is the contemporary occurrence of the facts it purports to explain. Second, as pointed out by Charles Darwin, group marriage cannot explain why an individual would apply the term for 'mother' to a plurality of females, since there is no uncertainty about motherhood.[7] We could envisage a situation where a boy reserves the term 'mother' for the woman who gave birth to him but extends the term 'father' to all men who cohabit with her. Third, although the terms are represented as though they express relations of consanguinity and affinity, they are in fact merely common salutations used in preference to personal names. They entail no duties or privileges, and are barren of consequences except as a code of courtesies.

Morgan replied a year later.[8] The value of his book, as he had stated in its introduction, lay not in its speculations but in the tabulated facts of kinship terminology. In choosing to describe the entire work as unscientific, Mr McLennan had invited a counter-attack that would otherwise not have been called for. Morgan thereupon levelled his sights on *Primitive Marriage* and, in a brief offensive on its most vulnerable parts, removed it from the battle. His adversary's criticisms, however, were not so easily disposed of. Admittedly, Morgan acknowledged, the concept of group marriage was hypothetical; but hypotheses to account for bodies of facts are indispensable to scientific progress and stand until superseded by better ones. With regard to the point that uncertainty may explain the joint classification of men as fathers but not women as mothers, Morgan replied lamely that the latter were 'mothers' because they cohabited with 'fathers'; they might be likened to 'step-mothers' in English. Last, but not least, if classificatory kinship systems were merely modes of address, without attendant rights and duties, the superficiality of their function would tend to make them variable and ephemeral. Whatever the ultimate fate of his speculations about group marriage, Morgan believed he had succeeded in establishing the uniformity of principles of classification over vast areas and, by implication, the centrality of classificatory kinship systems in the regulation of social life through untold ages.

Given the wide-ranging scope of Morgan's inquiries, as well as the evolutionist temper of his speculations, it is curious that *Systems of Consanguinity and Affinity* included no material on the Australian Aborigines whatever. One presumes that circulars were sent but not returned. Fortunately for Morgan, if not the Aborigines, an English missionary named Lorimer Fison belatedly received a questionnaire in 1869 while serving in Fiji. He immediately sent off data on the Fijian and Tongan systems, which Morgan incorporated as appendices. Soon afterwards Fison moved to Australia, where he obtained information on Aboriginal kinship and marriage from Rev. W. Ridley, a fellow-missionary, and Mr T.E. Lance, a pioneer settler. In 1871 he forwarded the material to Morgan, who within months had presented it in full to the Academy of Arts and Sciences.

It is not hard to understand why Morgan regarded Fison's communication as important. Till then he had merely postulated a prior state of group marriage as a means of explaining classificatory kinship of the kind prevailing among the Iroquois. The data newly arrived seemed to indicate that this very state of affairs existed among the living natives of Australia. Not only were the Aboriginal principles of classification basically the same as those already recorded for American Indians and Tamils but, according to Fison's informants, two pairs of inter-marrying divisions prevailed over wide areas of the continent. All members of a division called each other brother or sister; and they addressed all opposite-sex members of the paired division as 'spouse'. As Morgan informed the Academy, 'here we find, in a direct and definite form, communal marriage, or a legalized system of cohabitation in a great

41

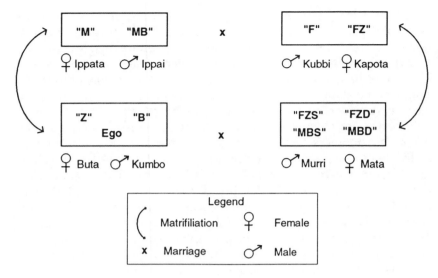

Fig. 3   Section system.

communal family, with the family itself as comprehensive as the range of conjugal privileges'.[9] It was but a step or two from total promiscuity, and represented the most archaic system of reproduction so far observed.

For want of a better word, Morgan referred to the inter-marrying divisions as 'classes'. Later anthropologists, in order to avoid hierarchical connotations normally associated with the term, preferred to call them 'sections'. As Morgan's exposition was understandably somewhat cumbersome, I have set out the principles of the system according to modern conventions (Fig. 3). The section names are those used by the Kamilaroi people of northern New South Wales, as recorded by Ridley and Lance.

As we see, the system comprises eight named groups, four male and four female. Morgan realized, however, that for analytical purposes these could be treated as four brother/sister pairs, each comprising roughly a quarter of the total population. If I am Buta or Kumbo, then all other members of Buta and Kumbo are my sisters and brothers. All members of Ippata are our mothers, and all members of Ippai are our maternal uncles. All members of Kubbi are our fathers, and all members of Kapota are our paternal aunts. All members of Murri and Mata are our cross-cousins.[10] The arrows show to which section the child of any woman belongs; in conjunction with the crosses showing marriage relationships, they enable us to determine the section affiliations of all Ego's relatives. For example, if I am Buta my mother and daughter are both Ippata, my mother's mother is Buta, my mother's mother's brother is Kumbo, my father's mother is Mata, my father's father is Kumbo, my brother's son is Kubbi, and so on.

It is possible that members of the Academy had difficulty following the finer points of the system. But Morgan's rhetoric should have left them in no doubt as to the import of the communication on a major issue of theory: group marriage was no longer a matter of speculation but an observed fact (viz. between Ippata women and Kubbi men, Ippai men and Kapota women, and so on). Rev. Ridley, it is true, had not said so in as many words. Mr Lance, however, was more explicit. He was a frontiersman who had lived for many years on cattle stations along the Darling River. In his letter to Fison he stated: 'If a Kubbi meets a stranger Ippata, they address each other as *Goleer* = Spouse... A Kubbi thus meeting an Ippata, even though she were of another tribe, would treat her as his wife, and his right to do so would be recognized by her tribe.'[11] If this is a privilege enjoyed by a man with strangers, Morgan added, then it must exist even more so within his own community. The conjugal rules thus sanction a domestic institution whereby one quarter of all males are united in marriage with one quarter of all females.

Following the pleasing reception accorded his initial report, Fison sought to extend the investigation to other parts of Australia. In June 1872 he published a long letter in a Melbourne periodical, appealing to gentlemen in contact with Aborigines in the State of Victoria to communicate with him on the burning theoretical issue of classificatory kinship. He received but one reply, from a government official in the Gippsland district named Alfred Howitt.[12] Eleven years earlier, as leader of a relief party sent to find the lost explorers Burke and Wills, Howitt had established contact with Aborigines in central Australia. More importantly, he had in recent years become interested in the customs of the Kurnai of Gippsland and, as local correspondent for the Aboriginal Protection Board, was able to gain valuable information from tribal elders. This he was only too willing to share with Fison. The collaboration, thus begun, flourished under the guiding hand of Morgan, who told his two antipodean disciples they were 'working at the very foundations of that great Science of Anthropology which is sure to come'.[13] Inspired by this encomium, and simultaneously fearful of plagiarism,[14] they decided to write a book.

Kamilaroi and Kurnai by Lorimer Fison and A.W. Howitt was published in 1880, with an introduction by Lewis Henry Morgan. Fison wrote the sections on the Kamilaroi, Howitt those on the Kurnai; and both authors presented previously-unpublished data on numerous other tribes sent to them by correspondents. Unfortunately, the testimony for group marriage as a living fact was less than might have been hoped for. Through some unexplained miracle, the Kurnai had skipped a number of evolutionary stages and were now unequivocally committed to polygyny[15] and individual families. Far from sharing rights of sexual access with other men, husbands jealously guarded their harems and sought to impose on their wives a regime of strict fidelity. Fison's data were more encouraging. The Kamilaroi, like the Kurnai, practised polygyny, but the constraints were looser and the old communal rights more liable to re-assert themselves. Thus, although most women were nominally the wives of the elderly men of the tribe, the latter were obliged to lend them to the younger men on stated occasions. Furthermore, friendly visitors from other tribes were accommodated with temporary wives from the appropriate sections. The explorer Eyre had been one of the first to note this practice in the course of his journeys in central Australia and thought it proper to report it in Latin. Many pages might now be filled with similar testimony, as a result of Fison's inquiries. For instance, a widely travelled Queensland native had told Mr Bridgman of Mackay that he had exercised his right to women of the permitted section in numerous tribes, 'though the places were 1,000 miles apart, and the languages quite different'. Surely, Fison commented,[16] where each woman is married to a thousand miles of husbands, we are in the presence of the most extensive system of communal marriage the world has ever known.[17]

Prior to the publication of *Kamilaroi and Kurnai* Fison had returned to Fiji, where his interests turned increasingly to the local inhabitants. Howitt, however, continued his work among the Aborigines of Gippsland, as well as his correspondence with observers living in contact with tribes in other parts of Australia. Of signal importance to the issue of group marriage was a growing body of information about the Dieri people of Lake Eyre, whom he had contacted briefly during his expedition in 1861. It was now apparent that in this area two distinct forms of marriage coexisted.[18] The first eventuated as a consequence of betrothal, whereby a girl would be promised by her mother and maternal uncle to a particular male relative. The second was subsidiary to the first and eventuated when a husband formally granted another man privileged access to his wife. The first relationship was known as *tippa-malku*, the second as *pirrauru*.

Pirrauru arrangements were allowed only between men related to each other as 'brother'. They could be either reciprocal, in which case two men agreed to share their respective wives with each other; or asymmetrical, in which case one man shared his wife with another man without enjoying a similar privilege in return. In either case the agreement was affirmed and proclaimed by a public ceremony. Where the arrangement was asymmetrical, two ridges of sand, representing the two men, were formed and combined into one. The man being offered *pirrauru* status then took sand from the merged ridge and sprinkled it over his thighs. Where the arrangement was reciprocal, a similar ceremony was carried out first, followed by a ritual in which two pieces of burning wood were brought together while simultaneously the names of the two pairs entering into the *pirrauru* relationship were announced.

For Howitt, wife-sharing between two brothers was a clear case of group marriage. Normally the two men lived together with their wives in a group of four. Although asymmetrical arrangements fell short of fully fledged group marriage, they nevertheless pointed in that direction. A common occurrence was the granting of *pirrauru* privileges by a married man to his younger unmarried brother, who reciprocated with gifts. When the elder brother was away for any length of time, the younger brother assumed the role of husband and protector. The *tippamalku* husband's prerogatives always took precedence over those of the *pirrauru* husband, so that when both were in camp together, wife-sharing in a sexual sense could occur only with the former's permission. The shared wife for her part often carried out her duties with touching solicitude, exercising surveillance over her *pirrauru* partner's movements, requiring him to be near at hand, and staying awake at night until sure he was asleep.

Institutionalized wife-sharing occurred in other circumstances. The needs of widowers, for instance, were often provided for through the generosity of married brothers. Guests from neighbouring tribes might likewise be accommodated. Not uncommonly, according to Howitt's sources, husbands offered their wives as *pirrauru* partners to men noted for their power and influence. Less commonly, women asked their husbands to offer them as partners to men noted for their sex appeal. Whatever the circumstances, *pirrauru* relationships, once established by public ritual, were approved by convention and favourably contrasted with the alternatives of unlicensed adultery and promiscuity. Even the Rev. Otto Siebert, one of Howitt's correspondents, spoke kindly of them: 'The practice of *pirrauru* is worthy of praise for its strength and earnestness in regard to morality, and in the ceremonial with which it is regulated...'[19]

In 1899 Howitt's account of *pirrauru* practices received powerful confirmation when two fieldworkers in central Australia, Baldwin Spencer and Frank Gillen, reported a similar institution among the Urabunna, northern neighbours of the Dieri.[20] Known in this case as *piraungaru*, the auxiliary relationship required authorization by the woman's elder brothers, as well as the senior men of the community, but otherwise was established without ceremonial. Although husbands were entitled to lend their wives to other men, they played no formal role in initiating their wives' *piraungaru* relationships. The institution conferred on other men rights of access that the respective husbands resisted at the risk of public ridicule. The number of *piraungaru* partners bestowed upon a man was a measure of his power and popularity. Women also often had *piraungaru* relationships with several men, and as a general rule husbands and wives together with their *piraungaru* partners were to be found living in the same group. Offspring were regarded as the common children of the men.

Further north, according to Spencer and Gillen, husbands in the Aranda tribe normally exercised exclusive rights over their wives, including the right to lend them, but *pirrauru*-type privileges were not in evidence. However, when a girl reached marriageable age, she was ceremonially deflowered and subsequently required to have coitus with men assembled for the purpose. She was then decorated and presented to the man to whom she had been promised as a wife. Again, when groups gathered for important rituals, several married women were detailed each day to attend the ceremonial ground, where they were sexually available to all the men present except their fathers, brothers or sons.

To Spencer and Gillen, as well as to Howitt, the theoretical implications were plain. Group marriage had once prevailed throughout the continent, and Australian systems of kin classification could not be satisfactorily explained on any other hypothesis. In at least two instances (viz. among the Dieri and Urabunna) a modified form of group marriage persisted up to the present day. Elsewhere, as among the Aranda, the old communal rights re-appeared symbolically on special occasions.

Spencer was Professor of Zoology at Melbourne University, Gillen the Postmaster at Alice Springs. Appropriately, they dedicated the book containing their findings to Fison and Howitt. A few years later, in 1904, Howitt brought together the results of his own inquiries and published them in a comprehensive work entitled *The Native Tribes of South-East Australia*. Unquestionably he was now the pre-eminent authority on the Aborigines, with Spencer the rising star. In the preceding years, Morgan's speculative theory of classificatory kinship had been the subject of extensive discussion and criticism, especially in England, and Howitt himself had not been spared. The new evidence now being advanced by Howitt and Spencer in support of Morgan inevitably provoked a reaction.

In 1906 Northcote W. Thomas, Fellow of the Royal Anthropological Institute and Corresponding Member of the Société d'Anthropologie de Paris, addressed the issues at length in a book called *Kinship Organisations and Group Marriage in Australia*. The arguments for the existence of group marriage among the Aborigines, he said, were of

46

two kinds: (a) from the terms of relationship; (b) from sexual customs in various tribes. In regard to the former, Thomas reiterated several points made by previous commentators. First, the fact that a man applied the term for 'wife' to a whole category of women (e.g. a Kubbi man in relation to all Ippata women; see p. 43 above) was no more evidence of a previous state of group marriage in Australia than the fact that the French word *femme* means both 'wife' and 'woman' would be an argument for a similar state of affairs in France. Second, the inference from terminology to behaviour required the absurd conclusion that, because a woman applied the same terms to her sisters' offspring as to her own, she must therefore have given birth to them; or, alternatively, that the whole group of women had produced the children through some kind of joint parturition. Through false logic, Morgan's method led not only to the hypothetical condition of 'group marriage' but 'group motherhood' as well, and zoologists would no doubt be interested to hear of it.

Turning to the *pirrauru* institution, Thomas suggested that it could be more satisfactorily explained in terms of its contemporary functions than as a survival of a previous state. In most of its manifestations, the *pirrauru* was more accurately described as 'adelphic polyandry' than group marriage, i.e. a situation in which several brothers shared the same woman. This was probably a consequence of the polygynous practices of older men, which created a shortage of women available to younger men. Polyandry through the *pirrauru* institution thus made provision for the sexual needs of a younger brother, while conversely it ensured that the older brother's wife would be protected during his absence, e.g. from abduction.

Thomas's book seemed like the *coup de grâce* for group marriage on behalf of the British anthropological establishment. Yet before the next year was out, one of the most influential members of the younger generation had sought to revive it. W.H.R. Rivers was a medical scientist who had gained first-hand experience of native cultures as a member of a Cambridge expedition to the Torres Straits Islands in 1898. In a paper written in honour of E.B. Tylor[21] in 1907, he took issue with the prevailing tendency among his colleagues to dismiss any scheme which suggested that human social organization might have begun with connubial arrangements of the kind suggested by Morgan. Far too much weight had been placed on Darwin's objection, on the basis of which Mr Thomas had jocularly proposed the notion of 'group motherhood' as a *reductio ad absurdum*. But if we take motherhood to encompass rearing as well as parturition, the notion is not absurd at all. On the contrary, it accords well with what we know of infant nurture in contemporary savage cultures, where groups of closely related females share in the tasks of child-care to the extent of suckling

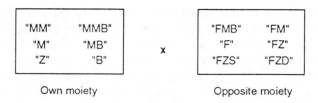

Fig. 4   *Group marriage between matri-moieties.*

each other's offspring. In circumstances of group marriage, individual motherhood would have as little significance for a child as individual fatherhood, and accordingly the use of common terms for 'mother and 'father' would arise naturally.

Although Rivers regarded certain aspects of Morgan's proposed evolutionary sequence as untenable, he nevertheless took seriously the possibility that classificatory kinship arose out of a state of group marriage. We know, he said, that dual division is a fundamental organizing principle of many contemporary primitive societies. Let us imagine, then, an archaic population divided into two moieties, each of whose active male members were jointly the husbands of the child-bearing women of the other. Let us assume that membership of these two original divisions depended on descent through females (given the greater certainty of motherhood) and that marriage within each division was forbidden. Individuals would thus belong to the division of their mothers (M), while their fathers (F) would belong to the opposite division. It would necessarily follow that mothers' mothers (MM) and their brothers (MMB) , mothers' brothers (MB), brothers (B) and sisters (Z) would all belong to one's own moiety; while fathers' mothers (FM) and their brothers (FMB), fathers' sisters (FZ), and fathers' sisters' children (FZS, FZD) would all belong to the opposite moiety (Fig. 4).

A comparison of Figure 4 with Figure 3 indicates close similarities between Rivers' hypothetical model for the origin of classificatory kinship systems and Australian section systems as described by Fison and Howitt. In the section systems, the grandparental generation in Figure 4 is classified with one's own generation, e.g. 'MM' = 'Z', 'MMB' = 'B', 'FMB' = 'FZS', 'FM' = 'FZD'; or, more generally, alternate generations within each moiety are classified together. We may note in passing that while Rivers' moiety model prohibits sexual relations between brothers and sisters, and between mothers and sons, it allows them in principle between fathers and daughters (since they belong to opposite moieties). Section systems prohibit sexual intercourse in all three cases.

Rivers speculated that the original relationship terms would have connoted age-grade status rather than consanguinity. Thus 'Z' initially meant 'female child of my own moiety'; 'M' initially meant 'child-bearing woman of my own moiety'; 'MM' meant 'old woman of my own moiety'; 'F' meant active adult male of the opposite moiety; and so on. This, he thought, would help to account for the fact that in classificatory systems the terms often express status relationships between broad social categories (e.g. as in the Hawaian system, see above p. 39). The difficulty, however, was that it would entail applying different terms to the same person at different stages of his or her life cycle, e.g. I would address a female of my own moiety as 'Z' while she is a child, as 'M' when she becomes a child-bearing adult, and as 'MM' when she grows old. Having investigated at first hand kinship systems in three exotic cultures (two in the Torres Straits, one in south India), Rivers knew full well that the application of classificatory kinship terms normally remains constant throughout life, e.g. my 'Z' is always my 'Z'. It was also apparent that the terms are not merely indicators of age-status but as well are invested with definite ideas of blood relationships and ties of marriage, even though the terms are frequently applied to individuals with whom actual links cannot be traced. Rivers therefore postulated a gradual evolution of kinship systems in terms of which they came to express status less and ties of consanguinity and affinity more. How the transition came about, he was unable to say.

In the following year Andrew Lang, a versatile man of letters from Scotland, addressed the British Academy on 'The Origin of Terms of Human Relationship'. He was not convinced by Rivers' attempt to evade the Darwinian objection: even if children were unable to discriminate their mothers from other nurses, mothers would always know their own children. Group marriage would accordingly be unable to explain why sisters applied the same term to each other's offspring, as they do in all classificatory systems. A more plausible explanation, in Lang's view, was that classificatory terminology is an *extension* of pre-existing kinship terms for larger-scale social purposes. The available evidence indicated that Aborigines were quite capable of distinguishing between 'actual' and 'tribal' fathers, mothers, brothers, sisters, wives, sons, daughters and so on. By extending the original terms to more distant relatives, along with at least some of the duties, privileges and restrictions normally associated with them, it was possible to integrate small kin groups into larger political units. This was no mere system of salutations and courtesies, as his compatriot McLennan had maintained, but the very framework of archaic society.

The tempo of the inquiry was quickening. In 1910 a Polish scientist named Bronislaw Malinowski arrived in London to study sociology at the London School of Economics. Here his mentor was Edward

Pl. 4   *Aranda family with possessions in front of a bough shelter. This photograph, taken by Baldwin Spencer in 1896, exemplified what Malinowski judged to be the typical Aboriginal family.*

Westermarck, who two decades earlier had published a definitive work on *The History of Human Marriage*; and he was also in regular contact with Rivers. Malinowski chose as the subject for his doctoral thesis 'The Family among the Australian Aborigines' (published as a book in 1913). His stated objectives were limited and, as befitted a beginner, modest: 'I shall avoid making any hypothetical assumptions, or discussing general problems which refer to the origin or evolution of the family. I wish only to describe in correct terms and as thoroughly as possible all that refers to *actual* family life in Australia.'[22] The repercussions, as it turned out, were far from parochial. By demonstrating how Howitt and Spencer, the two leading Australianists, had allowed their theoretical loyalties to distort their representation of the facts of Aboriginal family life, Malinowski sealed the fate of evolutionism in British social anthropology and simultaneously established the foundation for a new paradigm preoccupied with empirical description and the sociological function of contemporary institutions.

Through the influence of Morgan and other prominent evolutionists of the previous century, the attention of observers in Australia had been directed away from the actual functions of social mechanisms towards alleged survivals of fictitious primeval conditions. In the process, Malinowski said, the culture of the Aborigines had come to be regarded as a museum of sociological fossils. With regard to sex and reproduction, the impression had been given that the continent once housed vast systems of group marriage, whose vestiges were still clearly in evidence at the present time. But group sex, if it occurs, is not the same as group marriage. Marriage, as Westermarck had pointed out, is rooted in family, not the reverse; and, in addition to conjugality, family life entails a mode of living together, a recognizable pattern of household economics, and enduring bonds between parents and offspring. The first question to settle, therefore, was the extent to which these various earmarks occurred in Australia.

In Malinowski's judgment, the available data indicated that throughout the continent a man held an over-right to his wife's sexuality, including the right to grant privileged access to others. Husbands expected fidelity from their wives and punished them severely for alleged infractions. Family encampments typically consisted of a man, his wife or wives, and their pre-pubertal offspring. At night each family slept in the open around its own fire, separated from neighbouring families by a dozen yards or so; or, depending on climate and season, inside a temporary shelter. Husbands did not normally intrude into each other's camping areas, and on no account would a visitor from another community approach the fire of a married man unless formally invited to do so. Parental love was much in evidence; and children were protected, nourished and indulged by their fathers as well as their mothers. Marriage unions were expected to last until the death of one or other of the partners, and attachments between parents and offspring continued for a lifetime.

The weight of evidence was that the individual family, as characterized above, prevailed as the basic unit of social organization in all the tribes so far observed. The next matter to clarify was in what sense, if any, group marriage could also be said to occur. Applying Westermarck's definition of marriage, the issue was whether cases occurred in which a plurality of males and females constituted an identifiable residential unit, had regular sexual relations with each other, acted as parents to the offspring of the group, and contributed to the group's subsistence and welfare. If they did occur, they could reasonably be classed as instances of the group family, as compared with the individual family.

Malinowski had no hesitation in disqualifying all cases of ceremonial licence. These ephemeral liaisons conducted in the excitement of large tribal gatherings did not result in bonds of family, such as develop from living and eating together, and rearing children. The same applied to occasional sexual hospitality accorded to visitors. With regard to the *pirrauru* institution, while it must be conceded that it formalized a sexual relationship subsidiary to the primary marital union established through bestowal, its group character was problematic. Typically, a man cohabited with a *pirrauru* partner only during the absence of her husband; or when visiting a neighbouring community, especially on the occasion of a large ceremony. Spencer and Gillen, it was true, had reported that Arabunna *piraungaru* partners and their spouses lived together in a group, but evidence of common interests in subsistence and child-care was entirely lacking. No doubt the formalized wife-sharing arrangements of the Dieri and their neighbours came closer to group marriage than anything else so far reported; but, in Malinowski's view, even they fell a long way short of realizing the concept in the sense required by Morgan. Finally, as to whether shared access to women in any of its forms constituted evidence of a previous state of group marriage, Malinowski declined to offer an opinion. The question could lead only to sterile speculation.

With the phantom of group marriage now banished to the realm of science fiction, the way was clear for an explanation of classificatory kinship in terms of its contemporary social functions. In the same year that Malinowski published *The Family among the Australian Aborigines*, Radcliffe-Brown submitted the first results of his field research in Western Australia. This was followed by a series of articles on kinship and social organization in various parts of Australia, culminating in his comprehensive and classic monograph on *The Social Organization of Australian Tribes*. There Radcliffe-Brown not only rejected the evolutionist approach to the problem of classificatory kinship but offered a functionalist account in its place. In a final and decisive confrontation, using ethnographic materials from four North American Indian tribes, he confuted Morgan on his home ground.[23]

Radcliffe-Brown's disagreement with Morgan began in 1904, when he studied kinship theory at Cambridge under Rivers. Despite the evolutionist leanings of his mentor, he regarded the method of 'conjectural history' as futile and obstructive; in the case of classificatory kinship, it was demonstrably false. Morgan had assumed that, because vernacular kinship terms made no sense when translated into English, they must be relics of extinct marriage practices. But once we demonstrate that the terms make perfectly good sense within their own semantic systems, the resort to imaginary conditions in the past becomes an unnecessary obfuscation.

By 1930 Radcliffe-Brown had worked out a set of principles sufficient to explain all the main varieties of kinship classification found among the Aborigines, though later he refined some of his descriptions and designations. The most important principle was what he initially called 'the equivalence of brothers'[24] and then, more accurately, 'the unity of the sibling group'.[25] The principle requires that for the purposes of terminology Ego treats as equivalent any two individuals related to each other as either brothers or sisters (e.g. F and FB; M and MZ; FF and FFB; MM and MMZ). A corollary or extension of the principle requires that two siblings apply the same kinship terms to others, including their respective descendants (e.g. a man and his sister use the same terms when referring to his children, and the same terms when referring to hers; whereas husbands and wives use different terms). A second principle of great structural significance was 'the merging of alternate generations',[26] which requires that for the purposes of terminology Ego treats as equivalent any two individuals of the same sex who are two generations apart and who are connected by descent in the male line (e.g. for a male Ego: FF, B and SS; FFZ, Z and SD; FFF, F and S; FFFZ, FZ and D).

Through the application of these basic principles (in conjunction with others indicated by Radcliffe-Brown, which we may omit here), an indefinitely large number of relatives of varying degrees of genealogical distance are classified together under a small number of named categories. Thus an individual has hundreds of relatives whom he or she addresses as 'father', 'mother', 'brother', 'sister' and so on. For all relatives denoted by the same term, there is 'normally some element of attitude or behaviour that is regarded as appropriate to them and not to others'.[27] But there are also important distinctions within each category, especially between near and distant relatives. Every term in an Australian system of terminology may be regarded as having a primary meaning e.g. 'own father' as distinct from 'classificatory father'.[28] Indeed, the systems all depend upon the recognition of primary relatives constituting the nuclear family, whose existence Malinowski established beyond doubt in 1913. Kin classification, by extending the sentiments of family life outwards along lines dictated by the principles of classification, creates a framework for a wider social order (cf. Lang, see p. 49 above).[29]

What are the main implications for the regulation of sex and reproduction? Within the nuclear family there are four opposite-sex relationships: H/W, M/S, F/D, B/Z. Sexual intercourse is forbidden in the last three. Hence, as a concomitant of the system of kin classification, sexual intercourse is forbidden between males and their classificatory daughters, mothers and sisters; conversely, between females and their classificatory sons, fathers and brothers. If we return to the section system (Figure 3, p. 42), we see that the primary female kin of a male Ego (viz. M, Z, D) are in the three sections whose females are all forbidden to him (viz., respectively, Ippata, Buta and Kapota); conversely, the primary male kin of a female Ego (viz. F, B, S) are in the three sections whose males are all forbidden to her (viz., respectively, Kubbi, Kumbo and Ippai). The remaining quarter of the opposite-sex population in each case (viz. Mata, Murri) are available as spouses. In essence we could say that the system of reproduction has been generated by the intra-familial incest prohibitions in conjunction with the principles of kin classification.

Radcliffe-Brown considered Morgan's hypothesis of a prior state of group marriage to be 'one of the most fantastic in a subject that is full of fantastic hypotheses'.[30] That may well be so. Yet one wonders in what sense his own alternative approach ruled it out of court. Presuming that the principles of classification have a history, albeit conjectural, they would not be incompatible with the kind of arrangement imagined by Morgan. More to the point, if every kin term has a primary meaning and entails a common element of attitude or behaviour, what is there to rule out sex as the common element in the case of the classificatory term 'spouse'?

By adopting a legalistic approach to marriage, Malinowski and Radcliffe-Brown were able to argue successfully that everywhere in Australia the unit of reproduction and child-rearing was the individual family. Nowadays we might take more account of *de facto* relationships and their consequences. It is worth recalling that when Morgan invoked group marriage as an explanation of Iroquois kin classification he had in mind arrangements in which men related to each other as brothers co-habited with women related to each other as sisters. Although Malinowski relegated the matter of polygyny among the Aborigines to a brief addendum,[31] it is well attested that senior men often had two or more wives. Not uncommonly the wives were related to each other as true or close classificatory sisters. Wife-sharing between brothers has also been widely reported, not only by Howitt's correspondents in the last century but by twentieth-century professionals as well.[32] When *de jure* sororal polygyny is combined with *de facto* adelphic polyandry (as when, for example, a polygynous husband grants sexual privileges to his unmarried younger brothers), we have a situation at least approximating to group marriage in Morgan's sense. The same could be said of arrangements between two monogamous brothers to share each other's wives. Normally such *de facto* arrangements are entered into through tacit understandings or informal agreements. In the notable case of the Dieri, we appear to have ceremonial authorizations as well.

One of the subjects that particularly interested Malinowski was sexual jealousy.[33] Of its existence among the Aborigines he had no doubt: 'That... such instincts of jealousy are not absent, that they are, on the contrary, very strongly developed, is evident from nearly all the facts quoted...'[34] How was it possible, then, to reconcile such well-attested sexual jealousy with equally well-attested wife-sharing? Malinowski suggested that the instinct was modified in the Aboriginal case by culturally-endorsed values of generosity and hospitality; men shared because they were under public pressure to do so. No doubt this was so, but it should also be said that altruism was usually alloyed with self-interest. The *pirrauru* institution, as Northcote Thomas noted, provided a husband with a degree of insurance against his wife's abduction during his absences from home.[35] Furthermore, privileged access was presumably offered to trading partners and men of influence with an eye to economic and political advantage. In regard to the problem of sexual jealousy, the critical variable in most varieties of wife-sharing was conscious control of the woman's sexuality by her husband. Writing last century of the Port Lincoln tribes of South Australia, Rev. Schurmann recorded that: 'Although the men are capable of fierce jealousy if their wives transgress unknown to them, yet they frequently send them out to other parties, or exchange with a friend for a night.'[36] The observation may exemplify a general truth, at least for the Aborigines.

It seems clear in retrospect that *de facto* group marriage occurred on a small scale among the Aborigines, never as a total system of the kind postulated by Fison and Howitt but as an option, usually informal but sometimes formal, within regimes favouring polygyny. Undoubtedly kin classification of the Australian type was compatible with it, and might even be said to have been conducive to it. In the area where I did my research, the terms for 'wife' and 'mother' were respectively *mangga* and *ama*. If a man wanted to indicate that he did not regard a

particular classificatory 'wife' as a potential sexual partner (for instance, he might wish to affirm a relationship of trust with her
husband), he ceased addressing her as *mangga* and called her *ama*
instead. I learnt this during a period in my fieldwork when I would sit
with my mentor outside my tent, watching people pass by and asking
him what relationship term I should apply to them. Because he was
classified as my 'brother', I knew that (in accordance with the principle
of the unity of the sibling group) he and I should always use the same
terms. I was therefore puzzled when, on observing a young woman
walking past, he said: 'That woman is your wife, but she's my mother.'
After hearing the same formula applied to a number of other women, I
realized from his tone of voice that it was a kind of joke: '*You* could
have sexual relations with her, but the thought wouldn't enter my
head.' Eventually when, with growing confidence, I turned the joke on
him, he collapsed with laughter.

With reference at least to Australia, then, the proper treatment for
Morgan's theory may be to reject it and then turn it on its head: group
marriage does not explain kin classification, but kin classification may
help to explain group marriage. It is now clear beyond reasonable
argument that even if fully fledged group marriage in Morgan's sense
had once prevailed throughout the continent, it would not account for
some of the most conspicuous characteristics of the systems of classification (e.g. the merging of alternate generations). At best it would
account for the classification of some collaterals with lineal kin, but at
the cost of assuming a temporal disjunction between putative past
practices and contemporary terminology, especially in areas for which
there is no evidence of even *de facto* group marriage. The concept of
'cultural survivals out of tune with current practice' lacks conviction.
Hence nothing remains of the theory except the facts adduced in the
process of testing it. From this body of information we can conclude
that when principles of kin classification create broad categories of
males and females who address each other as 'husband' and 'wife',
sporadic crystallization of small-scale 'group mating' (or partner
sharing) may be facilitated. The discovery of this grain of truth does
little, of course, to rehabilitate Morgan and his loyal Australian
disciples on the issue of the evolution of marriage among the Aborigines. Nevertheless, it is probably better than being remembered for
one of the most notable fantasies in the history of anthropology.

4

The woman question

Early in 1868 *The Anthropological Review* published an essay by Paul Broca entitled 'Anthropology'. In the course of a state-of-the-art overview, Dr Broca touched briefly on the subject of women. In normal circumstances, he said, the mission of woman is to bring forth children, suckle them, and attend to their early education; the father's role is to provide for the family's subsistence. Everything that affects this normal order has consequences for the evolution of races. It follows that the condition of women in society must be carefully studied by the anthropologist.[1]

There was a good response. In December 1868 Luke Pike Esq. addressed Fellows of the Anthropological Society of London on the claims of women to political power. In general he thought they were poor. In June 1869 George Harris, Barrister-at-Law, discoursed on the mental and moral distinctions occasioned by the difference of sex. Although in both areas women had shown potential, their actual performance was disappointing. In a second paper on the same occasion J. McGrigor Allan confessed that when his attention was first directed to the 'woman question' he firmly believed that the mental and moral differences between the sexes could be removed by education. After fifteen years of personal experience and anthropological study he was convinced they were ineradicable.[2]

In general the papers were well received. Nevertheless, one or two of the Fellows thought the judgments passed on the ladies had been unduly severe. Dr Drysdale made a passing reference to the liberal views of John Stuart Mill. Mr Lewis preferred to think of woman not as inferior but as complementary. Mr Dendy thought the papers were moral exercises, replete with truisms and too diffuse for discussion. He was inclined to agree with them but wished they had set out something more on which to found an argument.

Two years later his wish was granted. In *The Descent of Man*, published in 1871, Charles Darwin argued that most of the higher divisions of the animal kingdom are characterized by two types of sexual struggle, one in which males try to drive off or kill their rivals, the other in which females seek to attract the most desirable males.[3] Qualities contributing to success tend to be preserved in succeeding generations and to constitute inherent differences between the sexes. The early history of our own species had undoubtedly been marked by conflict between competing males. Among the natives of Australia, for instance, women are the constant cause of war between tribes as well as conflict between individuals of the same tribe.[4] The 'law of battle' entailed that the strongest and boldest men acquired the most wives, procreated the greatest number of offspring, and hence propagated the characters that led to their own success. That is why man is more courageous, pugnacious and energetic than woman, and has a more inventive genius. He delights in competition, is naturally ambitious, and tends to be selfish. The competitive tendencies of woman, though undeniably present, are modified by her maternal instincts which, when generalized, give her temperament a tender and altruistic cast. Although overshadowed by man in physical strength and intellectual ability, she appears to be endowed with superior powers of intuition, rapid perception and imitation.[5]

Darwin acknowledged that sexual selection in human populations could be prevented or inhibited by certain practices said to be widespread among savages, viz. communal marriage, early betrothal, female infanticide and female slavery. Communal marriage would be an impediment because if 'no choice [is] exerted by either sex, there can be no sexual selection; and no effect will be produced on the offspring by certain individuals having had an advantage over others in their courtship'.[6] Early betrothal rules out choice by either partner on the basis of personal appearance. A similar consequence would occur where women are valued only as slaves or beasts of burden. Female infanticide might reduce the number of women to such a level of scarcity that considerations of beauty or ugliness would become inconsequential.

There can be little doubt that Darwin regarded the first of these impediments as potentially the most serious. It seemed that, for various reasons, anthropologists were in agreement that marriage in its earliest forms was communal. Three years earlier Mr L.H. Morgan had presented a case based on new discoveries about the nature of primitive kinship classification, and obviously the evidence had to be taken seriously.[7] All the same, Darwin found it difficult to believe that early man would be so radically different from modern man who in primitive communities typically acquires a plurality of wives and guards them jealously against rivals; or from quadrupeds who are armed with special weapons for gaining ascendancy over sexual competitors. The notion of communal marriage as the original human condition, mediating between non-human and later human forms, seemed highly improbable.[8]

Morgan replied briefly in his book *Ancient Society*, a discourse on the evolution of the family, property, and government published in 1877. The evidence for an evolving sequence of group-marriage forms, beginning with connubium between members of the same generation, was clearly embedded in kinship nomenclature. As to what preceded it, the logical inference was a general state of promiscuous intercourse, even though there was no direct evidence and despite the fact that such an eminent authority as Mr Darwin disagreed.[9] There the matter rested, and within a few years both Darwin and Morgan were dead. We should be clear, however, that Darwin's scepticism was directed against promiscuity not in the sense of an absence of marriage but in the sense that sexual relations were unconstrained by competition. Morgan certainly meant the former but it is not evident that he also meant the latter or that his theory required him to.[10] More importantly, Darwin's disagreement was by no means limited to the notion of random promiscuity at the beginning of human history; as well, it encompassed the putatively later and much longer phase of group marriage. Inasmuch as the concept of communal marriage meant sharing access to women as a matter of right, it presented an obstacle to assuming the normal operation of the principle of sexual selection, and hence to explaining observed physical and mental differences between men and women.

The notion of sexual communism as the original human condition would probably not have survived the Darwinian critique but for the fact that the Russian jurist Maxim Kovalevsky returned from a visit to the United States with a copy of *Ancient Society* and lent it to Karl Marx.[11] During 1880–2 Marx excerpted and summarized the book at considerable length, apparently with a view to presenting Morgan's findings within the framework of his own materialistic conception of history. Shortly after his death in 1883, his collaborator and literary executor Friedrich Engels discovered the notes and took it upon himself as a duty to complete the task Marx had begun. The result, published in 1884, was *The Origin of the Family, Private Property and the State*.[12]

In one vital respect Engels took the inquiry into an area left untouched by Morgan and Marx, namely the reproductive arrangements of animals, and in doing so confronted Darwin on his own ground. In Engels' judgment, the survival and evolution of mankind depended upon the formation of a social order above the level of the individual family. The main obstacle to its emergence was male sexual jealousy, which in higher vertebrates either dissolves the herd during mating time or makes herd life impossible altogether. The animal family stands in the way of social solidarity; and if we appeal to the possessive individual male in non-human species as a model for primal man, we render ourselves incapable of explaining how man transcended the anthropoid apes. The necessary condition for the formation of large and permanent groups for defensive purposes was mutual tolerance between adult males. The decisive transformation from beast to man thus occurred when sexual possessiveness gave way to sexual sharing. Human history began with the emergence of a society in which sexual intercourse was unrestricted and in which all adult males and females belonged to each other.[13]

Following Morgan and other scholars, Engels went on to argue that group marriage effectively ruled out the identification of natural fathers. In primeval society, therefore, the tracing of descent for social purposes was through mothers only, and the consequent formation of matri-lineages created economic and political conditions in which women were able to achieve a general and widespread supremacy. Their privileged position prevailed throughout the whole epoch in which humans lived by hunting and gathering, and came to an end with the rise of pastoralism and agriculture. Confronted with unprecedented wealth, men wished to pass it on to their own offspring. Accordingly, they abolished group marriage and restored the polygynous regimes of their animal forebears. Fatherhood was established through overlordship of the individual family, property was inherited in the male line, and political ascendancy passed to men. 'The downfall of maternal law', wrote Engels, 'was the historic defeat of the female sex.'[14] Not content with their victory in the wider political sphere, men seized the reins in the household, stripped women of their dignity, enslaved them, and used them as receptacles for the satisfaction of lust and machines for the generation of children.

The earliest writers on the English colony at Sydney noted that the native inhabitants subsisted entirely by fishing, hunting, and collecting wild fruits and vegetables. They also considered that the treatment of women among them was barbarous in the extreme. The typical manner in which men acquired wives was by theft from enemy tribes. Caught unawares in the bush, a woman would be stunned by a blow on the head, dragged back to the ravisher's home territory and forced to become his spouse. Thereafter she lived in a state of servility, fear and physical suffering. All women bore the marks of male brutality on their scalps, and elsewhere on their bodies. Sad to relate, it was often found that the victims of domestic violence had themselves contributed to the quarrels by irritating or inflaming the passions of their menfolk.[15]

The theme of marriage-by-capture persisted in descriptions of the Aborigines well into the nineteenth century. With growing familiarity, however, it became evident to observers that another, more civilized,

Pl. 5 Marriage ceremony. The original drawing for this picture was probably done by J. Arago, draftsman in Freycinet's journey around the world. The expedition spent some three months in New South Wales in 1819, but apart from the title ("Cérémonie préliminaire d'un mariage, chez les sauvages') there is no documentation. Whatever the basis for the representation, it nicely illustrates McLennan's conception of 'marriage-by-capture'.

method was also widely practised – the betrothal of infant females to adult males. In 1865 the Scottish legal scholar John McLennan, noting the contemporary coexistence of the two systems, argued that the more violent form had once prevailed alone, not only among the Australians but throughout the world as the original prehistoric method of acquiring a wife.[16] One of McLennan's main sources was George Grey, who indeed described abduction as the common fate of young, good-looking women. But far from regarding the method as primary, Grey explained it as a consequence of infant bestowal and the monopoliza-tion of sexually mature females by old men. In order to acquire a wife through betrothal, a man had to wait many years after reaching adulthood. Wife-stealing by abduction was an alternative frequently practised, notwithstanding the considerable risks to the abductor and the unavoidable damage to his prize.[17]

Grey was the first to note reciprocal obligations in bestowal arrange-ments and to appreciate their role in the aggrandizement of harems: men gave their daughters to each other, and the more daughters a man had, the greater his chances of acquiring additional wives.[18] Unfortu-nately the denial of marital choice to females, in conjunction with the presence of a virile and audacious bachelor class, created a chronic security problem compounded by the roving style of life and the opportunities provided by the Australian bush. A stern and vigilant jealousy was the trademark of every married man. When a husband detected or suspected infidelity, he subjected his wife to cruel and brutal punishment. If he felt able to inflict injury on her paramour, either through his own fighting skills or with the aid of kinsmen, he threw as many spears as possible before others restrained him. Men came to the aid of other men. No one came to the aid of a woman.[19]

Later in the century A.W. Howitt confirmed the primacy and ubiquity of infant bestowal.[20] Nevertheless, reports from various parts of the continent also corroborated the occurrence of marriage by capture as an alternative. The typical context was warfare between tribes, or even clans of the same tribe. It was important, however, to bear in mind two qualifications. First, class or section regulations applied even to captives; women taken in battle could not be appro-priated by men whose relationship with them would be classified as incestuous. Second, marriage by capture, which took place against the woman's will, had to be distinguished from marriage by elopement, which took place with her complicity. Both occurred frequently, and both resulted from the same basic cause: the monopoly of wives held by old men.[21]

By the turn of the century the condition of Aboriginal women was firmly established in the literature as 'abject'. Noting that various authors had described them as 'slaves', the Dutch ethnologist H.J.

Nieboer began his classic treatise on *Slavery as an Industrial System* (1910) by considering whether the usage was justifiable. On technical grounds he thought it should be classified as rhetoric. In any case, their condition was not as bad as commonly supposed. Girls' wishes in regard to marriage were sometimes listened to, elopement was often successful, women were clearly capable of speaking up for themselves, husbands did not enjoy complete freedom of action in relation to their wives (whose relatives afforded them some protection), and there was evidence of affection between marital partners. Although the lot of Aboriginal women appeared hard when viewed through Western eyes, experienced observers considered them to be, on the whole, 'fairly happy, merry and contented'.[22]

In 1913 Malinowski endorsed Nieboer's assessment in the course of his painstaking review of the nineteenth-century literature on Aboriginal domestic life.[23] As to obtaining a wife, it was now evident that throughout the continent the normal, legal and peaceful method was by bestowal. Once a commitment had been made, the husband was expected to give food and services to his parents-in-law; in many tribes he was also expected to arrange the gift of a bride to a member of his wife's family. By undertaking to discharge these contractual obligations, a man acquired a right of property over his wife. Upon his death she normally passed to his brother or some other close relative. Other methods of obtaining a wife were illegal and usually violent, since they necessarily encroached on existing rights. The elopement of betrothed or married women with bachelors was common, and inevitably led to conflict between the elopers and the aggrieved husband. Abduction of women during warfare no doubt occurred from time to time, but early reports of marriage by stunning-and-dragging could safely be dismissed as fanciful. Malinowski noted that it was only in marriage by elopement that males and females exercised personal choice. In the normal case they acted in accordance with arrangements made on their behalf by others.

Twenty-five years later Phyllis Kaberry submitted her doctoral thesis in Malinowski's department at the London School of Economics.[24] Published in 1939 as *Aboriginal Woman: Sacred and Profane*, with modest descriptive aims, it marked an important turning point in the study of male–female relationships. Whereas the all-male cohort of observers in the nineteenth century had pitied Aboriginal women as victims of male oppression, Dr Kaberry defended them against the misrepresentations and devaluations of male ethnographers. Far from being chattels and slaves, they had rights, privileges and complex social personalities on a par with men. The impression of drudgery and servility was superficial. Beyond the digging-stick and dilly-bag lay a rich social, sexual and spiritual life which so far had either escaped observation or been denied importance.

The sexual division of labour, in accordance with which men hunted and women foraged, had been noted from the earliest days of colonization. There was general agreement among observers that (a) women carried heavier burdens than men; (b) their work was more arduous, monotonous and time consuming; and (c) their contribution to family subsistence was greater than men's, partly because of the unreliability of hunting and partly because the hunter typically distributed game to others as well as his own wife and children. Kaberry accepted these assertions, with reservations; but she rejected the inference that, by compelling women to undertake the drudgery of foraging, men freed themselves for the joys of the chase. Men hunted because of their natural endowments of speed and strength; and by its nature hunting required them to be as unencumbered as possible. The life of the pedestrian hunter was full of hardship and disappointment; by comparison foraging was leisurely, dependable and leavened by the fellowship of female companions. Moreover, the unreliability of hunting conferred an advantage on women in domestic disputes that they were not slow to exploit. To counter the superior physical strength of the male, a wife could simply pack her belongings and move into the camp of a relative for a few days. With the withdrawal of his source of vegetable staples, as well as his transport for firewood, water and other heavy burdens, the husband soon came to his senses and sought reconciliation.

Much had been made of infant bestowal and child marriage to old men. Although this was repugnant to most Europeans, the system contained advantages for women that deserved to be mentioned. The girl's mother shared equal rights of bestowal with the father and received an equal share of the gifts made by the future husband following betrothal. Any suggestion that the arrangement entailed the brutal rape of a minor was totally misplaced. From the age of about nine the girl periodically visited her husband's camp and slept at his fireside. Full intercourse did not occur until after she reached puberty. All girls were thus eligible for a solicitous induction into sexual life. There were no spinsters in Aboriginal society, and an attitude to sex of healthy enjoyment was inculcated from an early age in girls as well as boys. Although women were often much younger than their husbands, they were usually able to combine the security of marriage with the excitement of clandestine affairs. If thoroughly dissatisfied with their marital partners, they took their chances and eloped. One woman at Forrest River had four successive husbands and helped the second to kill the first.

In a life that was not meant to be easy, Aboriginal women had

Pl. 6   Central Australian woman dancing for land. This photograph of Mona Heywood Nungarrayi was taken during a Land Claim hearing in 1981.

obviously worked out how to look after themselves; and though aspects of their existence might arouse our pity, there was also much to be admired and envied. But what of their alleged exclusion from spiritual life? The influential writings of Spencer and Gillen early in the century had given central Australian male secret cults a permanent place in the history of world religion, while relegating women's menstruation and childbirth rites to the category of 'Peculiar Native Customs'. More recently, in a book entitled *A Black Civilization* (1937), William Lloyd Warner had argued that through religion the men of Arnhem Land became progressively sacred, while the women remained forever profane. Their exclusion from the great dramatizations of cosmic forces performed by initiated men kept them at the same level of ignorance in religious matters as uninitiated boys. As Warner put it, 'the principle of the social bifurcation of the sexes has been used to create the lowest status, that of women and children'.[25]

Kaberry found this very difficult to accept. Aboriginal women everywhere shared with men a common religious heritage based on equal ownership of the land.[26] Within each clan all members, female as well as male, were linked without discrimination to the same founding ancestors through sacred sites and spirit centres on the clan's land. The benefits as well as the responsibilities were in principle the same for both sexes. It was true that men performed their ritual duties on a scale and with a flourish that women rarely matched. This was their choice; and though women were sometimes impressed by these vainglorious displays, they were never overawed. Male ethnographers had dwelt upon the centrality of cult icons for tribal religious history, and upon the fact that women were never allowed to see them. No one would deny the significance of these repositories of sacred tradition. But – and here Kaberry played her trump card – women had secret ceremonies of their own which, although largely ignored in the literature, were every bit as sacred as those of the men.

In the Kimberleys the main women's rite was known as *Yirbindji*. Young women were particularly enthusiastic; and on each of the five occasions she witnessed a performance, Kaberry was struck by the boldness with which the participants warned the men to stay away. Just as the latter's ceremonies were dangerous to the uninitiated, so was *Yirbindji*. But there was an interesting difference: whereas men ritually commemorated the foundation of the social and cosmic order in the Dreamtime, women attempted to throw off the shackles of the marriage system in the here-and-now. It was not merely that participants in the *Yirbindji* told Kaberry they wished to be free of their old husbands, nor even that they hoped by magical means to excite the interest of younger and more attractive alternatives. The truly subversive intent of the ritual was manifest in songs and dances specifying the tribal son-in-law as the illicit lover *par excellence*. By flagrantly inverting the taboo on this pivotal relationship, *Yirbindji* enabled women to give vent to rebellious feelings against the systematic control of their sexuality.[27] At the same time it gave them the opportunity to pursue particular object choices outside marriage, regardless of relationship categories. As the participants returned to the main camp, displaying phallic designs painted above their navels, young men grinned and joked with them; older men stood silent and subdued. Two of Kaberry's friends told her they had slept with their lovers on the night after the ceremony. Others lived in confident hope.

Not long after World War 2, when Catherine Berndt reported her findings on the *Yirbindji* in an adjoining area, she took issue with Kaberry for ascribing to it a purely love-magic function.[28] Its deeper religious significance was to be found in associations with men's fertility cults, in particular common links to the Munga-munga Sisters. The choice of the latter from the mythological repertoire was certainly appropriate for love-magic purposes, since the Munga-munga Sisters were renowned for their lasciviousness and promiscuity. And indeed the songs transcribed by Dr Berndt expressed the erotic wishes of the singers in sequence with invocations of ritually potent phallic symbols and accounts of the Munga-munga's Dreamtime adventures. It would seem, at least on the evidence presented, that the esoteric content was meant to intensify the love-magic purpose rather than to transcend it. And if, as appears to have been the case, women as they grew older placed increasing importance upon cosmic associations, perhaps it was because the erotic and dissident elements in the ceremony had not only lost urgency for them but had actually become inimical to their interests within the bestowal system.

The power wielded by Aboriginal women through contracts with the future husbands of their daughters was given its proper due a decade later in an article on Tiwi marriage by Jane Goodale (subsequently included in her book *Tiwi Wives*).[29] Among the Tiwi of Bathurst and Melville Islands the basic contract was what we might term 'mother-in-law bestowal', as compared with 'wife bestowal'. It was initiated on the occasion of a girl's menarche, normally by which time she was married. After the menstrual flow had ceased, her father placed a spear between her legs and then presented it to a man he had chosen as her son-in-law. The latter embraced it and henceforth addressed it as 'wife'. As holder of the spear, he was entitled to claim all the daughters produced by his newly acquired mother-in-law. In return he undertook to provide her with goods and services until she died. To that end he normally lived close to her (though observing a strict taboo on verbal communication) until his wife's birth, and often for a considerable time after. If he failed to serve his mother-in-law to her satisfaction before marriage, she was entitled to void the contract (a power not held by the girl's father). Men composed songs expressing the hope that their mothers-in-law would not go back on their promises, as well as anger at the power they held over them. Sometimes men quarrelled with their fathers-in-law; but no matter how hard-pressed they might be to fulfil the demands of their mothers-in-law, they kept their temper with them.

Goodale's article was not less important for the fact that, two years before its publication in 1962, two male anthropologists had described Tiwi bestowal almost entirely in terms of the benefits derived by men.[30] According to Charles Hart, who had lived with Tiwi bands in the late 1920s, and Arnold Pilling, who worked in the area twenty-five years later, the right of betrothal unquestionably belonged to the girl's father. Daughters were assets which a man promised in marriage to other men with a view to increasing his own wealth, influence and prestige. No mention was made of the spear ceremony at menarche or of any advantages enjoyed by the girl's mother (though the authors noted that commitments entered into by the mother's father might constrain the father's choice of son-in-law). In commenting on these omissions, Goodale insisted that the basic contract in the Tiwi marriage system was established when a man bestowed his daughter not as a wife but as a mother-in-law. She acknowledged that, in doing so, the father was usually hoping to further his own career. At the same time, he was indubitably furthering his daughter's career, since it was through the mother-in-law/son-in-law relationship that 'women gained a balance of power over a male'.[31] The birth of daughters consolidated her ascendancy and assured her of security and influence as she grew older. With rare exceptions, barren women were social nonentities.

Given that male anthropologists normally worked with men, and female anthropologists with women, discrepancies between their findings were probably inevitable. It was not always the case, however, that the role of the female anthropologist was to correct an undervaluation of women's power by her male counterpart. In 1970 my colleague Annette Hamilton reported that, whereas I had attributed a primary right of bestowal to mothers among the Gidjingali of northern Arnhem Land, the mothers themselves stoutly denied it. When she questioned a number of women on the point, none identified herself as the bestower of her daughter, and all maintained that mothers did not possess such a right. Some attributed the bestowal to the daughter's maternal grandmother, others to her maternal uncle, and others again to her father. Girls themselves usually stated that they had been given in marriage by their fathers.[32]

Hamilton's explanation for this puzzling contradiction was that, because marriage promises so often generated resentment and conflict, no one was particularly anxious to claim responsibility for them. It was an unfortunate fact of life that young women regularly objected to the choices made on their behalf. As the bond between mother and daughter played a key role in forming networks of mutually supportive matrilineal kinswomen, as well as being of lifelong importance in itself, women collectively had an interest in dissociating themselves from the disposal of their female offspring. For men likewise, promises entailed risks as well as benefits. In a situation where demand for wives always exceeded supply, claiming the right to bestow a girl in marriage was as potentially invidious as claiming the right to receive her. Accordingly, men insulated themselves against grievances by officially shifting responsibility for bestowals to their wives.

Contracts among the Gidjingali were in the nature of private treaties rather than public declarations of commitment. There was nothing comparable to the Tiwi spear presentation, and information about promises spread informally and not always reliably. When I asked men who had the right to bestow a girl in marriage, I was told it belonged to her mother and maternal uncles. Because a woman's reproductive life was taboo to her brother, and also because not all women had brothers anyway, informants tended to give central place to the mother. My chief mentor Gurrmanamana, who took it as a serious duty to instruct me in 'custom-law' regardless how people might behave in practice, insisted that the father had 'nothing to do with it'. The mothers questioned by Hamilton apparently wanted nothing to do with it either. Nonetheless, as both parents stood to gain by bestowals, we may suspect that both often took part in them, at least behind the scenes. The formal transposition of authority to the maternal uncle helped to resolve latent tension between male dominance and mother-right, while buck-passing in the forum provided a shield against charges of wrongful actions and outbreaks of generalized disaffection.[33]

The coalition of interests between a woman and her son-in-law was brought out vividly by Gurrmanamana in a text on pregnancy and childbirth dictated not long after he had described the rules of bestowal. The four characters are a man, his wife, his mother-in-law and his unborn male offspring. The young wife is portrayed for the most part as an instrument of procreation in the hands of her mother and husband. They feed her fish so that the baby inside may eat and grow bigger. Her husband commands her to take precautions against injuring the child. Her mother exhorts her during parturition to sit straight so that the baby's bones will not be broken, and she urges the child to come quickly so she can present it to her son-in-law. Seen in wider perspective, the text represents procreation as the outcome of investments by the father and his mother-in-law under the terms of unspoken understandings between them. The son-in-law has provided food for his mother-in-law in return for the promise of her daughter. The marriage, and now the birth, have consolidated her contribution to his status as a married man and father. The son-in-law for his part has been diligent in carrying out his responsibilities to both her and her daughter. He has thus earned the right to rear the child as his son.[34]

Hamilton's paper on Gidjingali bestowal practices was published in a collection of essays on *Women's Role in Aboriginal Society*, edited by Fay Gale.[35] In the same volume Nicolas Peterson suggested on the basis of his Arnhem Land field research that co-residence of patri-kin and in-laws was probably a regular feature of band composition throughout Australia.[36] The core of each band comprised senior men of the same patri-clan, their wives, some of their children, young sons-in-law, and possibly elderly mothers-in-law. The dynamic force under-lying this widespread formation, according to Peterson, was the need for older men to have access to the productive labour of younger women, e.g. their daughters. But we should note that older women also had needs; moreover, through their notable ability to produce female offspring, they had the means of satisfying them. The obligation of a husband to provide his wife's mother with a regular supply of meat was as much a part of the force that kept men within the ambit of their in-laws as the duty of a daughter to her ageing father.[37]

Clinching evidence for the active participation of women in bestowal arrangements was presented a decade later by Diane Bell in a paper called 'Desert Politics: Choices in the "Marriage Market"'. One of the unusual features of marriage promises in central Australia as described by male-orientated ethnographers was that men bestowed their daugh-ters in return for the privilege of circumcising their future husbands. When a boy reached puberty, his kinsmen (maternal as well as paternal) chose the man who would remove his foreskin. Several years after the operation, when the lad was about 18, his circumciser promised him his baby daughter in marriage.[38] What Bell discovered was that, during a women's segment of the ritual, the boy's mother formally chose his mother-in-law before the men announced the identity of the circumciser. The women then collectively communicated the decision to the men. As the mother's choice was made indepen-dently, it seemed she had effectively determined the men's choice of circumciser (i.e. the husband of the woman chosen as mother-in-law). After the decision (and often before it), the relationship between the boy's mother and his future mother-in-law was one of solidarity and mutual advantage. Through the arranged marriage of their respective offspring, the former gained a daughter-in-law who in later years would become a comfort to her, while the latter gained a son-in-law who would provide her with meat and other goods for the rest of her life.[39]

Female ethnographers have thus established beyond reasonable argument that Aboriginal women had a substantial stake in the bestowal system, and that their willingness and ability to deploy their assets in female offspring to their own advantage made them anything but slaves to male oppressors. Of course, as the advantage depended upon depriving their daughters of an initial choice of husband, a consequence of the demonstration that women shared power with men is that they were also implicated in its oppressive applications. Not all female ethnographers have felt comfortable with this outcome, or known how to deal with it. Bell, for instance, maintained on the one hand that the sexual life of young Aboriginal women had much to be said for it: they flaunted their sexuality and enjoyed extra-marital affairs, while simultaneously learning 'to appreciate the charms of an older husband as he wooed her with gentleness and love rituals'.[40] On the other hand, she deplored the fact that, in accordance with a policy of non-intervention in 'tribal matters', white male officials in central Australia declined to oppose Aboriginal elders in their efforts to force their promised child brides to take up residence with them.

Whatever moral dilemmas they raised for her, Bell's data showed clearly that the life histories of many desert women were characterized by resolute struggles to effect their own sexual choices within a system heavily weighted against them, especially during early adulthood. Young women endured beatings and crippling wounds rather than give up affairs with men of their own age. Often they eloped; and although this course of action entailed even greater risks, especially to the female partner, cases occurred in which the union was eventually accepted as a *fait accompli*. If a woman stayed with her first husband until he died, she was expected to remarry in accordance with the wishes of his brothers. Not uncommonly she defied them, as well as her assigned new husband, by eloping with a man of her choice or by conducting affairs from her base in the widows' quarters. In all these adverse circumstances love-magic was available as a helpful adjunct. In a later publication Bell described the sexuality of women of the desert as 'theirs to bestow as they please'.[41] With as much truth the same could be said of the punishments inflicted upon them by their husbands.

During the 1970s Gillian Cowlishaw carried out an extensive survey of the literature on infanticide in Aboriginal Australia.[42] The practice was widely reported for communities still or until recently subsisting as hunters and gatherers, and most commentators supposed that the basic reason was adaptive: mothers sacrificed a new-born babe in order to ensure the survival of an older unweaned sibling. This seemed plausible enough until the investigation established that the first-born child was in fact most at risk. In seeking to throw light on the problem, Cowlishaw suggested that a young mother might be torn between instinctive nurturing responses and a wish to retaliate against those who controlled her sexuality. An early source from South Australia stated that women customarily killed their first-born offspring in order to avoid the trouble of rearing them, or to take revenge on them for the sufferings of childbirth. If we put to one side the imputation of irresponsibility and consider the situation of young women pressed into unwanted marriages, the information can be interpreted to mean that the physical pain of parturition provoked primiparous mothers into attacking or abandoning the neonate as both symbol and agent of their continuing servitude. Infanticide thus defied the marriage system by upsetting the expectations of those hoping to gain from the perpetrator's reproductive powers and, simultaneously, by removing an impediment to her covert strivings for sexual independence.

Given that love-magic ritual threatened the interests of the male establishment, it is hardly surprising that men were not invited along to help with the performance. By contrast, the exclusion of women from the major revelatory ceremonies is curious, since the necessity of carrying them out was often expressed in terms of the spiritual and material well-being of the whole community. Whether the sacred symbols were memorabilia of totemic creators and their ancestral pathways, or representations of the Mother-of-All or Father-of-All,[43] why should women have been prevented from seeing them on pain of death? In 1970 Isobel White hazarded an explanation based on an apparent paradox. Men's secret cults were concerned above all with the origins, maintenance and reproduction of life. Indeed, they were often referred to as fertility cults. Yet the sex with the more elaborate natural endowment for reproduction and nurture was barred from entry. The reason, according to White, was that men, unclear about their physical contribution to new life, had developed a compensatory metaphysical role. Whereas women were equipped to produce the carnal forms of human beings, men provided them with souls.[44]

Even more intriguing than female exclusion were myths, documented at length by Catherine Berndt in 1965,[45] describing how ancestral men had stolen the symbols of transcendental power from women and made them the basis of their secret cults. What women once owned, women nowadays were forbidden to see. To compound (or justify) the felony, men deployed the appropriated power to bring about the symbolic death and spiritual rebirth of their sons; and throughout Australia, when boys were taken away to be initiated, their mothers went into ritual mourning. The youths, believing themselves about to die, were brought into proximity with the transcendental source of life itself. Then, not dying after all, they were reborn through symbolic processes utilizing the blood of initiated members of the cult.

In 1971 I brought together material from various parts of northern and central Australia suggesting that when secret male cults ritually transformed youths into men of mystical understanding they usually did so on a female generative model.[46] In other words, natural birth provided men with a metaphor of spiritual rebirth. A year later Kenneth Maddock made an important connection between induction of young men into religious cults and protection of the sexual interests of their mentors. The induction process might last ten years or more, during which time young men were often secluded for long periods and in general exhorted to refrain from sexual intercourse (since practically all mature females were already the wives of their seniors). Instinctual denial, as Maddock put it, was clothed as a religious demand for which a religious gratification was promised.[47] In 1978 Ian Keen demonstrated how control of religious knowledge enabled senior men to gain young wives at the expense of younger men.[48] To participate in secret ritual was not merely to witness cosmic power but to absorb it; to be excluded was to remain on the spiritual level of women and children. Young men were therefore prepared to pay for membership in the currency of discipline, suffering and self-denial.

Maddock's hypothesis, considered in conjunction with Kaberry's material, strongly suggested the existence of a causal nexus between secret cults and gerontocratic polygyny. On the one hand, by diverting the energy of bachelors into esoteric religious attainments, male cults aided senior men in acquiring and protecting their monopoly of marriageable females; on the other hand, female cults defied the rights of venerable husbands and sought to re-focus the bachelors' minds on sex. This is a line of argument that I myself have pursued.[49] It is important to note, however, that not all anthropologists have found it persuasive. In her book *Daughters of the Dreaming*, published in 1983, Diane Bell set out to redress what she saw as an undue emphasis on competing sectional interests in the interpretation of Aboriginal religion, by drawing attention instead to its integrative function. In a chapter entitled 'We Follow One Law' she argued that, through their respective ceremonies, men and women worked on an equal footing towards maintaining society in accordance with laws laid down during the mystical period of creation known as the Dreamtime. Men stressed their creative power, women their role as nurturers. Far from being subversive, women's secret rituals were concerned with the well-being of the land, good health for all, and emotional management in the interests of social harmony.[50]

In 1980 Annette Hamilton, who had shifted her interests from

Pl. 7 Mangaridji family, East Alligator River. This photograph, taken in 1912 by Baldwin Spencer in sub-tropical Arnhem Land, shows a man with an unusually large polygynous household. Spencer was unsure whether the man had seven wives and three children, or six wives and four children. Either way, it would be a matter for astonishment to people of the Western Desert.

subtropical Arnhem Land to the Western Desert, foreshadowed Bell's findings on the relative independence of desert women without at the same time representing it as functional complementarity for the common good. Given the relative scarcity of large game, men would have had difficulty in surviving on their own products alone; women by contrast regularly exploited good supplies of eggs, birds, lizards, burrowing animals and grubs in addition to vegetable foods. A critical element in production technology was the heavy grindstone and mill used by women to produce meal from grass seeds. Men were thus unusually dependent on women's labour (as compared, say, with their counterparts in Arnhem Land), and nowhere was this more in evidence than in the provisioning of their major secret ceremonies. Though perhaps other factors were at work as well, the marked indispensability of women in desert economic life seemed to have provided them with a foundation of self-reliance and self-esteem upon which to build strong cult ideologies of their own. Through their secret ceremonies they sought to promote the physical aspects of human reproduction, the growth of girls, sexual morality, good health, and harmonious relations among women. Whereas love-magic in better-watered areas often seemed to be a subversive reaction to male dominance, in the Western Desert it was integrated into a religious complex affirming the right of women to pursue their sexual interests on a basis of gender equality. In Hamilton's opinion, cult-based solidarity in defence of women's interests was largely responsible for an unusually low rate of polygyny: among the people she lived with in north-west South Australia, two wives were possible but not common, three a matter for astonishment.

Towards the end of the decade, in a review of recent literature on gender in Aboriginal social life, Francesca Merlan expressed surprise at the degree to which Diane Bell had played down the sexual content of women's ritual. Female anthropologists before her had represented it as fundamental. Annette Hamilton, for instance, had written that the 'big secrets' of women's ceremonies in the Western Desert were statements about female sexuality that the participants communicated to each other but never to men. Merlan herself considered that some women's rituals placed 'a tremendous emphasis ... upon the constitu-tion of sexuality as a power conferred by the ceremony'.[51] No doubt men and women worked together for shared ends. The fact remained that men regularly sought to gain control of female sexuality for their own purposes, including that of cultivating relationships with other men;[52] conversely, women used secret rituals in an attempt to manip-ulate the sexuality of men.[53]

The work of Hamilton and Bell in desert regions undoubtedly focussed attention upon special conditions in which Aboriginal women had been able to develop unusually strong traditions of independence and cultural autonomy. Nevertheless, inequalities in the scale of male and female ritual, in male–female cooperation, and in sanctions against violation of secrecy raised serious difficulties for any suggestion of Australia-wide gender parity within a framework of complementarity. Nowhere were there to be found female equivalents to the great inter-tribal gatherings organized by men.[54] Men regularly pressed women into provisioning male secret ceremonies and participating in them as auxiliaries (by dancing or responding to men's calls from the secret ground). Sometimes their subordinate status was dramatized in 'rites of exclusion'.[55] No such demands or indignities were ever imposed on men. Finally, sanctions against women for discovering male secrets included rape and death. Male intruders into the ritual domain of women risked mystical retribution, but physical reprisals against them were unknown.

It is apparent from our review that the Australian data give no more support to Engels' assertion that women reigned supreme in early human history than to the associated hypothesis of communal mar-riage.[56] By the same token, Darwin's assumption that the acquisition of wives was largely a matter of strength and boldness among rival males is also untenable. Although such traits might well have contributed to success, they need to be assessed within cultural contexts where the 'law of battle' was heavily constrained by the 'rule of law'. Everywhere in Australia sexual availability was limited by wide-ranging incest prohibitions; and in respect of any female of an eligible category, some men had better claims than others on the basis of legally recognized genealogical connections.[57] Bestowers of girls were obliged to respect these rules. Within the range of choice available to them, no doubt they preferred men best able to contribute to the security, nourishment and well-being of the bestowers, the bestowed and, in due course, the latters' offspring. Some selective pressure may thus have been exerted on certain heritable characters, including fighting and hunting skills.

Similar skills would have conferred advantages on males when bestowed females reached puberty and began making alternative, though illicit, choices for themselves. It should not be forgotten, however, that men who sought to capitalize on such preferences needed strength and boldness not merely to resist the physical retalia-tion of injured husbands but to overthrow the weight of the law as well. What little evidence we have on this point suggests that obeying the law contributed at least as much to reproductive success as defying it.[58] The best results were probably achieved when Darwinian traits were combined with deference and genealogical good fortune. For example, in tribes where males had marriage rights to the daughters of their maternal uncles, the prospects for a youth with good fighting and hunting skills, respect for authority, and numerous maternal uncles would have been excellent. If in addition he developed political skills as he grew older, his success was virtually assured.

Just as Darwin's 'law of battle' applies up to a point,[59] so too is there a grain of truth in Engels' speculations. Although there is no evidence to suggest that all men ever shared sexual rights to all women within an Aboriginal tribe, the rules defining prohibited and eligible categories (especially as articulated in section and subsection systems) did establish a broad equality of opportunity. Ironically, the higher-level social formations whose emergence Engels thought depended on the elimination of sexual jealousy have been recently attributed by a modern Darwinist to the invention of law, whose function was 'to regulate and render finite the reproductive strivings of individuals and subgroups within societies, in the interests of preserving unity in the larger group'.[60]

While women may never have gained ascendency in prehistoric times, the Aboriginal evidence suggests that their procreative ability provided a basis for political power in two inter-related ways. First, in a context where the demand for wives was always likely to outstrip supply, men were prepared to invest in futures through contractual relationships with individuals classified as potential mothers-in-law. The latter's privileges as producers of female infants were protected by various male partners, especially their husbands and brothers, who gained advantages for themselves in return. Second, men compensated for their nebulous role in physical procreation by developing a metaphysical counterpart on a female procreative model. The exact terms on which initiated males participated in the spiritual reproduction of life were concealed from females, and revealed gradually to junior males in return for respect and subordination. Idiomatically the secret cultivation of mystic power was referred to as 'men's business', whereas pregnancy and parturition were designated by men as 'women's business'.[61] The power of men and women increased with seniority, in the one case through control of ritual knowledge and in the other through deployment of the products of procreation. Through a coalition of interests in restricting the freedoms of the young, Aboriginal societies thus developed as neither patriarchies nor matriarchies but double-gendered gerontocracies.

5

People without politics

In 1883 Prince Peter Kropotkin, an anarchist and Russian exile, was sentenced by a French court to five years imprisonment for associating with members of a proscribed political organization. During his incarceration he received a copy of a scientific paper by Karl Kessler, Dean of Zoology at the University of St Petersburg, who argued that mutual aid in animal species was as important in evolution as competition and struggle. This accorded not only with Kropotkin's political philosophy but with his observations of wildlife in Siberia as a young man. Following his early release in 1886 he took refuge in London, where he earned a humble living as a science writer.[1] In 1888 the monthly periodical *Nineteenth Century* published an essay by Thomas Huxley, setting out necessary conditions for the survival of the British economy: in brief, competitive labour-costs plus law and order. Kropotkin responded in a series of articles which he later published in a book called *Mutual Aid: A Factor of Evolution*.[2]

Huxley had long been the pre-eminent authority on Darwin's theory of evolution. Like Darwin, he had visited Australia as a young man and seen Aborigines at first hand. In extenuation of his low opinion of them, one of his biographers has observed that 'if like many Victorians he thought of them as children, at least he regarded them steadfastly as human beings'.[3] But only just. In the opening section of his 1888 essay, entitled 'The Struggle for Existence: A Programme', Huxley divided humanity into (1) 'ethical man', the member of society or citizen, and (2) 'non-ethical man', the primitive savage or man as a mere member of the animal kingdom. The latter, like any other animal, fought out the struggle for existence to the bitter end. He appropriated whatever took his fancy and, if he could, killed anyone who got in his way. In such circumstances the weak and stupid went to the wall, while the strong and cunning survived. Civilization is an attempt to moderate the struggle for existence by imposing a code of ethics on human behaviour, limiting the freedom of action of each man so that he does not interfere with the freedom of action of others. When men substituted mutual peace for the war of each against all, they created society out of anarchy.[4]

With all his undoubted mastery of nineteenth-century developments in biology, Huxley's conception of the political life of the savage was hardly more than a rehearsal of the archetypal European myth articulated by Thomas Hobbes two centuries earlier.[5] Working from first principles, Hobbes deduced that it was in the nature of men to compete for gain and glory and to defend their possessions and reputations. Unless constrained by a sovereign power, they quickly resorted to violence in order to achieve their objectives and habitually lived in a state of war of every man against every man, either in actual combat or readiness for it. In such circumstances, industry and arts were unable to flourish, and life was solitary, poor, nasty, brutish and short. One need not assume, Hobbes added, that this condition is located merely in antiquity. The savage inhabitants of many parts of America have no government whatsoever and to this very day live in the brutish manner described.

A century later, meditating in the forest of Saint-Germain, Jean-Jacques Rousseau conceived a contrary myth.[6] The life of original man was solitary but healthy, happy, good and free. Initially a lone hunter and forager, he came eventually to build a hut for himself and his mate, and in doing so created the sweetest sentiments known to the human male – conjugal and paternal love. Primitive man was inherently peaceable, restrained by natural pity from doing harm to anyone. Government did not exist in a state of nature because it was unnecessary. The state of war described by Hobbes came into being with the invention of metallurgy and agriculture: 'iron and wheat ... civilized men and ruined the human race'.[7] Natural inequalities, previously imperceptible, were magnified by heightened productivity; notions of private property in land and goods came into being; inequalities of wealth were consolidated by inheritance; avarice, envy and ambition became the driving forces of social life, while dominance and subordination characterized its form. Society itself created and reproduced the evils that Hobbes had ascribed to a state of nature.[8]

In Kropotkin's judgment, the flaw common to both scenarios was a specious individualism: 'one against every one' as contrasted with 'one against no one'. Man had evolved from the beginning as a social animal; society was anterior to man, not his creation. Although it is true that Darwin had dwelt upon competition between individuals of the same species, he had also acknowledged the importance of cooperation. Communities with the greatest number of mutually sympathetic members would flourish best and rear the greatest number of offspring. Huxley, in common with numerous lesser exponents of Darwinism, stressed the selfish aspects of social life in animal species to the virtual exclusion of altruism. In his article in *Nineteenth Century* he had gone so far as to liken nature to a gladiator's show, where the weak succumb and the strong and cunning live to fight another day. In Kropotkin's opinion, such a view had as little claim to scientific validity as Rousseau's idyll of love, peace and harmony. Beak-and-claw undeniably exist, but competition predominates neither in the animal world nor in mankind. It undoubtedly flourishes in harsh conditions, but the operative principle in the evolution of social life is that conditions can be improved by replacing competition with mutual aid.

Huxley's representation of primitive communities as agglomerations of unruly, brawling savages was, Kropotkin argued, manifestly untrue. No better proof of human social instincts could be imagined than the section organization of Aboriginal Australia, where countless communities lacking any form of government nevertheless conformed to complex systems regulating marriage eligibility.[9] To describe such people as creatures devoid of ethical principles could be pardoned only on the grounds of lamentable ignorance. Altruism and hospitality abounded, and within the tribe the principle of 'each for all' reigned supreme. The same sociability and spirit of solidarity characterized primitive communities everywhere. As Darwin had argued (and Huxley apparently forgotten), man's intelligence, combined with his capacity to give and receive aid from his fellows, more than counterbalanced his shortcomings in strength, speed and natural weaponry and laid the foundations for his ascendancy.

Huxley offered no reply. In 1883, the year after Darwin's death, indignation among English intellectuals at Kropotkin's imprisonment had led to the drawing up of a petition for his release. The signatories included Wallace, co-discoverer with Darwin of the principle of natural selection. Huxley, however, declined to add his name. History records that Kropotkin never bore him any personal animosity for his decision and, despite a belief that his later writings were dangerous distortions of Darwin's theory, always praised him for the courage, learning and intelligence with which from the first he had defended Darwinism against the orthodoxy of the church.[10]

Captain Watkin Tench was an officer in the fleet that established the British settlement in Sydney Harbour. Aged about 30, he had received a sound education in classical and English literature and, following a sojourn in France, could quote Rousseau from memory. In 1789 and again in 1793 he published accounts of the colony, including descriptions of Aboriginal life that can fairly be regarded as the foundation stone of Australian ethnography. Several times in his narrative he alluded to Rousseau's views in order to repudiate them. The realities of native life had been better described by Hobbes: 'Too justly, as my observations teach me, has Hobbes defined a state of nature, to be a state of war.'[11]

Yet parts of Tench's account would have pleased Rousseau very well indeed. One of the earliest injuries inflicted on the Aborigines was the pilfering of their spears and fishing gear by convicts, who sold them to sailors with access to the artefact trade. It was not long before potential thieves began receiving some of the coveted objects between the ribs. Faced with deteriorating relationships, Governor Phillip issued a proclamation forbidding the sale of native goods. He also decided to capture some of the natives in order to convince them the colonists intended no harm. On the last day of 1788 a truly noble savage named Arabanoo was seized by the marines on Manly beach and delivered to Government House, where he remained as the governor's guest until he died from smallpox five months later. The following is from Tench's obituary:

> Although of a gentle and placable temper, we early discovered that he was impatient of indignity, and allowed of no superiority on our part. He knew that he was in our power; but the independence of his mind never forsook him. If the slightest insult were offered to him, he would return it with interest.[12]

A few months after Arabanoo's capture, fifteen convicts were flogged for allegedly setting out to plunder a native encampment at Botany Bay. The reason for the punishment was communicated to Arabanoo, who was brought along to witness it. He was not impressed; instead of expressing gratitude to the authorities, he evinced only disgust and terror. When a large group of Aborigines was assembled two years later to watch the lashing of a convict caught in the act of stealing fishing tackle, all reacted with abhorrence to the brutishness of the spectacle. One of the women went so far as to snatch a stick and menace the flogger. Tench noted that on a previous occasion when a bundle of stolen spears had been recovered and placed on the beach, an old man came up and singled out his own from the rest: 'and this honesty, within the circle of their society, seemed to characterize them all'.[13] Sharing, moreover, was commonplace and spontaneous, as evidenced by Arabanoo's gifts of food not only to his countrymen but to the colonists' children who flocked around him.

Tench's anecdotal observations on the ethics and temper of the Aborigines of Sydney foreshadowed a more general characterization some half-century later in the report of the United States Exploring Expedition of 1838–42.[14] During 1839 six ships of the United States Navy anchored in Sydney Harbour, and in the course of a brief stay members of the expedition, including the chief ethnologist Horatio Hale, encountered Aborigines in various townships and mission stations. The official report, published in 1846, described the natives of

New South Wales as proud, self-sufficient individuals who acknowledged no superiors among themselves and regarded the ranked order of colonial society with disdain. They treated the highest officers as equals, paid deference to no one, and on entering a room seated themselves while others remained standing. Confidence in their own worth gave them an air of haughtiness and insolence. They refused to work for white masters, and all attempts to govern them by threats and violence had failed. They responded to kindness, but on receiving insult or injury they returned immediately to their wandering life in the bush.

Regarding the indigenous polity, Hale maintained that there were no tribal chiefs or legal authorities; no words in the language for 'command' or 'obey'; and no distinctions of rank. Nevertheless, later in the report we learn that custom required young men, following their initiation, to obey their elders, stay away from young women, and abstain from eating certain prized items of food. Furthermore, the colonists had adopted the practice of rewarding particular natives for their services by giving them brass breast-plates inscribed with a royal title (plate 8).[15] Initially the recipients were greatly pleased with the distinction conferred upon them. But, on becoming commonplace, the medals fell into disrepute, and those eligible sought hard cash instead. We might infer that though manifestations of rank were not visible in the indigenous culture, a taste for them was nonetheless latent.

The report attributed to the Aborigines a total absence of selfishness. Various observers had been struck by their custom of freely sharing with each other gifts received from the colonists, manifesting 'a disinterestedness that is seldom seen among civilized nations'.[16] Social life, nevertheless, was neither an unqualified state of peaceful cooperation nor a continual struggle of each against every other. There were limits to the ethic of generosity, especially in sexual matters, and conflict over adultery and the acquisition of wives was endemic. However, where the early observers had represented the situation as one of unregulated violence, the report of the expedition drew attention to accumulated testimony on ritualized combat and collective punishment. If a man killed his wife or her lover, he was obliged to defend himself with a shield while the victim's tribal relatives threw spears at him:

> Such punishments are inflicted with great formality, upon an appointed day, and the whole tribe assemble to witness it. The person most injured has the first throw, and it depends upon the feelings of the tribe respecting the offence committed, whether they endeavour to do injury to the culprit or not; and thus it may be supposed that there is some judgment evinced in this mode of punishment.[17]

Pl. 8   King Mickey Johnson of Illawarra. c. 1896.

The contrast between a system of punishment in which the offender was given a sporting chance to minimize injury and one in which he was simply bound and flogged barely needs comment, but it may help to explain why Arabanoo and his compatriots found the latter so barbarous.

Inter-tribal battles were also conducted with formality, in accordance with agreed principles and an established code of honour. The two

83

Pl. 9 Trial. This picture by John Heaviside Clark first appeared in a supplement entitled 'Field Sports etc. of the Native Inhabitants of New South Wales' to a book on 'Foreign Field Sports, Fisheries, and Sporting Anecdotes', published in 1814.

sides assembled after an exchange of messages, and the tournament began with the hurling of insults by senior women. A warrior from one side then advanced and launched several spears. A warrior from the other did the same, and so on. Such combats, according to the report, seldom resulted in loss of life and often became reduced to a duel between the most determined rivals.[18]

Two years before the United States expedition arrived in Sydney, an English expedition put George Grey ashore in wild country on the other side of the continent. Led on by the geographers' myth of a great river draining an inland sea, he discovered instead remarkable galleries of rock paintings expressing the Aboriginal myth of the rain-making *wonjina*.[19] Unfortunately the conditions for exegesis were unfavourable, and Grey barely escaped with his life. Heading south, he spent the next few years in more settled areas around Perth and Albany, and in 1841 published his journals of exploration, including a lengthy section on the Aborigines.

Where Hale and his colleagues highlighted a bold egalitarianism, Grey chose to emphasize radical inequality. The natives of Australia, he said, rejected all idea of the parity of persons or classes. Throughout the continent the female sex, the young and the weak were subjugated by superstitions and traditions conferring benefits upon the old and the strong. Aboriginal people would be unable, in Grey's opinion, even to comprehend the meaning of the question 'Are all men equal?' Yet if the term 'men' is understood narrowly to mean adult males (especially those regarded as socially mature), the assertion loses its rhetorical force as well as its sharp contrast with the observations of the Americans. One could say without internal contradiction both that an egalitarian ethos prevailed among mature adult males, among whom no distinctions of rank were acknowledged, and that these same males collectively deemed themselves superior to females and junior males, and enjoyed powers and privileges institutionally denied to them.

While Grey's journals were at the printing-house, his compatriot Edward John Eyre was in the process of becoming the first man in history to walk across the Nullarbor Plain. By then Grey was Governor of South Australia; and, upon returning to Adelaide, Eyre accepted an appointment as Resident Magistrate and Protector of Aborigines of the Murray River District. The region was a trouble-spot, having been the scene of recent bloody clashes between the natives and white over-landers bringing stock from the east. During the next three years Eyre travelled widely among tribes whose previous contact with Europeans was minimal. In 1845, following Grey's example, he published his ethnological observations as part of his journals of exploration.

Eyre's numerous encounters had left him with a high regard for native character. The indigenous inhabitants were by nature cheerful, magnanimous, hospitable, punctilious, tactful, polite, honest, and courageous. Many times during his travels he had been received in the kindest and most friendly manner.

> Nor can a more interesting sight well be imagined, than that of a hundred or two hundred natives advancing in line to meet you, unarmed, shouting and waving green boughs in both hands, men, women, and children, the old and the young, all joining in expressing their good feelings and pacific intentions.[20]

The people gave freely of their aid and possessions not only to the white visitor in their midst but habitually among themselves; and in the division of food, convention required them to be both formal and generous. Nevertheless, Eyre had watched men on the River Murray devour the entire product of a morning's net-fishing, then return empty-handed to the camps to share in what had been procured by the women. He had seen conscientious, skilful hunters forced by custom to share a meagre catch with a group of 'expectant sharks'.[21] He was neither the first to remark on the high value placed by Aborigines on a readiness to share, nor the last to complain of unfair advantages taken of it.

Eyre agreed with Grey that, through custom's irresistible sway, the young and the weak (including the generality of women) were held in willing subjection to the old and the strong. Nevertheless, in his view this did not in any meaningful sense constitute a form of government. Among none of the tribes yet encountered were chiefs acknowledged, though in all of them men of influence existed. Usually they were between 45 and 60 years of age, physically active and strong, courageous, good counsellors, prominent in ceremonial life, and from powerful families. Male elders generally discussed issues of importance in council; and, not infrequently, influential men harangued the whole tribe. But no one was in a position to issue a command and have it obeyed. Proposals were urged and the merits of alternative courses of action publicly debated, but in the end people had to form their own judgments and decide what to do for themselves.[22]

When Eyre claimed that chiefs were not known to exist, he meant throughout the continent. Yet just a few decades later, the Reverend George Taplin discovered them at the mouth of the Murray River, less than a hundred miles south of Eyre's headquarters at Moorundie. According to Taplin, each of the eighteen bands making up the Narrinyeri nation had a chief whose title was *Rupulle*, meaning 'landowner'. The chief was elected to his position by family heads within the band, who gave backing to his authority and constituted a governmental body under his leadership. He was expected to reside at all times on the clan's land. He led the clan into battle and was carefully protected against injury by his clansmen.[23]

Although it is hard to judge the extent to which Taplin's statement set a fashion, several similar reports appeared soon after its publication in 1874. The Reverend J. Stahle of Lake Condah in Western Victoria maintained that, before the arrival of whites, the headman of the Gournditch-mara people had the power to settle disputes within his own tribe and to declare war on others. His authority was absolute. He kept the best spoils of war for himself, and his subjects provided him with food and luxuries. The office was hereditary in the male line.[24] James Dawson, also from Western Victoria, wrote that every tribe had its chief whose subjects treated him with unquestioning respect and obedience. Six young men formed his retinue, while eight young women waited upon his wife. Their children were of superior rank to the common folk and also had servants. Chiefs and chiefesses were addressed only by their titles and only after they had spoken first. They were entitled to appropriate any of their subjects' possessions that took their fancy. Mr Dawson, we should note, was a prosperous landowner who employed Aboriginal servants. According to his preface, his main source of information about past traditions was his sable friend, 'the very intelligent chiefess Yaruun Parpur Tarneen, whose knowledge greatly exceeded expectation'.[25]

Although despotic and monarchical images of this kind seemed incompatible with the egalitarian portrayals of Hale and Eyre, they were not entirely without precedent. William Thomas, Protector of Aborigines in the early days of Melbourne, wrote:

> Their government is patriarchal, the head of each family having control over his household... Each tribe has a chief who directs all its movements, and who, wherever he may be, knows well where all the members of the community are...Besides the chiefs, they have other eminent men, as warriors, counsellors, doctors, dreamers who are also interpreters; charmers who are supposed to be able to bring and drive the rain away...[26]

Some thirty years later, in 1878, R. Brough Smyth embellished Thomas's formulation and extended it to the whole of Victoria:[27]

> There are the doctors or sorcerers who under some circumstances have supreme power; there are the warriors who in time of trouble are absolute masters; there are the dreamers who direct and control movements of the tribe until the divinations are fulfilled or forgotten; there are the old men – councillors – without whose advice even the warriors are slow to move; and finally there are the old women who noisily intimate their designs, and endeavour by clamour and threats to influence the leaders of the tribe.

Smyth went on to speak of a 'principal man of the tribe', whose role was to put into effect what the experts had previously determined. He commended the indigenous polity to nations claiming to be more civilized.

The mounting contradiction between libertarian and authoritarian perceptions of Aboriginal political life came to a head shortly afterwards. In 1886, in his book entitled *The Australian Race*, E.M.Curr directed a lively polemic against certain gentlemen who, by crediting the Aborigines with formal institutions of government, had elevated them to a stage of progress they notoriously had not yet reached. Unlike Mr Brough Smyth, the early writers had actually observed native tribes at first hand and had consistently noted the absence of chiefs and headmen. Mr Dawson, notwithstanding opportunities for gaining knowledge as an early settler in Western Victoria, had allowed his retainers to represent as indigenous a number of conceptions they had in fact derived from their association with Europeans. The Rev. Taplin had encountered chiefs in a region where thirty years earlier, before the modifying influence of colonization had taken hold, Eyre declared them not to exist. Curr claimed to have in his possession reports on over a hundred other tribes, all asserting an absence of government. By government he meant the 'habitual exercise of authority by one or a few individuals over a community or a body of persons'.[28] In general, good conduct in Australian tribes was achieved not through the personal authority of political leaders but in consequence of fear of the impersonal power of sorcery.

Three years later A.W. Howitt brought the issue before the Royal Society of Victoria.[29] It was not surprising, he said, that early observers of Aborigines had denied the existence of government among them, for the simple reason that insignia of office and rank were almost entirely lacking. Families were seen wandering apparently at will over the countryside, and each man appeared to be a law unto himself. On closer acquaintance, however, it became evident that behaviour was constrained and regulated in every tribe by a body of laws and customs, some of them of a most intricate and complex kind. Mr Curr was correct in arguing that fear of supernatural sanctions was an important factor in obtaining conformity. The diffuse power of public opinion was another. But in addition to these 'impersonal' forces there existed very definite and concrete forms of secular authority vested in persons by virtue of their office. It was the intention of the author to present examples of such executive powers from his own personal observations and experience.

Howitt went on to describe various forms and contexts of governance among the Kurnai, Murring, Kulin and Wotjobaluk of southeastern Australia, as well as the Dieri of central Australia. The information may be summarized as follows. Each local subdivision of a tribe included a man who, by virtue either of age or distinction (e.g., as a warrior, orator, or medicine-man), was designated by a term which Howitt translated as 'headman'. In several cases the term literally meant 'great man'. Headmen, together with other elders, formed a Tribal Council, which was presided over by either the oldest headman or one who was particularly distinguished or forceful. The office of headman was not hereditary, though the son of a headman commonly developed qualities enabling him to follow in his father's footsteps. A headman had the power to despatch messengers on matters of war and peace. He stopped fights, presided over ritual punishments, passed death sentences on murderers and sorcerers, and sent armed parties on revenge expeditions. He played a leading role in the ceremonial life and, most notably, organized and directed the initiation of young men.[30]

Ten years later Spencer and Gillen came out on Howitt's side against Curr in their book *The Native Tribes of Central Australia*.[31] The authority of the headman, or *alatunja* as he was referred to in the Aranda language, though admittedly of 'a somewhat vague nature', was nonetheless real. His most important function, according to Spencer and Gillen, was to act as custodian of his clan's sacred paraphernalia and to preside over its main ceremonies. In this capacity he convened meetings of the male elders of his local group and despatched messengers to neighbouring groups. The council of elders also discussed what to do about serious offences and had the authority to order punitive expeditions against other groups. In such matters the voice of the *alatunja* depended on his personal qualities rather than the power of his office. He held no disciplinary rights over individuals in his own group or beyond it. The post of *alatunja* was normally transmitted from father to son, and men of forceful personality undoubtedly used it to strengthen and extend their influence. There was no one, however, who could be described as a chief or leader of the tribe as a whole.

In 1910 Gerald Wheeler, a post-graduate student in sociology at London University, published what his teacher Edward Westermarck described as 'the first monograph on intertribal relationships among uncivilized peoples'.[32] It was devoted entirely to the political life of the Australian Aborigines. After reviewing the available evidence Wheeler concluded that, notwithstanding the negative inferences of the early observers, it now appeared that there existed in many tribes 'the rudiments of a regular government over and above the mere authority belonging to the head of each family'.[33] Each local group had its headman and assembly of elders and, for the most part, was politically autonomous. Tribal unity was slight.

During the same year Alfred Brown was elected to the Anthony Wilkins Studentship in Ethnology at Cambridge University, enabling him to carry out fieldwork in Western Australia. In his initial report he characterized political organization as follows:[34]

> The tribe is distinguished from its neighbours by the possession of a name, a language and a defined territory. There is no tribal chief, nor any form of tribal government....The country of a local group, with all its products, animal, vegetable and mineral, belongs to the members of the group in common....The whole territory and everything on it belongs equally to all members of the group.

Before going to Cambridge, Brown had been befriended by Kropotkin, who advised him to study primitive society before trying to improve his own.[35] As a student he was known as 'Anarchy' Brown. Though he lost his nickname and in time adopted a hyphenated surname,[36] Radcliffe-Brown held consistently to an anarchist perception of the Aboriginal polity. His monograph on *The Social Organization of Australian Tribes,* written after he became the inaugural Professor of Anthropology at Sydney University, included not a solitary reference to chiefs, headmen, or councils of elders.[37] In two articles for the *Encyclopaedia of the Social Sciences,* one on 'Social Sanctions', the other on 'Primitive Law',[38] Australian Aborigines were introduced only to exemplify institutions regulating private vengeance.

Without reading too much into his intellectual priorities, we can say that the theoretically important question for Radcliffe-Brown was not whether the Aborigines lacked or possessed the rudiments of centralized government, measured on some ascending scale of political evolution, but how they had managed to develop a wide-ranging and complex social order *without* an over-arching apparatus of authority. The answer, he argued, lay in their deployment of family kinship as a conceptual microcosm for the social universe at large. In our own culture we are familiar with the adoption of kinship terms for non-kin (e.g. 'father', 'brother') to promote relationships of protectiveness and amity. No known society, however, has applied the formula as systematically as the Aborigines. Through the operation of a small number of simple principles, identified by Radcliffe-Brown with labels such as 'the equivalence of brothers' and 'the combination of alternate generations', terms designating primary relationships of blood and marriage were extended outwards along ramifying genealogical networks to everyone whom an individual encountered or was likely to encounter in his or her lifetime.[39] Thus a man might classify and address all males in his own and neighbouring tribes as either 'father', 'brother', 'father-in-law' or 'brother-in-law'; and all females as either 'mother', 'sister', 'mother-in-law' or 'wife'. A precondition of a social relationship was an assumption or determination of the kinship idiom in which it had to be conducted; and, at least notionally, expectations of behaviour appropriate to the assigned kinship roles were thereby generated. Since kinship was equated with amity, the extension of terms and their associated sentiments beyond the narrow confines of closely related families created a wider polity within which peace, hospitality and goodwill were pursued as an ideal even if not always achieved in practice.

The effect of Radcliffe-Brown's formulation was profound. Since the organizing principles and integrating framework of Aboriginal society were cast in the idiom of kinship, it followed that the scientific understanding of Australian tribes must depend largely upon the development of kinship theory. Thus the study of kinship, pursued on the basis of genealogy and classificatory principles, came to be seen as the master-key of Aboriginal anthropology, relegating other subject domains to a status of dependency or insignificance. Government, as a category in its own right, virtually disappeared. In 1938 A.P. Elkin, in what may be regarded as the first university textbook on the Aborigines, found no use for the word and acknowledged the existence of headmen and councils of elders in less than a paragraph.[40] Even this was too much for his American colleague Lauriston Sharp, who complained that by perpetuating such outmoded nineteenth-century concepts the ethnographic literature was giving Aboriginal groups an appearance of political organization and government that in fact they did not possess.[41]

Sharp presented his view in a paper entitled 'People without Politics'. In the course of his fieldwork in North Queensland, carried out under Radcliffe-Brown's patronage, he had encountered neither headmen nor councils of elders nor any other institutionalized form of authority above the level of the family. Social interaction was regulated not from above but in accordance with highly standardized kinship roles which individuals played over and over again throughout their lives. That is not to say that social relationships were conducted on a basis of equality: greater age conferred seniority of status, and recipients of wife-bestowals deferred to donors. However, while no man dealt with another as a formal equal, in roughly half of his relationships he was superordinate and in the other half subordinate. In these circumstances, Sharp argued, no one could be absolutely strong or absolutely weak. The structural asymmetry built into all relationships acted as a barrier to the emergence of a fixed hierarchy, and any attempt to extend and consolidate authority beyond defined kinship limits would be treated by North Queensland Aborigines as intolerable.

The structural impediments to institutions of government were probably not as substantial as Sharp imagined. After all, the President of the United States could pay deference to his father and shrink from his mother-in-law yet satisfactorily carry out the duties of high office. The question remained whether enduring frameworks of political and administrative authority had arisen anywhere in Aboriginal Australia independently of the kinship system. In 1964 M.J. Meggitt, following fieldwork in the Northern Territory and a review of the literature, maintained that they had not. The explanation for their absence was that they were functionally unnecessary and ideologically unacceptable. Religious master-plans based on ancestral precedents allocated organizing and performance roles to particular kin for the purpose of dealing with recurrent life crises (birth, initiation, death, revenge and so on). The personnel changed from one occasion to the next depending on kin connections with focal subjects (the woman in labour, the initiand, the deceased, the injured party and so on). No one emerged as a paramount leader or universal organizer for the simple reason that individual citizens performed their kinship duties religiously and guarded their kinship prerogatives jealously.

Meggitt, who had graduated in the department established by Radcliffe-Brown at Sydney University, on occasion wryly described himself as a 'Tory anarchist'. In describing how Aborigines conducted their civic affairs, he attributed to them a deep conservatism in their reliance upon ancient tradition and an intense egalitarianism in their resistance to domination. That is not to say he denied the existence among them of differences in knowledge, skill and ability. Individuals excelled as warriors, yet war parties lacked a hierarchy of military command. Each man possessed weapons and stood ready to defend his interests, but systematic warfare for the purpose of territorial conquest or seizure of property was unknown. Some men achieved great prestige as healers, others for their religious knowledge; yet outside their fields of expertise, their opinions and wishes carried no more authority than those of ordinary citizens. Age generally commanded respect, especially in the case of men, but male elders did not constitute a solidary body with the power to assert its will over other sections of the community. In short, local communities conducted their internal and external affairs on the basis of religious tradition and kinship. They lacked, and neither needed nor desired, (a) formal apparatuses of government, (b) permanent political leaders, (c) enduring hierarchies of authority.[42]

In 1965 I published the results of my field inquiries into fighting and violence in northern Arnhem Land carried out a few years earlier.[43] Like Meggitt, I found little evidence of conflict over land or food supplies. Everyone was a member of a land-owning clan, and clan territories were roughly the same size. Within communities, and between neighbouring communities, people shared magnanimously in times of abundance, dutifully in times of scarcity. Altruism was enshrined as a central value (to be good was to be generous); when necessary, it was activated by appeals to kinship (classificatory as well as primary). Clearly, the struggle for existence had been moderated most admirably, by an ethic of generosity operating in conjunction with an elaborate system of extended kinship.

The problem of allocating resources in women had been dealt with rather less successfully. In principle all men were born with marriage rights to daughters of women in specified kinship categories, and therefore each man ought to have been guaranteed a wife. In practice polygynous aspirations and the bestowal of infant females upon adult males created chronic shortages between demand and supply. Broadly speaking, senior males monopolized sexually mature females at the expense of their juniors, who were fortunate if they acquired a wife before they reached the age of thirty. Furthermore, some men benefited from genealogical good fortune, as when women defined as their mothers-in-law produced numerous daughters; while other men were disadvantaged because their potential mothers-in-law produced few daughters or none at all. Although the ethic of generosity was supposed to moderate such structurally induced inequalities, and to some extent did, they nevertheless provided a fertile ground for grievance, manipulation, breach of promise, infidelity and, all too frequently, accusation, mounting tension, aggression and violence.

Although no formal courts existed to hear plaints and allegations, grievances were publicly aired, usually at night as families sat around their camp fires, and people formed opinions as to the rights and wrongs of a case. Nevertheless, no one had the authority to impose a judgment on behalf of the community or even to articulate it. While public opinion undoubtedly influenced outcomes, the main avenue available for peaceful redress of injury or restoration of rights was by private negotiation through intermediaries. If satisfaction was not achieved in this way, injured parties frequently took up arms in prosecution of their own interests. Once a fight began, three discernible groups emerged: (a) attackers (e.g. an aggrieved party supported by close male kin), (b) defenders (e.g. the accused, similarly supported), and (c) people with divided loyalties, or no strong commitment to either side, who hampered the warring parties and sought energetically and at some risk to themselves to bring the outbreak of violence under control. Once peace was restored, interested parties took stock of their positions. Sometimes disputes were settled by agreement (for example, through compensation to the injured party), sometimes they fizzled out, sometimes they festered.

In regard to the organization and direction of public affairs, again my findings confirmed the general description advanced by Meggitt. The keynote of the daily food quest was individual enterprise on a basis of free exchange of information and mutual aid when needed. Decisions about community movements were reached by an informal consensus. The organization of public rituals, such as initiation and death ceremonies, proceeded in accordance with clearly defined kinship responsibilities which changed from one occasion to another. It was true that some individuals became renowned for their skill and zeal in staging ceremonies, and for the scope and authority of their ritual knowledge. Yet men of eminence in the realm of the sacred were accorded no special powers or privileges in secular domains. There were no headmen or councils of elders for public administration or law-and-order; and no semblance of a priesthood or ecclesiastical hierarchy for public religion or secret cults. External affairs were conducted on the basis of kin connections, personal trust, traditional formalities and an ethic of hospitality. Hostilities between neighbouring tribes broke out sporadically, typically when death in one community was attributed to sorcery in another, and sometimes resulted in blood feuds. Expiation was available through the institution of the *makarrata*, in which those who had killed or maimed submitted to ritual punishment at the hands of the victims' kinsmen.

Like Meggitt, I had learnt my anthropology at Sydney University. In fact, he was one of my first teachers. Both of us were influenced by the realist philosopher John Anderson, whose anti-authoritarianism spawned a lively anarchist and libertarian movement in Sydney in the post-war decades. In the mid-1960s Kenneth Maddock, an anarchist thinker from Auckland, joined the Sydney department as a doctoral student and undertook field research in the Northern Territory near Katherine. Subsequently, speaking generally of the Aboriginal polity, he stressed its freedom from institutions of enforcement and its dependence upon self-reliance and mutual aid. It was, he said, 'a kind of anarchy, in which it was open to active and enterprising men to obtain some degree of influence with age, but in which none were sovereign'.[44]

Maddock's description, published in his influential textbook *The Australian Aborigines* in 1972, brought the anarchistic representation of Aboriginal political life to its apogee. Two years earlier, while apparently carrying its banner, Theodore Strehlow dramatically undermined it from within. Strehlow, the son of a Lutheran missionary, grew up with members of the Aranda tribe studied by Spencer and Gillen. On the basis of his deep knowledge of the peoples of central Australia, he proclaimed that Aborigines before European conquest had achieved an anarchistic utopia of the kind described by William Morris in *News from Nowhere*.[45] According to Strehlow, the autonomy conferred on patrilineal clans by mystical links with sacred sites on their own territories prevented the emergence of centralized authority above the level of the local group. The population could not be tyrannized by hereditary rulers, priestly castes or bureaucrats; large-scale warfare for territorial conquest was impossible. Men and women lived in a state of freedom and social equality.[46]

Paradoxically (not to say regrettably), the mystical framework that guaranteed freedom from tribal overlords was sustained by a reign of terror within the local community. In each territorial clan a ceremonial chief, supported by a council of elders, held the power of life and death over his subjects, and from time to time inflicted capital punishment for alleged acts of sacrilege. Strehlow gave a number of examples. (a) Three young men who accidentally broke a ritual object in the course of preparing for a ceremony had their necks broken by order of the ceremonial chief. No one dared raise a voice in protest. (b) A woman suffering from thirst took a short cut to a spring and passed within sight of trees in which men's sacred icons were stored. Her tracks were discovered and she was speared fatally through the chest. (c) A youth accidentally dropped a stone icon while bringing it down from a mountain cave. He was speared to death several months later. (d) Four youths were executed by order of the elders when they allowed a bushfire to damage a tree in which sacred stones were hidden. Some of their relatives refused to accept the verdict of culpable negligence and avenged the deaths by killing the men who had carried out the execution orders.

A condition of admission to the sacred mysteries was voluntary submission to the excruciatingly painful operations of circumcision, subincision, scalp-biting and wrenching out of finger nails. Any sign of resistance was met by special punishments, such as requiring the recalcitrant novice to perform in the blazing heat or to kneel and sit on stony ground until the skin was lacerated. The authority of the old men was not confined to the custodianship of secret knowledge and sacred objects. When an Aranda boy stole some meat given to certain elders in payment for religious instruction, the aggrieved elders had him thrown into a flooded river, in which he drowned. Rebellious or disrespectful youths could be charged with sacrilege and executed on a hunting expedition by young men acting under orders. Ceremonial headmen, Strehlow averred, were not only venerated for their control of ritual progress; they were also feared as sorcerers. Obviously, it was not wise to offend them. Although breach of promise, adultery and other domestic matters in theory lay outside their province, it was prudent to suppose that power in the sacred sphere had ways of penetrating the secular.

Following the publication of Strehlow's essay, fieldworkers began to find ceremonial headmen, or 'big men', nearly everywhere. In Cape York Peninsula, where in the 1930s Sharp had encountered an unequivocal and pervasive egalitarianism, John von Sturmer identified the pursuit of ritual pre-eminence as a driving force in the political life of men. Among the Kugu-Nganchara, fame as a ceremonial 'boss' depended on gaining and maintaining control of an important site, typically one located near a naturally favoured camping area capable of sustaining large numbers of visitors. Such sites were normally transmitted from father to son, but an inheritance had to be protected against pressures from forceful rivals. Special training for 'big man' status included periods of celibacy and fasting, submitting to humiliations and indignities, and instruction in the performing arts. Through a combination of inherited advantage and personal effort, certain individuals made reputations as ceremonial leaders and, correlatively, as men of note in the public forum. The 'big man' was an arbiter of what constituted correct or incorrect knowledge. After others had expressed their views, he spoke and people heard.[47]

On the other side of the continent, in the Kimberley region, Erich Kolig glossed a vernacular term for a religious leader as 'great man'.[48] A few years earlier, in south-eastern Arnhem Land, John Bern described at length a nexus between land, ceremony and politics. In a culture where much time and energy were devoted to 'men's business', i.e. secret cult activities, it was an accolade to be referred to as a 'business man'. Men achieved prominence as entrepreneurs by acquiring rights to stage major ceremonies, which in turn depended upon establishing or defending their credentials as custodians of the territorial sites to which the ceremonies were mythologically linked.[49] Further north, among the Yolngu, several observers affirmed the existence of clan leaders as well as ceremonial 'big men'.[50] Ian Keen went so far as to suggest that asymmetrical kinship systems of the kind found in north-eastern Arnhem Land helped to generate social inequality by enabling some individuals to acquire a disproportionately large number of wives.[51] Their male descendants formed the core of fast-growing and ultimately powerful clans which were able to acquire defunct neighbouring estates through a process of ritual custodianship and accretion.[52] The senior men of such clans, with their ample resources in land, wives and warriors, were well placed to become citizens of note. Not uncommonly, they embellished their reputations by becoming patrons and practitioners of the arts.

In 1979, notwithstanding his origins in the Sydney Department, John Bern re-entered the arena to despatch the weakened anarchist position with a Marxist *coup de grâce*.[53] The representation of Aboriginal politics an an embodiment of ordered anarchy could be sustained, in his opinion, only by ignoring the existence of adult females and junior adult males. Far from being free and equal, these two categories (as noted by George Grey a century and a half earlier) were subservient to senior males. In Aboriginal society wealth and prestige were defined in terms of ritual property and knowledge, and both were accessible only to men as they grew older. Religion was not, as Meggitt and Hiatt had maintained, a separate political domain which just happened to be premissed on hierarchy, command and exclusion; rather, it housed the ruling ideology in which relations of domination for the social formation as a whole were articulated and justified. By virtue of the central cosmic and social value accorded to the major cults, senior men were able simultaneously to appropriate the products of women's labour and to subject junior males to discipline and domination. In giving precedence to issues concerning the existence or otherwise of specialized organs of government, such as headmen and councils of elders, anthropologists had allowed themselves to be distracted by trivialities.

Bern's point seemed so undeniable that as soon as possible I not only conceded it but tried to show that a dim awareness of it could be discerned in my own early writings.[54] By 1986, however, the argument had shifted to a higher plane. According to Fred Myers,[55] the issue was not whether Aboriginal political life was hierarchical or egalitarian, since the evidence for both characteristics was now overwhelming. The task, rather, was to interpret the terms of their coexistence. Among the Pintupi of the Western Desert (near-neighbours to the Aranda), equality was in fact a product of hierarchy. Just as mothers reared their offspring to physical independence, so male elders subjected novices to religious disciplines in order to transform them into free and autonomous men. In one case the source of nourishment was food; in the other, knowledge.The apparent authoritarianism of senior men was in fact a form of nurture. The cultural construction of authority through the symbolism of nurturance provided a means of sustaining hierarchy within an essentially egalitarian framework.

In Myers' account, daily life in the Western Desert was free, untrammelled and anarchic. Political leaders and governmental structures were conspicuous by their absence; and, within a broad framework of rules and guidelines, citizens negotiated their relationships civilly and with due regard to the feelings and interests of others. The desire to dominate or give orders was entirely foreign to them. If there was a semblance of gerontocracy, it was because elders were respected for their wisdom and acknowledged to be the ones best fitted to look after the welfare of the community as a whole. Inasmuch as each generation had the responsibility of caring for those that followed, inequality in Pintupi society was to be measured in terms of sacrifice rather than gain. Social hierarchy existed not as a correlate of differential access to scarce resources but of graded levels of civic responsibility.

The life history of the Pintupi male could be represented as a progression from the unbridled egoism of childhood to the cultivated altruism of adulthood, mediated by the discipline of initiation. In inflicting the pain necessary to effect the transition, those responsible did so with solicitude and compassion. Afterwards, during a lengthy period of seclusion, the initiated youths began their apprenticeship in the expanding ritual universe of adult males. In retrospect, when describing the experience to Myers, men likened it to both 'high school' and 'prison'. Under the constraints of disciplined learning, however, they formed powerful affective bonds with each other and an enduring attachment to the corporate life of the cult. In time subordination and humility matured into autonomy and self-respect. It was true that, within the cult, a status hierarchy existed, based on graduation from one level of religious knowledge to the next. It was also true that, as men grew older, they extended their contacts through ritual and took pride, some more than others, in their reputations as 'business men'. Ultimately, however, all men stood equal before the imperatives of the Dreaming. Their common worth as human beings was guaranteed by induction into its mysteries and dedication to its values.

Myers disposed of Bern in a footnote.[56] The question for anthropologists was not to determine either men's dominance or women's equality but to examine how they impinge on each other's lives and how their respective activities are integrated within the totality of the social structure. Strehlow was admonished for a positivistic emphasis on geography and local groups, which ignored the real stuff of Aboriginal politics in the form of interconnecting links and associations.[57] Ritual mutilations and punishments were passed over with the observation that, in combination with revelation of sacred knowledge, they produced marked changes in personality.[58] The Pintupi polity was neither an agglomeration of discrete autocracies nor a sadistic and sexist oligarchy. It was better understood as 'a temporary jurisdiction of relatedness among autonomous equals'.[59]

We may wonder what the Anarchist Prince would make of this apparent reprieve. No doubt, if forced to choose, he would prefer the benign paternalism of the elders to the malignant paternalism of slave-owners; the temporary subordination of youth to the permanent subjugation of classes; and the brotherhood of the cult to the big brotherhood of the state. We can be sure, however, that he would not accept equality before the externalized authority of the Dreaming as an earmark of the anarchist condition. It was his compatriot Bakunin, after all, who said that even if it turned out that God existed, he would have to be abolished. The equality of men who obey the same master, of this world or any other, is not the same as the equality of men who bow to none. Nor is the freedom to come and go the same as the freedom to think. The doctrines of the Dreamtime were cosmological and moral orthodoxies; its imperatives, as mediated by the authority of the cult, were constraints on critical inquiry and social experiment. No doubt a Marxist would be justified in representing them as mystifications advancing sectional interests in the name of the common good. But to a Darwinian that issue might, in the long run, have been less important than whether they helped to maintain a system highly vulnerable to external challenge and susceptible to internal collapse.

On the positive side, few peoples can have placed higher value on altruism and mutual aid than the Aborigines of Australia. The genius of the Australian polity lay in its deployment of the goodwill inherent in kinship as a central principle of organization for society as a whole. Government in these circumstances was otiose; its absence, Kropotkin would say, was to be regarded not as a low level of political evolution but as a luminous peak. Natural resources and the land itself were equitably distributed among descent groups; appropriation of clan estates by force was unknown, and theft of private property a rarity. The business of everyday life was conducted informally through unspoken understandings, quiet consensus or noisy agreement. In general the authoritarian mode in public affairs was discountenanced. Vanity and self-importance were mocked. Nearly everywhere men insisted on speaking for themselves and, conversely, evinced a reluctance to speak on behalf of others. Such characteristics belong to the anarchist tradition. The tenacity of their roots, embedded deeply in the indigenous polity and temper, has helped to make assimilation of Aboriginal communities into the imported structures of British government a task of notorious difficulty.[60]

6

High gods

In the pantheon of late nineteenth-century anthropology, Edward Burnett Tylor was Zeus. The son of a prosperous Quaker manufacturer, Tylor joined the Ethnological Society in 1867, and in 1870 presented a paper on 'The Philosophy of Religion among the Lower Races of Mankind'. The following year, coinciding with the formation of the Anthropological Institute, he published a book called *Primitive Culture*, which became one of the great formative texts of anthropology. He was twice elected president of the Institute, became the first professor of anthropology in Great Britain, and by the time of his death was acknowledged throughout the world as the towering figure in the science of culture.

Towards the end of 1891, during his second term of office as president, Tylor delivered an admonitory address to Fellows of the Institute 'On the Limits of Savage Religion'.[1] Over the last forty years some observers had shown a regrettable tendency to attribute to the lower races of mankind religious and philosophical conceptions of which they were in fact not capable. Of particular concern was a readiness to regard certain beliefs and sentiments found in low tribes as evidence of monotheism. This was certainly going beyond the limits: all such instances upon examination turn out to be consequences of ideas implanted in the minds of the natives by missionaries.

The case of the Australian Aborigines, Tylor thought, was especially instructive. Early descriptions hardly mentioned religious ideas among them. Then, following the arrival of missionaries, we were presented with a host of alleged native names for the Supreme Deity. Indeed, observers on the Australian continent were currently reporting theological conceptions as to the formation and conservation of the universe that, if truly indigenous, would place the blackfellow on a par with his white supplanters. Such a conclusion was unnecessary. The alleged native deities were nothing more than adaptations of indigenous beliefs to ideas obtained from civilization. Misunderstandings and confusions on both sides were the result of difficulties in communication and translation. For instance, in accordance with an English literary convention, missionaries and colonists capitalized the names of various Aboriginal spirits and demons, thereby conferring on them a higher status than they deserved. Conversely, words allegedly signifying native gods might well turn out to be attempts by missionaries to translate the concept of the Christian God into native dialects.

Tylor reverted to the matter soon afterwards in his presidential address, when reviewing proceedings of the Institute for the previous year. With uncharacteristic neglect of syntax he expressed concern at the harm being done to anthropological theory by the spread of civilization:

> On my own paper on the limits of savage religion I need only say that it is high time that such papers should be written, for the accounts of religious ideas among the lower races, as representing stages of religious development among mankind, are being so spoilt by native religious ideas becoming mixed with those borrowed from civilized men, and especially from missionaries, that only the most laborious and stringent criticism can bring them down to their original state.[2]

In order to appreciate the reason for Tylor's indignation, we must first understand the nature of the enterprise he undertook a quarter of a century earlier. The subtitle of *Primitive Culture* was 'Researches into the Development of Mythology, Philosophy, Religion, Language, Art, and Custom'. Of these various topics, religion commanded the greatest attention, practically the whole of the second volume and part of the first as well. Tylor approached the subject through an unusually broad definition. Let us, he said, for the purposes of the inquiry define religion simply as the belief in spiritual beings.[3] In that sense the phenomenon is a property of all cultures for which we possess an adequate record. Religion, it would appear, is a universal element in human history.

Now we can take it for granted that the religious beliefs of savage and barbarous races are mistaken. In other words, the spiritual beings they describe do not exist. We should therefore, as scientists, try to explain how such beliefs could have arisen. Once we have done that, the next step is to account for the various forms taken by religious conceptions in their subsequent evolution. By treating religion as a natural phenomenon and proceeding in this fashion, we may eventually be able to write its natural history.

Tylor felt that a technical term was needed for this basic and general belief in spiritual beings. 'Spiritualism' would be an obvious choice, except that it was already in service for table-tapping seances and other unorthodox methods of communicating with the dead in civilized society. He proposed the word 'animism' instead. Animistic doctrines, according to Tylor, have their roots in two great enigmas of human experience: death and dreams. By inferring that every human is animated by a ghost-soul capable of independent existence, primitive rational philosophy solved them both at a single stroke. In dreams we see the spirits of fellow human beings, including the departed dead. Death itself is to be understood as a permanent departure of the soul from the body.

The doctrine of souls is the seed from which religion in all its rich variety subsequently grew. Interaction between the living and the dead, including various magnifications of ancestral human powers, was an obvious development. But by extending the theory from its human locus of origin, animistic thinkers succeeded in peopling the whole world with invisible agencies. 'Spirits', as Tylor put it, 'are simply personified causes.'[4] So theories of spiritual links between humans and animals came into being, giving rise to totemism. Spirits were said to inhabit trees and even stones and other apparently inanimate objects, forming a category of religious belief known as fetishism. The heavenly bodies were personified, especially the sun and moon; and celestial phenomena such as thunder, lightning and rainbows were regarded as impressive demonstrations of spiritual activity in the sky. As population density in the spirit world increased, functional specializations (fertility, health, war, love, etc.) and hierarchies of importance appeared. Sky dwellers usually fared well in these departmentalized elites, though denizens of the underworld also achieved distinction, not to say notoriety. The full flowering of polytheistic traditions occurred whenever one member of the pantheon was recognized as superior to all the rest. Finally, in a few rare and relatively recent instances the distinctive attributes of deity were denied to all except the Supreme Being, and polytheism gave way to monotheism.

Tylor discreetly excused himself from the task of contemplating the full bearing of his researches upon the philosophies and creeds of Christendom. But the implications were clear enough. If there is an unbroken line of development from animism to monotheism, and if the former is a fallacious system of human reasoning, then the claim of the latter to be revealed truth must surely be undermined.

Although Tylor named no names, there can be little doubt that his paper 'On the Limits of Savage Religion' was directed mainly at Andrew Lang, one of his ex-pupils. Four years earlier, in a book entitled *Myth, Ritual, and Religion*, Lang had attributed to the Aborigines religious beliefs in a 'power that makes for righteousness in this world and the next'; he had expressed the view that whatever heights the ancient Greeks may have reached in philosophy, much of their art, myth and ritual was not different in kind from that of the Kamilaroi of

New South Wales; and, in a final heresy, he had maintained that even the lowest known savages, in hours of awe and need, 'lift their hands and their thoughts to their Father and to ours, who is not far from any of us'.[5]

A decade later, despite Tylor's remonstrations in the meantime, Lang directly assailed the thesis that the idea of God is a late outcome of the doctrine of souls.[6] On the contrary, he said, the evidence indicates that the concept of a Supreme Being, in the sense of a first cause or creator of the universe, exists among the lowest savages *simultaneously* with beliefs in souls, ghosts, demons and other spirits. We may therefore infer that it did not evolve out of animism but arose independently of it. Furthermore, since the idea has been found among people living in the most rudimentary social conditions known to anthropology, we may assume that it is of very great antiquity rather than one of the hallmarks of civilization.

Confronted with this explicit challenge, Tylor assumed the role of a *deus otiosus* and rose above the battle. He was not, as Lang remarked in a tribute to him some years later, a man who enjoyed controversy.[7] Late in 1898 Mr Sidney Hartland, lawyer, civil servant, and President of the Folk-Lore Society, took up the gauntlet for him. Professor Tylor's theory that religion had its origin in a doctrine of souls was not, he said, beyond criticism. But in maintaining that notions of a Supreme Being had emerged autochthonously among the most backward peoples in recorded history, Mr Lang was placing himself in opposition to a wide consensus of scholarly opinion. The critical case was that of the Aborigines. This was the arena in which the arguments must stand or fall. As foreshadowed in the title of his article, Hartland proposed to examine the evidence for and against 'The "High Gods" of Australia'.[8]

The earliest reference to a "High God" among the Aborigines appeared in the records of the United States Exploring Expedition of 1838–42.[9] Although only half a century had elapsed since the arrival of the first British settlers, the Aboriginal tribes of the Sydney area were virtually extinct. Horatio Hale, the chief ethnologist, travelled several hundred miles inland to a new mission at Wellington, where he was told that the natives believed that the world had been made by a deity called Baiame. In the years that followed, information recorded by colonists elsewhere indicated that Baiame was by no means a peculiarity of the Wellington Valley.By the end of the century it could be said that, while given different names in different regions (such as Bunjil, Daramulun, Nurelli), the High God of the tribes of south-eastern Australia was uniformly conceived as a Sky God referred to as 'Our Father', who created the earth and instituted culture, and whose presence is manifest in the rumbling of thunder.

Hartland, like Tylor, found it hard not to believe that at least some of these characteristics had come out of the Bible. Apart from that, it was not unreasonable to expect any Supreme Being worthy of the name to be eternal, omniscient and moral. Yet in Hartland's judgment the evidence from Australia was disappointing on all scores. Indeed, once we begin to look carefully at the myths and legends, comparison with civilized conceptions of divinity becomes embarrassing. Daramulan is a cannibal whose name means 'leg-on-one-side' or 'lame'. Bunjil, with his two wives and six sons, was blown into the sky by wind released from bags by an angry man who later became a bird. Baiame tripped and fell on his face one day while pursuing an emu. In mystery cults he is shown carved in the earth in this humiliating posture, together with a print of his hand left in the ground when he tried to break the fall. Such childish tales bear no comparison with the sublime conception of the Creator as set forth in the book of Genesis.

When Lang read Hartland's critique, he 'bounded on his chair'. Later, on surveying the damage in calmer mood, he was relieved to discover that his main position had been left unscathed. In the next issue of the journal of the Folk-Lore Society[10] he charged Hartland with having failed to appreciate the critical point, namely, that personified conceptions of a cosmic creative force may coexist with oral traditions depicting the deity as all-too-human. The classical exemplification of this notorious truth is Ancient Greece. Two moods have been evident in the history of religion, one of earnest contemplation and submission, the other of playful and erratic fancy. Why it should be so, we do not know. But the Aborigines are no exception; and, behind the articulated trivialities and obscenities of their myths lies a mute striving, most clearly evident in their sacred rites, to express the idea of an exalted and transcendent Power, a Father, Master and Maker.

With regard to the borrowing hypothesis, Lang made the following points. First, Aboriginal High Gods have been recorded in circumstances strongly suggesting that the beliefs were in existence prior to contact with Europeans. The missionaries at Wellington were told about Baiame and the songs in which he was worshipped shortly after they arrived. Further north, in 1844–5, in a frontier region well beyond direct Christian influence, a settler named John Manning (inspired by a conversation with Goethe) studied native customs and made extensive notes on Baiame's similarity to the Christian God. In order to maintain that Aboriginal notions of deity are the product of proselytization, one would have to assume that Christian beliefs caught on at their points of introduction and (like smallpox) travelled ahead of the invaders. Second, detailed information about Aboriginal High Gods has consistently come from initiated adult males, on the understanding that it should not be divulged to women and children. If it were true that the deities of the male cults were borrowed from the missionaries, how would we reconcile the men's desire for secrecy with the fact that knowledge of Christian doctrine is freely available to all? Furthermore, male elders in Aboriginal society are notoriously conservative. Why, especially in the matter of religion, should they be so ready to abandon old beliefs and embrace the new?

In a brief rejoinder, Hartland sought to foster a mood of compromise.[11] Victory was not his aim, nor presumably was it Mr Lang's. In the search for truth, a dialectic triumph may be a scientific disaster. Progress in the present matter is hindered by inconsistencies and infirmities in the record. What we need, above all, are more facts.

Unbeknown to Hartland, or perhaps too recently for his perusal, a large consignment had just arrived: *The Native Tribes of Central Australia* by Spencer and Gillen.[12] Spencer had attended lectures by Tylor while an undergraduate at Oxford. Not long after becoming Professor of Biology at Melbourne University, he was invited to join the Horn Scientific Expedition to Central Australia where he hoped to build on his promising studies of the giant Australian earthworm. Instead, after meeting Gillen, he became increasingly interested in the Aborigines, and in the summer of 1896–7 the two men spent four months observing and discoursing with members of the Aranda tribe living near the Alice Springs telegraph station. The manuscript of their first major work was published in 1899.

In mid-1897 Spencer had begun corresponding with James Frazer, a distinguished classical scholar at Cambridge University who for some time had been speculating on the evolution of religion and was particularly interested in the Aborigines. Like Tylor, Frazer subscribed to the view that beliefs in the supernatural had evolved through a number of stages, though his theory proceeded along somewhat different lines. Of key importance was a distinction between (a) magic, in which men sought to harness or coerce impersonal supernatural forces for their own ends; and (b) religion, in which they supplicated personalized supernatural beings to help and protect them. In the history of the human race, according to Frazer, the first came before the second, and the Australian Aborigines had failed to develop beyond it. Their thinking was almost entirely magical. The formulation of the idea of a Supreme Being would be beyond their unaided mental powers.[13]

During 1898 Frazer read the proofs of *The Native Tribes of Central Australia* and was particularly struck by the authors' account of ceremonies performed by the Aranda to increase their food supply. Each clan was associated with one or more natural species, and at regular intervals clansmen mimed or otherwise re-enacted stages of the creature's life cycle. The Aranda believed that these ritual procedures replenished the supply of spirits located in sites on the clan's territory and activated them so that they went abroad and generated new life. What puzzled Frazer, however, was that in accordance with a strict tribal taboo each clan was prohibited from eating its own totem species. How could one reconcile the voluntary investment of magical effort with a necessity to forgo its benefit? In a long letter to Spencer, Frazer surmised that the taboo originated in a belief among earlier generations of Aranda tribesmen that their magical techniques would not work unless magicians identified sympathetically with the species whose members they were attempting to multiply. Although when regarded narrowly this seemed to defeat the purpose of the ritual, everyone gained from the efforts of others. Taken together, the 'increase ceremonies' of the Aranda formed a remarkable system of cooperative magic for the benefit of the whole tribe.[14]

As befitted a desert landscape, Aranda religion was thus represented as a collective survival strategy orientated to the production of food. Spencer endorsed this conception enthusiastically, and also agreed with Frazer that beliefs in High Gods formed no part of Aboriginal mystical thought anywhere. In a letter written from the Gulf of Carpentaria after a journey through the interior, he told Frazer that: 'We cannot find a trace of any belief right through the Central tribes from Port Augusta in the south to the Gulf in the north in a being who could be called a deity.'[15] Then, in July 1902, he wrote as follows:

> I feel more than ever convinced that, judging from our Australian tribes as a fair sample of savages, your theory of magic preceding religion is the true one. It is so easy to render into English what a native tells you with regard to an individual such as Baiame or Daramulan so as to give an idea of a belief in a Supreme Being. Howitt, whom Lang quotes time after time, only made his statements on this matter as a result of talking to natives who were so civilized that they said the young men were spoilt by their intercourse with the whites... I do not believe that any native Australian has the slightest idea of anything like an 'All-Father'.[16]

All the same, when Spencer revised *The Native Tribes of Central Australia* in 1927 after a return visit to Alice Springs, he added a section devoted to a Being known as Numbakulla. The Aranda regarded Numbakulla as 'the supreme ancestor, overshadowing all others'.[17] He created the mountains and rivers, the plants and animals, the increase ceremonies, and the sacred icons used in them. Afterwards, he rose into the sky and disappeared forever. In providing scholars with this new information, Spencer felt no need to correct any earlier impressions he may have given. By 1927 the High God controversy, like most who had participated in it, was dead.

The spadework for its burial was done mainly by the French sociologist Emile Durkheim in his celebrated work *The Elementary Forms of the Religious Life* (published first in French in 1912). In Book I, conceived by the author as a graveyard for the theories of his predecessors, Durkheim argued that the basic flaw in Tylor's doctrine of animism was evident in the definition of religion itself. There are, he pointed out, religions – indeed, great religions – from which beliefs in spiritual beings are entirely absent. The best-known example is Buddhism. The Buddhist rejects the idea of a divine creator, since the cosmos is eternal. His only aim is to escape from suffering by suppressing desire. The way is through uprightness, meditation, and wisdom. Ultimately, the individual must make the journey alone. Gods, if they exist, cannot help him and therefore are of no interest.

We can see that, between them, Lang and Durkheim held Tylor in a pincer. At the alleged lower end of religious evolution, the Scottish critique had dwelt on evidence of gods 'where nae gods ought to be';[18] at the upper end, the Gallic intervention now drew attention to religions where gods ought to be but aren't. The evolutionist framework was under siege. At the very least, a surrender of Tylor's definition was called for.

In the meantime, Durkheim proposed an alternative.[19] All known religious beliefs, he said, presuppose a division of the world into two categories, the sacred and the profane. Sacred things, it is true, are often associated with spiritual beings; but their sacredness does not necessarily derive from them. The four noble truths of Buddhism are sacred, even though Buddhist doctrine in pure form is atheistic. Moreover, even in deistic religions, there are rites and interdictions whose sacredness is independent of gods and spirits. We may therefore define religion as a unified set of beliefs and practices relative to sacred things. By sacred we normally mean set apart and in some sense forbidden. A religion typically unites its adherents into a single moral community.

If sacredness exists independently of beliefs in spiritual beings, from where or what does it obtain its force? To find the answer to this question, Durkheim turned to what he regarded as 'the most primitive and simple religion which is actually known',[20] namely, that of the Australian Aborigines. Drawing on the work of Spencer and Gillen (though with a different end in view from Frazer's), he focussed attention upon a category of highly sacred ritual entities known as *churinga*. A *churinga* is an engraved object, made of stone or wood, and normally oval or oblong in shape. It is the religious property of one clan, and one only, and may be said to represent the clan's existential essence. Typically it is conceived as a tangible relic of the clan's totemic ancestry, that is to say, its descent from a primordial power responsible for the reproduction of both the clan and its associated natural species. It is kept in a secret place, whose holiness spreads beyond its confines to the area around it, and is seen and touched only by initiated males. It is the central object of worship in the religious life of the clan.

In Durkheim's view, the *churinga* is best understood by approaching it in the first instance as a kind of flag. In this capacity it symbolizes the corporate identity and continuity of the clan; and it acts both as a stimulus for sentiments of love and loyalty, and as a nodal point around which they crystallize. But it also represents the totem god, and it is from this source that ostensibly it draws its religious character or sacredness. In reality, no such god exists. May we not infer, therefore, that the power from which the symbol actually draws its sacredness is no more or less than the social solidarity of the group itself? The god, in other words, is the clan 'personified and represented to the imagination under the visible form of the animal or vegetable which serves as totem'.[21]

Durkheim went on to argue that the same basic principles, so conspicuous in the case of Australian totemism, form the foundations of the religious life everywhere. But before leaving the Aborigines he briefly reviewed the High God controversy. As to the provenance of the beliefs, he agreed with Lang that they were beyond reasonable doubt autochthonous. There was no need, however, to regard them as in any sense extrinsic to totemism, and certainly no need to attribute them to some mysterious intuition of a cosmic creator and universal legislator. On the contrary the High Gods of Australia represent a transposition of the principles underlying clan totemism to higher levels of social organization. They are 'the logical working-out of these beliefs and their highest form'.[22]

The characteristic form of totemism is egalitarian. Each clan within a language area or tribe has the same status, rights and obligations as all the others. Correspondingly, the totem god of each clan is on a par with all other totem gods. Nevertheless cases occur in which particular totems rise to a position of special esteem within the ceremonial cult life (for example, the Wild Cat totem among the Aranda). This may be accompanied by a tendency to aggrandize the creative powers of a particular clan ancestor and to emphasize his human form, or even to attribute to him an unqualified humanity. Here we would have an incipient High God, who was merely a clan god with a higher prestige ranking than others.

The critical step towards a true High God in Australia depended upon a surrender of some degree of clan autonomy in the interests of coalition and tribal unity. An integral component in this development was the organization of male initiation at a level beyond the individual clan. Above all else, according to Durkheim, Australian High Gods are tribal gods of initiation. Initiation rites were not inaugurated in order to worship High Gods; rather, High Gods were invented in order to authorize the rites. Typically the god of the initiatory cult is human, though vestiges of totemism remain (for instance, in associations with carnivorous birds such as the eaglehawk and the crow); and myths relate how the All-Father transcended the milieu of parochial totemism through conflict and struggle. In south-eastern Australia, initiation cults are not confined to a single tribe but incorporate varying numbers of neighbouring tribes. The unusually high status enjoyed by gods such as Baiame is a consequence of internationalism and religious confederation. We may say (though Durkheim did not put it quite this way) that the height of the god depends on the breadth of the polity.

Durkheim's book on religion was published in the same year that Andrew Lang died. We can assume that, although Lang would have been pleased to read that Australian High Gods are without a doubt indigenous, he would not have welcomed the view that they are merely a product of totemism and political evolution. After all, Hartland[23] had dismissed Baiame as the apotheosis of a tribal headman, and Durkheim's formulation was essentially a sophisticated version of the same opinion. A more serious matter was Durkheim's description of Lang's position as 'theological', as contrasted with the 'sceptical' hypothesis of Tylor.[24] In his reply to Hartland, Lang explicitly denied that he attributed beliefs in a Supreme Being to divine revelation. The basis on which early man had formed such a conception could only be a matter for conjecture, but Lang's own guess was that once humans formed the idea of making, through making things themselves, it would not be long before they arrived at the idea of a divine Maker. If the lowest savages are capable of explaining dreams and death through a theory of souls, as the doctrine of animism asserts, why would they not be equally capable of postulating a World Creator on the model of everyday human manufacture?

Lang may or may not have had a hidden agenda. According to one biographer, he was an essentially religious man who wished to demonstrate that belief in a powerful, kind and righteous deity is part of the heritage of people everywhere.[25] However that may be, his arguments were embraced not long before he died by a scholar whose religious convictions were unmistakable. In 1908–9 Wilhelm Schmidt, a Roman Catholic priest of Vienna, defended Lang against Hartland in the journal *Anthropos* and shortly afterwards began publishing a series of volumes that he described as a continuation of Lang's work on High Gods.[26] However, whereas Lang dissociated himself from revelation, the assumption implicit in Fr Schmidt's project was that men have formed the idea of a Supreme Being because a Supreme Being exists. A primordial intuition of God is evident in all religions, even though it is frequently overtaken by a corrupt and degenerate mythology. The essential truths revealed in the Bible are pristine and universal.

Durkheim referred to Schmidt's alliance with Lang in a footnote. He had no objection to the description of Australian High Gods as eternal, omnipotent, omniscient guardians of the moral order so long as such adjectives are understood in a relative sense (e.g. having more power or knowledge than other sacred beings). But 'if they want to give these words meanings which only a spiritualistic Christian could attach to them, it seems useless to discuss an opinion so contrary to the principles of the historical method'.[27]

In the wake of this magisterial aside, further preoccupation with High Gods was left by and large to theologians. The expression itself virtually dropped out of use in scientific writings on the Aborigines for about sixty years, when it was re-introduced by the eminent student of comparative religion Mircea Eliade in his book *Australian Religions*.[28] In the meantime the field of study was captured almost entirely by Durkheim and his followers, with the result that research was directed primarily to elucidating the relationship between religion and society. In professional writings on the Aborigines, religion and totemism became synonymous and interchangeable.

The most influential exponent of Durkheim's views in British anthropology was Radcliffe-Brown. At the Fourth Pacific Science Congress in 1929 he presented a paper entitled 'The Sociological Theory of Totemism',[29] in which he summarized Durkheim's analysis and commended it to the audience as the most valuable treatment of the subject to date. On one important matter, however, he found himself in disagreement. Durkheim had accounted for the sacredness of the totemic emblem in terms of its role as a symbol of corporate identity, but he had failed to give a convincing answer to the question why it should be based on a natural species. He merely supposed that, because animals and plants lent themselves to artistic representation, they made good emblems. The choice was a matter of convenience.

Such a view, in Radcliffe-Brown's opinion, misunderstood and trivialized the relationship between Aboriginal man and nature, not only in Australia but among hunting and gathering peoples in general. Where survival depends on wild animals and plants, nature as a whole is regarded as in some sense sacred. Totemism is to be understood as a special development of this general relationship, in which particular social segments become correlated with particular *sacra*, i.e. natural species. No doubt the sacredness of the totemic emblem is intensified by sentiments of collective identity, but it is not created by it. The emblem is sacred because the species it represents is already sacred.

The process by which a body of *sacra* becomes differentiated through social segmentation is, Radcliffe-Brown observed, by no means exclusive to totemism. Take, for example, the saints of the Roman Catholic Church. The saints are sacred to members of the church as a whole, but each local congregation is placed in a special relationship to a particular saint to whom its chapel is dedicated. Likewise, while nature in general is sacred to members of an Aboriginal tribe, each clan has a special ritual relationship to a particular species, which we designate in anthropological jargon as its totem.[30]

Now this is undoubtedly an interesting and helpful analogy. But how far can we take it? We know that the saints of the Catholic Church occupy exalted places in a heavenly hierarchy with God at the apex. Is there anything over and above the totems in Aboriginal religious doctrine? Or is it on this point that the analogy breaks down? If such questions occurred to Radcliffe-Brown, he passed over them in silence. Three years earlier, however, he had published a short paper in the *Journal of the Royal Anthropological Institute* that might have seemed to contain the outlines of an answer. It concerned a meta-totemic entity known throughout Australia as the Rainbow Serpent.[31] In 1930 Radcliffe-Brown published a second paper on the subject, this time following a period of field research in New South Wales. The significance of the Rainbow Serpent in Aboriginal religion is summarized as follows: "The rainbow-serpent as it appears in Australian belief may with some justification be described as occupying the position of a deity, and perhaps the most important nature-deity...The rainbow-serpent may be said to be the most important representation of the creative and destructive power of nature, principally in connection with rain and water.'[32]

In his writings on Aboriginal religion, Radcliffe-Brown evinced little interest in the High God controversy, perhaps because he considered the matter had been settled by Durkheim. However, in a lecture on 'Religion and Society' presented in London in 1945, he made several noteworthy points about Baiame. First, he placed greater emphasis than earlier fieldworkers on Baiame's role as a law-giver, and agreed with Andrew Lang and Fr Schmidt that 'Baiame thus closely resembles one aspect of the God of the Hebrews.'[33] Second, Baiame's powers are not believed to include the control of nature. That function is held by another deity, the Rainbow Serpent, whose sinuous image is sculpted in earth at the sacred ceremonies of initiation inaugurated by Baiame and held in his honour.

By bringing together these various statements, we could summarize Radcliffe-Brown's position as follows. The basis of Aboriginal religion is an attitude whereby the whole of nature is regarded as sacred by the whole of society. In many parts of Australia, the Rainbow Serpent is conceived to be a transcendent symbol or ruler of Nature. In some parts, notably south-eastern Australia, a Father-God is conceived to be the creator and ruler of Culture. At lower levels of organization, ritual responsibilities for divisions of nature (e.g. species) are undertaken by correlated divisions of society (e.g. clans). From the perspective of parochial religious history, divisions of the land (e.g. clan territories) are attributed to the creative activities of totemic ancestors ('Dawn Beings'), on whom the various natural species and their human counterparts depend for their existence and reproduction.

In 1926, the year Radcliffe-Brown took up his appointment at the University of Sydney, Lloyd Warner arrived from America to work under his auspices in the Arnhem Land Aboriginal Reserve. In the north-east corner where he established his base, the Rainbow Serpent was known as Yurlunggur, or 'Great Father'. The central narrative in vernacular religious traditions concerned a cataclysmic meeting between Yurlunggur and two women known as the Wawilak Sisters. During a primordial journey of creation the latter, with their two infant sons, camped by Yurlunggur's waterhole. One of the sisters accidentally profaned the sacred pool with her menses. Yurlunggur rose from the depths, drawing up the water with him and flooding the earth. He swallowed the women and their children, regurgitated them, repeated the process several times, finally retained the boys but spewed up their mothers, who turned to stone. The spirits of the Wawilak Sisters later taught men the songs and dances they have performed ever since in their mystery cults.

Whereas in southern Australia the Rainbow Serpent and Baiame were distinct Beings (albeit closely associated), Yurlunggur seemed to be simultaneously a meta-totemic Nature God and an 'international' God of Initiation. Thunder was his voice, lightning his tongue, and the rainbow his body. Each year he sent the north-west monsoon and flooded the land. When boys approached puberty, they were told by senior men: 'The Great Father Snake smells your foreskin. He is calling for it.'[34] Soon afterwards the lads were taken from their mothers and circumcised.

Warner described four great initiatory rites associated with Yurlunggur, of which the most powerful and dramatic was a cult called Kunapipi (an alternative name for the Rainbow Serpent). Late on the final night of the ceremony, the novices were placed on the concave side of a crescent-shaped trench, representing the generative organs of the Wawilak Sisters. Enormous symbols of Yurlunggur then emerged from the darkness and moved slowly towards the trench. The ceremony ended as they rose and fell above it, then went into it. A notable feature of the Kunapipi was the use of a bull-roarer[35] to simulate Yurlunggur's voice. Warner rendered its name as Muit, which was also another name for Yurlunggur himself. Half a century earlier Howitt had recorded virtually the same name for the bull-roarer used in the Father-God initiatory cults of south-eastern New South Wales, some 2000 miles away.[36]

Radcliffe-Brown's successor at Sydney University was Adolphus Peter Elkin, clergyman-turned-anthropologist. In 1939, two years after the publication of Warner's book *A Black Civilization*, Elkin received a communication from a legendary bushman named Bill Harney about a Kunapipi cult in southern Arnhem Land.[37] The intriguing fact was that whereas among the northern tribes the name Kunapipi referred to a deity manifest as the Rainbow Serpent and known as 'Great Father', here it was the name of a deity spoken of as the 'Old Woman' or 'The Mother'. Moreover, the bull-roarer, typically a symbol of male thunder-gods, was in this case said to be the Mother's womb. The climax of the ceremony was the symbolic rebirth of novices from an earth trench, also said to be her womb. Elkin was convinced that Harney had discovered for the first time in Australia a genuine Mother-Goddess, originating perhaps in Hindu beliefs brought to Arnhem Land by pre-Islamic Indonesian fishermen.

Unbeknown to Elkin, so it would seem, his younger colleague W.E.H. Stanner had witnessed initiations into a fully fledged Mother-Goddess cult four years earlier, some 300 miles to the west at Port Keats.[38] The details did not become available until 1959, when Stanner published the first article in his Oceania Monograph, *On Aboriginal Religion*. Among the Murinbata, whom he visited in the second half of 1935, the Old Woman or 'The Mother of All' was known as Karwadi. The induction of novices followed their circumcision and extended over a period of several months. On the third day after the youths were taken to the secret ground, they were anointed with blood and told they were about to be swallowed alive by Karwadi. Concealed men approached the ceremonial ground swinging bull-roarers to signify the awesome proximity of the Mother. Then, as tension reached a peak, they sprang into view. Following this climactic introduction to Karwadi, the novices spent a lengthy period of seclusion and instruction away from women and children. At the end of the ceremony they re-entered the general community by crawling towards their mothers through a tunnel of legs formed by initiated men.

As well as witnessing the Karwadi ceremony, Stanner made another remarkable discovery. The Murinbata knew the Rainbow Serpent as Kunmanggur, conceived as a man of great size and superhuman powers, whose mythology impinged 'more widely and deeply on the mystical beliefs of the Murinbata than any other'.[39] He was described as the First Man, who 'made us all', whose spit was the rainbow, and whose image remained in ancient rock-paintings. Yet within living memory no ceremonies were performed in his honour, and no cult existed in his name. Stanner conjectured that as colonization progressively dislocated and demoralized the Murinbata, they turned away from the Father towards the Mother in search of succour and renewed vitality.[40]

It is interesting that Elkin and Stanner independently attributed the emergence of Mother-Goddesses to external impacts and historical contingency. As the spectrum of data widened after World War 2, however, another possibility came into view, namely that the apotheosis of the reproductive and nurturing properties of *both* sexes was a generative principle inherent in Aboriginal religious thinking throughout the continent, and therefore probably of great antiquity. For reasons that are not clearly understood, the degree of prominence given to one sex compared with the other differed from time to time and place to place. Thus we have Father-Gods eminent in the south of the continent, and Mother-Goddesses conspicuous in the north; and, if Stanner's conjecture is correct, a Father-God displaced by a Mother-Goddess within the same culture. But there is a further manifestation of the principle that may provide the best key of all to its inner dynamics: the *conjunction* of male and female reproductive powers, residing either in deities of opposite sex or, more intriguingly, in a single deity of indeterminate sex.

Shortly after the war Elkin made arrangements for two of his students, Ronald and Catherine Berndt, to begin fieldwork in Arnhem Land. The location chosen was east of Warner's base and north of Harney's. Here Ronald Berndt was able to study male secret cults intensively, and in the early 1950s he published his findings in two books, one called *Kunapipi*, the other *Djanggawul*. As expositions of sexual conjunction in myth, rite and reality, they are probably without peer. Whereas Warner had reported that Kunapipi was the Rainbow Snake, and Harney said it was 'The Mother', Berndt maintained it was both: 'In north-eastern Arnhem Land, the name Kunapipi expresses a dual concept: on the one hand it refers to a Fertility Mother, or Mothers, and on the other to the great Rainbow Snake. This is the symbolism of the Uterus and the Penis, natural instruments of fecundity.'[41]

The formulation has an immediate appeal. Unfortunately, however, there are certain features of the Penis that can only be described as problematic. First, the sex of the Rainbow Snake in north-eastern Arnhem Land is usually said to be female. Berndt writes reassuringly that this 'does not affect its role as a Penis symbol',[42] but we are left to wonder why not. Second, while the swallowing of the Wawilak Sisters symbolizes coitus, regurgitation signifies rebirth.[43] The Rainbow Snake, it seems, contains within itself the generative properties of both sexes. Third, as well as expressing the dual concept of Rainbow Snake and Fertility Mother, the word *kunapipi* also means 'subincised penis'. As the incised urethra allegedly simulates the vulva, the male organ symbolically acquires the bisexuality of the Rainbow Serpent. It becomes, so to speak, an instance of the Rainbow Serpent.[44]

In the year following the publication of Berndt's *Kunapipi*, a German anthropologist named Andreas Lommel presented an account of the Rainbow Serpent among the Unambal people of Western Australia.[45] According to the Unambal, the Rainbow Serpent is a bisexual snake named Ungud who, with the help of the Milky Way, made the world. Natural species came into existence when Ungud dreamed itself into their various shapes. In the same way Ungud created clones of itself, known as *wonjina*, and deposited them in various places, particularly waterholes. The *wonjina* in turn generated the human spirits that enter women and become babies (Plate 10). Ungud is thus above all an archetype of life itself – an All-Soul, perhaps, rather than a Father-God or Mother-God.

Representations of the *wonjina* have excited the interest of anthropologists and others since they were discovered on rock walls by George Grey in 1838.[46] The Unambal say they were left there by the *wonjina* themselves. They usually appear as figures with strongly delineated heads and truncated bodies, though in some cases bodies are missing altogether. The faces are always mouthless (Plate 11). It would be consistent with the description of Ungud as bisexual if the apparent facial configuration of the *wonjina* was meant in fact to represent the male genitalia (testicles and penis) inside the vagina. The horizontal segmentation of the 'nose' would then be explicable as a differentiation of the glans from the shaft, and the absence of a mouth would no longer be a mystery.[47]

What are the properties of rainbows and snakes that have attracted Aboriginal thinkers in their search for godhead? Since the formulations are ancient, we have no sure way of telling. But we may reasonably presume that the quest, by its very nature, leads the mind away from the known (whose existence is the object of explanation) into the unknown. Cosmologically, the unknown worlds nearest at hand and most accessible to the imagination lie in the regions above and below the earth's surface – the sky and the underworld. Rainbows appear in the former, and snakes emerge from the latter. Their unification in the concept of the Rainbow Snake constitutes not merely an imaginative connection between the two domains of mystery impinging on the everyday world but a theory of an external source of the latter's Being.[48]

It is true that snakes are not the only things that emerge from the ground, nor are rainbows the only things that appear in the sky. Two points, however, are in their favour. First, they share a rough similarity of shape, so that the notion of the rainbow as a huge snake rising from the ground into the sky has a basis in empirical observation. Second, snakes are tubes that enter holes and have the ability to extrude objects as well as ingest them. They thus have properties that, at the level of analogy, combine in a single creature the salient activities of the human male and female generative organs. By an act of intellectual transposition of the observed conditions for the production of individual lives, the Rainbow Snake is equipped with the means for the production and reproduction of Life itself.[49]

Can we say, then, to bring this small segment of anthropological history to a tidy ending, that the High (or Highest) God of Terra Australis was the Rainbow Serpent? Not unless we want to start another argument. In a brief but challenging essay published in 1978 Kenneth Maddock maintained that the notion of a single, well-defined mythological entity known throughout the continent as the Rainbow Serpent is an anthropological fiction. The accumulated evidence indicates that there is no constancy of form, powers or role among the mythological creatures who manifest themselves as the rainbow. As well as snakes of various species, there are also crocodiles, lizards, and amalgamations of features of different species. Sometimes the Rainbow Serpent is ritually important, sometimes inconsequential. Even within a single culture it is often unclear whether it is one or many, male or female, serpent or human. And in many tribes the most important deities have little or no connection with the rainbow at all.

Nevertheless (and here Maddock would agree), we can still speak of a genre, a suite of fleeting forms connected with the rainbow through which the philosophers of Aboriginal Australia have sought to express the idea of an underlying reality. Metaphysical abstractions, being hard to grasp, lend themselves to vulgarization; and the ontological quest easily lapses into the pleasurable and useful pastime of telling fireside stories to frightened children. But in the higher reaches of serious reflection, we find a persistent intuition of a presence or power whose Oneness is felt to account for the plurality and impermanence of the sensible world and those who live in it. Totemic archetypes achieve this effect within specific limits. The concept of a cosmic One is naturally less well articulated, since it is the archetype of everything and therefore indescribable. Verbally, mortals can do little more than give it a name, such as Ungud, and affirm its existence. The impotence of language forces inquiry to call on other helpers, particularly art, music and dance. It is through these forms, elaborated and reworked in a rich mosaic of religious history, that men have reached towards the One and tried to become part of it and to make it part of themselves.

Pl. 10   Wonjina and spirit-child.

Pl. 11   Wonjina at Mushroom Rock. We can see here, adjacent to the large central wonjina, a partially overlaid wonjina with an ithyphallic 'nose'.

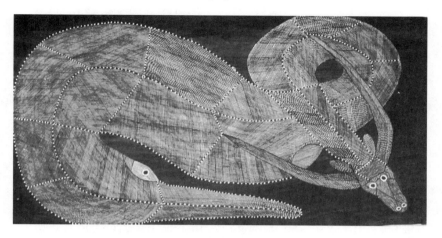

Pl. 12 Buffalo-headed Rainbow Serpent.

In 1990, sixty years after the appearance of Radcliffe-Brown's *Oceania* article on the Rainbow Serpent, Luke Taylor published an essay entitled 'The Rainbow Serpent as Visual Metaphor in Western Arnhem Land'. Kunwinyku artists of western Arnhem Land use the English word 'rainbow' to describe two distinct Beings: Yingarna, the first mother, and Ngalyod, her son. Both are thought of as bisexual, and both are typically represented as a combination of elements drawn from different species, including the feral water buffalo introduced in post-colonial times. The paintings, in Taylor's view, 'express the generalized message that the diversity of life masks an ultimate relatedness'.[50] In sharper contemporary focus, they also express the political relatedness of all Kunwinyku. The need to fashion a wider unity in the face of white domination was affirmed recently when a painting of the rainbow by a Kunwinyku artist was adopted as a logo by the Northern Land Council, representing Aboriginal interests throughout the Top End of the Northern Territory. On an even larger stage, devised to proclaim pan-Aboriginality on the two-hundredth anniversary of the colonization of Australia, urban Aborigines performed against the backgound of a Kunywinku painting of the Rainbow Serpent in the Rainbow Serpent Theatre at World Expo in Brisbane. Durkheim would have approved.[51]

7

Conception and misconception

In 1905 Sir James Frazer announced to the scientific world that he had discovered the origin of totemism.[1] There had been several false starts, and the search had been a long one. In 1886 his colleague and friend William Robertson Smith had invited him to write the entry on totemism for the *Encyclopaedia Britannica*. In the event he wrote a short book, setting out the available data and suggesting that a totem was a kind of strong-box, external to the body, in which a man deposited his soul for safe-keeping.[2] It was a theory that Frazer modestly, but quite accurately, judged to be of little importance. Then, in 1899, he had acted as midwife to Baldwin Spencer's presentation of central Australian totemism as a system of cooperative magic designed to increase the food supply.[3] Without abandoning these notions as interpretations of later developments, he now believed that the origin of totemism was to be found in ignorance of the role of the father in procreation. This had been reported by Spencer and Gillen in 1899 for the Aranda tribe of central Australia.[4] Conceptional totemism, Frazer told readers of the *Fortnightly Review*, 'furnishes an intelligible starting-point for the evolution of totemism in general. In it, after years of sounding, our plummets seem to touch bottom at last.'[5]

Conceptional totemism was Frazer's designation for the Aranda dogma that women became pregnant when totemic spirits entered their bodies. During the Dreamtime, the ancestors of contemporary natural species wandered the countryside and subsided at last into the ground at particular locations. They took with them their sacred stones, called *churinga*, which continued to generate spiritual power and life essence. Notable features of the landscape (such as rocks and waterholes) represented discrete totemic centres, each of which was associated with a single ancestral form. For instance, Witchetty Grub ancestors deposited stones not far from a picturesque gap in the mountains near Alice Springs, and Witchetty Grub spirits dwelt in various conspicuous rocks and ancient gum-trees in the vicinity. If a woman conceived a child after being in this locality, it was assumed that a Witchetty Grub spirit had gone into her womb. It was immaterial whether the mother herself was an incarnation of a Witchetty Grub spirit, or of some other totemic form. The father's conceptional totem was likewise irrelevant. For instance, the mother might have been conceived at an Emu site, the child at a Frog site, and the father at a Witchetty Grub site.[6]

As regards knowledge of the physiology of procreation, the facts seemed quite clear. Time after time Spencer and Gillen had questioned their Aranda informants on this point, and always the answer was that pregnancy was not the direct result of sexual intercourse. Sexual cohabitation merely prepared the mother for the reception and birth of an already formed spirit child.[7] Such profound ignorance of natural causation, Frazer supposed, must date from a time immeasurably remote. Accordingly, we may infer that conceptional totemism was antecedent to systems in which totemic affiliation was transmitted matrilineally or patrilineally (i.e. in which the child belonged to the same totem group as its mother or its father). Indeed, it could be safely asserted that central Australian conception beliefs represented totemism in its earliest surviving form.[8]

Andrew Lang saw Frazer's article as he was reading the proofs of his own account of the origins of totemism, due to be published towards the end of 1905.[9] The two theories were irreconcilable. Totemism, according to Lang, began when men bestowed animal and plant names upon discrete human groups in order to differentiate them. As the Scots used to say, 'the name goes before everything'. In time the purely semiotic purpose was forgotten, and beliefs developed about mystical connections between the group and the natural species whose name it bore. Such mythologies inevitably gave rise to assumptions about common descent from a totem ancestor, shared kinship, and the need to prohibit marriage within the group. Initially totemic descent was conceived to be through females, since sexual relations were likely to have been promiscuous and paternity difficult to establish. Patrilineal transmission of the totem was a later development and indicative of evolutionary progress.

Confronted with Frazer's assertion that conceptional totemism predated inherited totemism, Lang immediately drafted a polemic and added it to his book as the final chapter. Much of his discussion concerned the question whether Aranda culture as a whole was more archaic than other Australian cultures where the system of totemism was hereditary rather than conceptional. Appealing to criteria such as sexual arrangements, complexity of kinship organization, religious beliefs and inheritance of office, Lang succeeded in throwing doubt not only on Frazer's evolutionary sequence but on his own as well.[10] The critical difficulty was that in south-eastern tribes with matrilineal descent of the totem, men not only were apparently aware of paternity but stressed its importance relative to maternity. According to Howitt,[11] they claimed that children originated solely from the male parent and that the mother was merely a nurse. In south-eastern Australia matriliny thus coexisted with knowledge of paternity, whereas in central Australia ignorance of the male role coexisted with patrilineal inheritance of ritual and political office. In order to save his theory, Lang contested the alleged nescience and suggested that the Aranda had merely subordinated their awareness of the facts to an over-riding doctrine of reincarnation of the perpetual souls of Dream-time ancestors, in itself a sign of advanced intellect.

While the futile argument between Lang and Frazer heralded the end of a purely evolutionistic approach to totemism, it marked the beginning of a controversy about conception beliefs in Australia and elsewhere that has yet to be put finally to rest. By 1937 Malinowski had declared the alleged primitive nescience of paternity to be 'the most exciting and controversial issue in the comparative science of Man'.[12] Thirty years later British and American scholars were at war over Malinowski's own contribution to the subject.[13] Twenty years further on, a seminal article on the cultural construction of paternity provided the focus for an entire *Festschrift*.[14] Even if Malinowski's superlatives now seem excessive, there is no doubt that the issue has proved to be one of the agonistic evergreens of twentieth-century anthropology. Why it had so much life in it is still not clearly understood.

In 1894, the year that Baldwin Spencer made his first visit to Central Australia, Sidney Hartland published a three-volume treatise on the myth motif of supernatural birth, beginning with the legend of Perseus and ending with the conception of Christ.[15] As a result of his survey, it could now be said that the miraculous birth of superhuman culture-heroes was widely distributed in folklore, and might possibly be universal. No doubt the idea was facilitated by an imperfect knowledge of paternity, but the force of a belief in supernatural birth obviously depended upon a notion of natural or ordinary birth. The importance of the Aranda, as Frazer put it in 1899 when lauding the discoveries of Spencer and Gillen, was that they constituted 'the first case on record of a tribe who believe in immaculate conception as the sole cause of the birth of every human being who comes into the world'.[16]

It was soon evident that the Aranda were not unique. In 1903 Walter Roth, a medical officer in North Queensland, reported that the Tully River Aborigines did not acknowledge sexual intercourse as the cause of conception in humans, although they conceded that it accounted for procreation in animals.[17] In 1904, following an expedition to Central Australian tribes north of Alice Springs, Spencer and Gillen stated that conception beliefs in all cases were essentially the same as among the Aranda. Indeed, whereas the Aranda were initially credited with the belief that sexual intercourse prepared the way for the entry of a spirit-child into the womb, it now appeared that, along with their northern neighbours, they believed that pregnancy could occur without coition.[18] In 1913 the legendary Daisy Bates informed a meeting of scientists in Sydney that the natives of the Kimberley region of Western Australia insisted that sexual intercourse had nothing to do with procreation. They believed that conception occurred when a baby appeared to its father in a dream and then entered the body of its mother.[19] In 1914 Spencer published results of further fieldwork among tribes in the Top End of the Northern Territory, where once again he found that knowledge of physical paternity was lacking.[20]

As these reports reached the armchairs of Europe, two opposed scholarly positions began to emerge. One, initiated by Frazer, was that the statements of the natives were to be regarded straightforwardly as expressions of genuine ignorance. However, opinions differed as to the appropriate construction to be placed on such a state of affairs. Frazer saw it simply as indicative of an abysmally low level of mental development.[21] By contrast Arnold van Gennep, the eminent French folklorist, considered it to be little different from the ignorance of procreative mechanisms still prevailing among the masses of Europe. In any case, given that Aboriginal girls go to their husbands before reaching puberty, it is a matter of empirical observation among them that sexual intercourse does not necessarily lead to conception. Why should ignorance of physical paternity be a symptom of arrested mental evolution when a proper understanding of fertilization was not achieved by Western science until the nineteenth century?[22]

The opposing position, initiated by Lang, was that native testimony on the subject is not to be taken at face-value; at some level the connection between coition and conception is apprehended, but officially it is denied in favour of a doctrine of spiritual causation. In a book entitled *Sexual Antagonism*, published in 1913, Walter Heape expressed disbelief that such keen observers as the Aborigines would fail to note the gross facts of biological reproduction. Fortunately, Roth had made it clear that in at least one tribe the facts were acknowledged in the case of generation among animals. More importantly, he had explained that they were denied in the case of humans in order to affirm the superiority of man over beasts. But there was likely to be more to it than snobbishness. Could it not be that professed nescience and the doctrine of spirit-conception were female creations enabling adulterous pregnancies to be cloaked behind mystifications? The attribution of conception to chance supernatural causes shielded women from suspicion of extra-marital natural causes. Simultaneously, it liberated men from the embarrassments of cuckoldry.[23]

In 1918 Carveth Read reviewed the two rival viewpoints, lending his weight to the thesis that the natives possessed real knowledge of paternity but repressed it in favour of religious dogma. Although a psychologist as well as a philosopher,[24] he used the term repression without allusion to its burgeoning psychoanalytic connotation and meant simply the suppression of the truth by indoctrination. A decade later a gift from Princess Marie Bonaparte of Greece enabled a young Hungarian psychoanalyst named Geza Roheim to go to central Australia and study the Aborigines at first hand.[25] With the help of his wife, who worked with the womenfolk, and of his own natural talent as a linguist, he plumbed depths that in 1905 Sir James Frazer would not have dreamed possible.

On 5 August, 1929, Roheim made an entry in his field notebook that subsequently bore much of the weight of his interpretation of Aranda conception theory. That day, while watching children play with some toys he had given them, he observed a boy named Wili-kutu placing a paper trumpet over his penis and then thrusting with it. Later Wili-kutu put a ball into the trumpet and took it out, saying 'This is how semen comes out'. He repeated the process with a toy serpent, saying 'The child comes out of the penis.'[26] Roheim took this as clear evidence that small boys were aware of the connection between copulation and conception, even if grown men disowned it. At some stage the knowledge was banished from consciousness, where its place was taken by a doctrine of mystical conception. How do we account for this retrogression from fact to fantasy? According to Roheim, we are dealing with the repression of the Oedipus complex, in particular the procreative role of the father. To know that children are produced by coitus is to acknowledge not only that my mother (whom I love) has sexual intercourse with my father, but that I am its product. In the case of Aboriginal males, this painful fact was gradually repressed into the unconscious, while the myth of spirit-entry and reincarnation extinguished (or at least diminished) the carnal role of the father and allowed the son to represent himself as the agent of his own conception.[27]

Without doubt the most formidable and tenacious champions of the rival position were Malinowski and his protégé M.F. Ashley-Montagu. In 1913 the former reviewed Australian conception beliefs and concluded that over most of the continent the father's share in procreation was not known.[28] Three years later he reported an equally profound nescience among the natives of the Trobriand Islands,[29] thus forging in world anthropology an enduring link between the Australians and the

Trobrianders as the two prime exemplars of primitive ignorance of paternity. In *The Father in Primitive Psychology* (1927) and *The Sexual Life of Savages* (1929), he insisted that the answer to the question, 'Are the natives really ignorant of physiological fatherhood?', was 'unambiguously and decisively' in the affirmative. According to Trobriand metaphysics, a woman became pregnant when a spirit-child entered her belly. Systematic inquiry had shown conclusively that men sincerely believed sexual intercourse not to be necessary for pregnancy, and semen not to be implicated in the formation of a foetus.[30]

In 1929 Montague Ashley-Montagu, a student at University College, acted on a suggestion by Malinowski that he might present a seminar paper at the London School of Economics on the procreative theories of primitive man. It was the beginning of a lifetime of prodigious scholarly output. Later the same year Ashley-Montagu's paper appeared as an article in *The Realist*; by 1937 it had blossomed into a large book entitled *Coming into Being among the Australian Aborigines*. After reviewing the now-impressive body of data, Ashley-Montagu came to essentially the same conclusion as Malinowski had a quarter of a century earlier: 'From the evidence thus presented the conclusion is clear that in Australia practically universally, according to orthodox belief, pregnancy is regarded as causally unconnected with intercourse.'[31] Malinowski expressed satisfaction with the outcome in a lengthy foreword. It was true that a few dissentient opinions had been expressed, but the author had effectively disposed of them. There could be no doubt that Dr Ashley-Montagu's judgment would remain as the ultimate conclusion of science.[32]

For the purposes of his argument, Ashley-Montagu divided the continent into four broad regions: (1) Central Australia (2) Top End of the Northern Territory (3) North Queensland (4) Western Australia.[33] His review of each region began with a recapitulation of the 'classical' report of nescience viz. Spencer and Gillen for Central Australia; Spencer for the Top End; Roth for North Queensland; and Daisy Bates for Western Australia. This was followed by summaries and discussions of more recent reports, with particular attention to those conflicting with the paradigm. The three major dissenters, as identified by Malinowski in his foreword, were Lloyd Warner, Donald Thomson and Geza Roheim. Let us consider the nature of their dissent and the manner of its disposal.

In an article published in 1931 Warner recounted an anecdote that in the event undermined the ascription of nescience more than any other statement in the entire controversy.[34] During his first field trip to Arnhem Land, he became convinced that the Murngin had no understanding of the physiological nature of conception whatever. Speaking of their own experience as fathers, numerous men told him that their children had come in the form of spirits during dreams. After seeking directions to their mothers, they entered the latters' vaginas. During his second trip, an occasion arose in which Warner was able to ask several old men to explain the function of semen. They looked at him with incredulity and replied that semen 'was what made babies'. Warner went on to explain that his initial false assumption had been the result of his failure to appreciate his hosts' intellectual priorities. For them, the spiritual origins of the self were much more important and interesting than mundane details like copulation and semen. An intruder from Mars would probably have made a similar error had he arrived among the Puritans of colonial Massachusetts and recorded their belief that babies come from heaven.

The question raised was whether the Murngin were to be put to one side as an isolated case, or whether the assertion of a general procreative nescience among the Aborigines was based on superficial inquiry of the kind that led to Warner's initial false inference. Whereas Warner inclined to the latter view, Ashley-Montagu urged the former. The coastal tribes of Arnhem Land had for centuries been visited by Malay fishermen from Macassar in search of trepang. There was a distinct possibility, therefore, that the beliefs of the region were not strictly indigenous. In Ashley-Montagu's view, the question whether the Aborigines were ignorant of the facts of procreation could be settled only through research on tribes uncontaminated by foreign influences.[35] Malinowski for his part treated the anecdote as inconsequential. Warner's field location was 'on the periphery of Australian culture', and the value of his material was marred in any case by a tendency to confuse orthodox belief with 'random statements of irrelevant opinion'.[36] Presumably the latter included statements by old men on the procreative properties of semen.

Donald Thomson was a Melbourne field biologist who developed an interest in Aborigines in the early 1930s. Unaware that Warner had declared war on the nescience camp from his base in Arnhem Land, he published a similar challenge a few years later from Cape York Peninsula. Among the eastern tribes, men insisted that babies were produced by *tall'all*, the seminal fluid of the father. There were no beliefs in spirit entry or reincarnation, and the mother's role in procreation was regarded as unimportant. Women used certain plants as contraceptives in the conviction that they closed the genital passages and thus prevented semen from entering. Among the Wik Monkan of western Cape York, Thomson was informed that the embryo developed through a build up of seminal fluid in the uterus. A single act of sexual intercourse was deemed insufficient for pregnancy to ensue. Accumulated semen was said to block the flow of menstrual blood, thus allowing pregnancy to begin. The elderly become infertile because they are unable to copulate frequently enough. Humans die because in ancestral times they spurned the Moon-Man's offer of semen. He drank it himself, and that is why he is able to regenerate himself each month.[37]

In Thomson's opinion these facts showed conclusively that knowledge of physical paternity existed among the coastal peoples of Cape York. On the strength of his observations he therefore threw down the gauntlet to the nescience school and in particular its 'most fervid advocate', Professor Malinowski.[38] Yet in the same passage he adverted to his own earlier demonstrations of substantial cultural diffusion to north Queensland emanating from Papua via the Torres Straits Islands. Not surprisingly, when Ashley-Montagu came to review Cape York he graciously complimented Thomson on the extraordinary interest of his material and simultaneously accepted the offer to regard it as irrelevant.[39]

The case of Roheim required a different treatment. A charge of 'contamination' could be a double-edged weapon, since the Aranda in Spencer's day had already been subject to considerable European influence. Roheim, moreover, claimed that some of his most critical evidence had come from Luritja tribesmen who had never seen white men before. These informants stated that the human embryo passed from a *churinga* into the body of the father, and thence through his penis into the mother's womb.[40] Ashley-Montagu thought it possible that white influences were at work even here. Nevertheless, he conceded that Roheim's report could not easily be dismissed. At the very least it suggested a notion that intercourse was necessary to prepare a woman for spirit entry. As to Roheim's assertion that children know the facts of procreation and subsequently repress them, the simulation of intercourse may merely reflect the adult belief that the penis transmits the spirit-child. It does not necessarily indicate an understanding of the role of semen.[41]

Although Warner, Thomson and Roheim were the main dissenters, they were not the only ones. From Alice Springs, Olive Pink wrote that contrary to accepted anthropological opinion the Aranda understood physical paternity and believed that the spirit entered at the time of 'quickening' after the body of the baby had been produced conjointly by its mother and father.[42] Ursula McConnel reported that the tribes she had studied in north Queensland 'quite definitely consider sex-contact to be necessary to child-bearing', though they admitted they did not know in what way.[43] In Western Australia Radcliffe-Brown discovered a ritual for increasing sexual desire which was carried out explicitly for the purpose of increasing the population. It was true that in the same area Aborigines also associated conception with spirit entry following gifts of food from a hunter, but inconsistencies of this kind in folk belief were just as common among uneducated Europeans as among Aborigines and should not surprise us.[44]

In all the recent material reviewed by Ashley-Montagu, the strongest affirmation of nescience came from W.E.H. Stanner. Among the Murinbata of Port Keats 'sexual intercourse has an erotic significance only'.[45] It was not associated with conception, except inasmuch as defloration was acknowledged to be a precondition. Spirit children existed in various forms and made their presence known to a father by tweaking his hair, whispering in his ear, or setting his muscles twitching. They normally entered a woman's body through her toe nail. Stanner recorded these facts in 1935, within months of the arrival of the first missionaries. He had previously lived among neighbouring tribes whose cultures had been disturbed in various degrees by European intrusion. In some, the mystical theory of conception had been abandoned in favour of confused versions of white statements on the subject, while in others traditional and introduced theories coexisted and could be elicited by framing the same questions differently.[46]

A similar though slightly less unequivocal report of nescience came from Lauriston Sharp. In a letter to Ashley-Montagu written in 1936, he referred to 'a vague recognition of a very general relationship between intercourse and conception'. People admitted that if a woman never had intercourse, she would not find a spirit-child. There was no suggestion, however, that semen played a role, or even that regular sexual relations were necessary. After all, sex was a pleasant and exciting pastime in which all men and women engaged, but not all women had babies. Having lived among the Yir-Yiront for almost three years, Sharp failed to see why their lack of detailed knowledge of reproductive physiology should be treated as evidence of retarded intelligence.[47]

In bringing his survey to an end, Ashley-Montagu declared that its chief purpose was to assemble the classical and recent accounts so that readers might form judgments for themselves. His own conclusion, as we have seen, was that in orthodox Aboriginal belief pregnancy was regarded as causally unconnected with intercourse. We have also seen that the words 'orthodox' and 'causally' were used as devices to protect the proposition against falsification. Whenever the author was faced with beliefs implying awareness of a connection between intercourse and pregnancy, he argued that they were unorthodox (e.g., of alien provenance), or that the connection was not necessary and sufficient (e.g., it lacked a notion of fertilization). The outcome was, on the one hand, an artificial uniformity and, on the other, a criterion of knowledge that if applied consistently throughout the world would deprive the Aborigines of the special place reserved for them in the gallery of procreative nescience.[48]

In the thirty years' peace that followed the publication of Ashley-Montagu's book, fresh evidence confirmed his survey of previous material in one notable respect: conception beliefs in one area were not necessarily the same as in another. Some fieldworkers reported ignorance, others reported knowledge. In 1939 Phyllis Kaberry maintained that, despite contact with Europeans over several generations, the people of the East Kimberley 'still had no idea of the true relation between sexual intercourse and conception'.[49] Coitus was an erotic pastime whose only relevance for reproduction was that it prepared the way for the entry of a spirit-child 'found' by the father. Women were adamant that semen had nothing to do with the formation of a child, though several thought the embryo might float on it like a water-lily. Professor Elkin, drawing on his own extensive experience, endorsed these observations in his foreword. A year earlier in another context he had warned against upsetting the Aborigines' spiritual view of nature, including notions of pre-existence and spirit-conception. Nevertheless, he thought that if men were instructed in the biological facts of fatherhood they might be induced to give up certain customs objectionable to us, such as wife-lending and ceremonial licence.[50]

Not long after the publication of Kaberry's book two of Elkin's pupils set out for Ooldea, a siding on the Transcontinental Railway in South Australia. In their preliminary field report Ronald and Catherine Berndt expressed the opinion that Aborigines would only discuss intimate matters when a complete intimacy existed between field-worker and informant, a fact that helped to explain why so many previous observers had failed to realise that spiritual belief existed side by side with a more or less accurate knowledge of paternity. The Aboriginal people of Ooldea were a case in point. They said that semen built up in the uterus following a number of ejaculations until it stopped the flow of menstrual blood. The latter mixed with the semen and formed the foetus, which was then animated by a spirit entering through the women's vagina.[51] A few years later Mr and Mrs Berndt discovered basically the same theory of procreation two thousand miles to the north in western Arnhem Land, with the interesting elaboration that the husband ejaculated the spirit-child into an 'egg' formed by a coagulation of menses and semen.[52]

By the time Mervyn Meggitt published his monograph on the Walbiri of Central Australia in 1962, it was apparent that there might be subjective and contextual factors operating in the investigative process itself. Answers to questions on sexual topics might reflect not only cultural differences among Aborigines but sub-cultural and individual differences among the investigators. Perhaps it was significant that Professor Elkin found nescience wherever he worked, whereas the Berndts mostly found knowledge. There was also the possibility, so far not taken seriously, of a considerable variety of opinion within a single community. For instance, all the older men with whom Meggitt discussed conception maintained that, while copulation was a necessary preliminary to spirit entry, the latter was more important because it animated the foetus and determined the personality. One man volunteered that the foetus was a mixture of semen and menses. Another claimed that semen transmitted the father's clan-spirit into the child. Walbiri women, on the other hand, told Mrs Meggitt that copulation and menstrual blood were the important factors and that spirit entry merely gave the child an identity. Meggitt concluded that responses to inquiries about procreation depended on who was asked and in what circumstances.[53]

While ethnographers in Australia were doing their best to clarify the problem at an empirical level, war broke out again among theoreticians in the northern hemisphere. The provocation was allegedly the result of an example taken at random. In 1961 Edmund Leach, Fellow of King's College, Cambridge and subsequently a knight of the realm, published an essay designed to prove that J.G. Frazer, erstwhile Fellow of Trinity College and author of the best-selling paperback *The Golden Bough*, was in fact a pedestrian, unoriginal scholar who happened to have powerful friends and an ambitious French wife. To make matters worse, Sir James was an unabashed racist who, in the name of literary elegance, distorted the statements of observers upon whose writings his own almost entirely depended. To illustrate some of these points, Dr Leach invited his readers to compare Frazer's paraphrase of Roth's report of conception beliefs among the Tully River Aborigines with the original in Bulletin No. 5 of *North Queensland Ethnography*. It was evident that the intention of Frazer's additions and modifications was to magnify the 'childlike ignorance' of the natives. Admittedly, Roth himself said the latter were ignorant of the connection between copulation and pregnancy, but there was nothing in his text to warrant such an inference. The modern interpretation would be that in this society 'the relationship between the woman's child and the clansmen of the woman's husband stems from public recognition of the bonds of marriage rather than from the fact of cohabitation, which is a very normal state of affairs'.[54]

Given that (a) much better exemplifications of the racist assumptions underlying Frazer's conception theory of totemism were available, (b) the 'modern interpretation', as presented, was somewhat less than self-evident, and (c) the assertions appeared in the journal of the American Academy of Arts and Sciences (a publication not normally read by anthropologists), Leach's contribution to the conception debate might easily have passed without notice. Such was not to be the case. Two years later Melford Spiro from the University of Washington held it up to an audience on Dr Leach's home ground as an example of the peculiar notion advanced by some structuralists that, regardless of their ostensible meaning, 'religious explanations are concerned almost exclusively with phenomena of social structure'.[55] After dissecting Leach's 'modern interpretation' in a lengthy paragraph, he discarded it as being of no value. The vernacular statements quoted by Roth were, in Professor Spiro's view, not symbolic expressions of structural relationships but literal attempts to explain a biological phenomenon whose true cause the Tully River Aborigines did not know.

Spiro's sally into British social anthropology was met by the full force of the 1966 Henry Myers Lecture at the Royal Anthropological Institute.[56] By this time Leach had read Ashley-Montagu and was able to inform his adversary that their respective positions on the issue were already of some antiquity. Spiro was a latter-day apostle of the Frazerian view that the savages were truly ignorant, whereas Leach belonged to the Lang tradition of assuming that their formulations expressed the priority of religious dogma over prosaic knowledge. Adherents of the nescience school were, as Leach put it, 'positively eager' to attribute stupidity to native people in order to affirm their own superiority. Nearly all the recent evidence on the Aborigines led to the conclusion that 'the formally expressed ignorance of physiological paternity is a kind of religious fiction'.[57] The reports of Stanner and Kaberry were anomalous and hopelessly biased.

The title of Leach's lecture was 'Virgin Birth'. For Professor Spiro's enlightenment, he traced the 'modern interpretation' of Tully River conception beliefs through sixteen centuries of Christianity to the Gospels of Matthew and Luke. There the dogma of the Immaculate Conception was set down side by side with a pedigree placing Jesus in a direct line of patrilineal descent from David *through Joseph*. Likewise the Aboriginal dogma of spirit entry coexisted with filiation through the mother's husband. Neither dogma entailed ignorance of the facts of physiological paternity. By defining God or the Totemic Ancestor as the genitor, both dogmas affirmed that for jural purposes descent was to be traced through the child's legal father, regardless who happened to be its natural father.

Spiro was not impressed. In a reply published in *Man* in 1968,[58] he argued that Dr Leach's interpretation of the Virgin Birth as a charter for patrifiliation was at the very least eccentric. For the generality of Christian worshippers, the doctrine of Incarnation meant that, through the agency of the Holy Ghost, God impregnated a human female named Mary and thus begat his only son Jesus. Its central message was that God became flesh for the salvation of the world. According to Judaic prophecy, however, the deliverer of the Jews would be a patrilineal descendant of David. The pedigree of Christ was therefore included in the Gospels in order to advance his credentials as the Messiah. This solved one problem only to create another: how could Jesus simultaneously be the son of God and the son of man? According to Spiro, of all the attempted resolutions of this dilemma in Christian theology, only one had proposed that the Davidic pedigree was justified on the ground that Joseph was the sociological (as distinct from biological) father of Jesus. It was therefore perverse to argue that the dogma of the Virgin Birth was a cultural validation of the principle of filiation through males. It would be nearer the truth to say that it undermined the genealogical basis of patrilineality by rendering the paternal status of the mother's husband highly equivocal. As Leach himself had noted, medieval Christians regarded Joseph as a cuckold.

Spiro offered refutations on two subsidiary points. First, Leach's reading of the recent evidence from Australia was tendentious and misleading. Second, his reiterated attributions of a racist ideology to his opponents were gratuitous, obsessive and false. It was not the case that assertions of ignorance necessarily imply irrationality, childishness or stupidity. Numerous scholars had insisted that, although the Aborigines were ignorant of physical paternity, their alternative theory of reproduction was entirely rational and in no sense reflected a low level of intelligence. The shining example of this tradition was Ashley-Montagu himself, and for Leach to include him in his denigrations was nothing short of extraordinary. Within a few years of stating his conclusions on Aboriginal conception beliefs he had written his most famous and influential book – *Man's Most Dangerous Myth: The Fallacy of Race*.[59]

Spiro ended his paper by comparing two rival interpretations of Australian conception beliefs: the cognitive-explanatory view espoused by Malinowski and Ashley-Montagu, and the psychoanalytic view advanced by Roheim.[60] Both made better sense of the data than the so-called 'modern interpretation' advanced by Leach. In a letter to the editor in the following number of the journal, Leach admitted that the 'true relation' between sexual intercourse and conception was just as mysterious to him as it was to the Aborigines of Australia. He acknowledged that Professor Spiro had raised various questions for him to answer, but unfortunately their contents evaporated on being reduced to basic English. For the most part he was happy to let readers compare the two essays point by point, checking back to the original evidence. In a two-line rejoinder conceding nothing, Spiro bowed out on the same note.

The joust between Spiro and Leach generated a certain amount of comment. One of the contributors to the correspondence pages of *Man* was R.M.W. Dixon, a linguist from University College, London, who had recently documented the Dyirbal language of the Tully River region. Whereas Roth had recorded conception beliefs only at a mystical level, Dixon had encountered them at a more basic level as well, where the role of copulation was acknowledged to be exactly the same in human as in animal conception. Awareness of this fact was encoded in the Dyirbal verb *bulmbinyu*, which meant 'to be the male progenitor of' and which had clear reference to the particular act of copulation that induced a conception.[61]

A decade later Harold Scheffler of Yale University published an extensive analysis of Australian kinship systems, in which he sought to confirm that the basis of Aboriginal kin classification was genealogy (rather than, say, group membership).[62] To clear the ground, he briefly outlined the rival positions on conception beliefs and claimed that two recent statements had settled the issue beyond reasonable doubt in favour of those who affirmed the coexistence of secular knowledge and religious dogma. One was Dixon's letter, the other was an account of Aranda conception theology by T.G.H. Strehlow. Together they constituted an empirical refutation of the nescience view at its twin points of origin. It was now apparent that the Aborigines of central Australia and north Queensland traditionally held two complementary theories on procreation. One was about biological reproduction, the other about the implantation of immortal souls in ephemeral bodies. The naturalistic theory maintained that sexual intercourse was necessary for conception; that semen, either alone or in combination with uterine blood, contributed to the formation of the foetus; and that, therefore, the link between father and offspring was in part physical. The metaphysical theory explained how a foetus came to life and how an individual acquired an inalienable identity.

In my view the two refutations are not as straightforward as Scheffler supposed. Let us take the Tully River linguistic evidence first. Twenty years after the 'Virgin Birth' controversy, Dixon published a description of the Dyirbal kinship system in which he gave some additional information about the verb *bulmbinyu*. Although the word normally had 'father' as its subject and 'child' as its object, other subjects were possible viz. father's brother or father's sister. The full meaning of the verb should therefore be rendered as 'beget as a father does, either directly or through a brother'.[63] This raises some problems. First, what construction are we meant to put upon the notion of begetting 'through a brother'? Perhaps it is a euphemism for fraternal cuckoldry. Second, if the verb (a) means 'to beget', (b) has clear reference to the particular act of copulation that induced a conception, and (c) is clinching evidence of knowledge of physical paternity, what are we supposed to make of the fact that it may be used with a female subject?

In 1967 I encountered a similar concept in the Gidjingali language of northern Arnhem Land.[64] The verb *-bokama-*, which I initially glossed as 'to beget', could be used with either father or father's sister as singular subjects. It could also be used with father and father's sister as joint subjects. For example:

nguna-anya nguji-bapa nguna-birrin-bokama-rra
   my   F   my FZ   me   they   ?   past tense

If we translate *-bokama-* as 'to beget' (thus, 'my father and my paternal aunt begat me'), we imply that the speaker was begotten incestuously by his father and father's sister (OED *beget*, procreate, usu. of father, sometimes of father and mother). This is not the intention of the utterance, since it is used conventionally to indicate a normal state of affairs, not a reprehensible one. The translation would be both mis-leading and offensive.

In his article on Dyirbal kinship Dixon included another 'verb of begetting', viz. *gulngga-*, meaning (a) 'to breastfeed', (b) 'to give birth to'. In the latter sense, the subject was normally the baby's mother but again 'extensions' were possible, viz. mother's sister, mother's brother. Dixon's expanded gloss was 'to give birth to as a mother does, either directly or through a sister'.[65] Once again problems arise. What is indirect parturition? How does a maternal uncle give birth?

The Gidjingali verb *-ngichi-* (*-yichi-* when preceded by n) means (a) 'to tip out', (b) 'to give birth to'. From an early point in my genealogical research I used it to establish mother/child relationships. Subsequently (as with *-bokama-*) I discovered that it could also be used with a joint brother-sister subject. For example:

nguj-ama nguna-gula nguna-birrin-yichi-nga
   my M   my MB me   they ?   past tense

Obviously we cannot appropriately translate this utterance as 'my mother and my maternal uncle gave birth to me'. How, then, do we translate it?

In order to fathom the meaning of these expressions, we need to take into account a fundamental characteristic of Aboriginal systems of kin classification, viz. that siblings of both sexes act as a unit in applying kinship terms, not only to relatives in ascending generations (as in English) but in descending generations as well.[66] Commonly, the terms used by a father for his children differ from those used by their mother. The father's siblings use the same terms as the father, and the mother's siblings use the same terms as the mother. For example, if I am a Dyirbal male I address my son as *galbin*, and my brothers and sisters also address him as *galbin*. My wife, however, addresses him as *daman*, and so do her brothers and sisters. In the Dyirbal and Gidjingali cases it would seem that the conceptualization of the relationships between siblings and their offspring is homologous with the conceptualization of procreation. In both cases kin-term usage expresses simultaneously the unity of siblings in regard to their respective offspring and a disjunction between paternal and maternal sibling sets. The same can be said of the 'verbs of begetting'. A single principle is being expressed in two different, though related, modes.

Suppose, then, that there exists in Dyirbal and Gidjingali culture a model postulating (a) that members of a sibling set share a vital essence; and (b) that individuals derive part of their essence from their fathers and part from their mothers. On that basis the 'verbs of begetting' might mean respectively, 'to transmit the patrilineal essence' and 'to transmit the matrilineal essence'. The transmission might be thought of concretely or metaphorically, individually or collectively. In that case we could say that the vernacular conceptualization is more akin to genetics than physiology.

Let us now turn to Strehlow's account of conception theory among the Aranda. Whereas it has been common for one ethnographer to be in conflict with another, Strehlow in this instance is in conflict with himself. In *Aranda Traditions* (1947), he reported that pregnancy was normally attributed to the entry into a woman of a totemic ancestor or some object associated with him, such as a bull-roarer. The Southern Aranda believed that the spirit-child was fully formed before it found its way into its mother's body. Strehlow made no reference to sexual intercourse as a contributing factor, and his description of circumstances associated with conception strongly suggested that spirit entry was regarded as both necessary and sufficient.[67] However, in *Songs of Central Australia* (1971), he maintained on a number of grounds that the Western Aranda traditionally had knowledge of physical paternity. First, people often remarked on physical and mental similarities between fathers and their sons. Second, they translated the verb *tenama* (used only with a male subject) as 'to make a child'. Third, all old men had full knowledge of the causal connection between intercourse and conception, even though they expounded only the doctrine of spirit reincarnation for general consumption. Fourth, the embryo begotten by its father was regarded in exactly the same way as the young plant that had burst forth from the seed cast by the wind upon a sacred site. It was only after the embryo formed that a spirit made its entry.

Scheffler based his judgment largely on Strehlow's later account. In comparing the assertions made in *Songs of Central Australia* with those in *Aranda Traditions*, two points should be borne in mind. First, the assumption attributed to the Western Aranda of a natural formation of the foetus as a pre-condition of spirit entry seems to be an inference on Strehlow's part rather than direct testimony. The mother experiences symptoms of pregnancy; it would 'therefore seem to be a natural assumption that the soul or spirit of the ancestor entered into an embryo or foetus that had already come into existence by the natural means of procreation'.[68] But, given the belief system reported previously in *Aranda Traditions*, why should the mother not assume that she has been entered by an ancestor, his bull-roarer, or a fully formed child? Second, Strehlow stated in *Songs of Central Australia* that mature Western Aranda men rejected the notion of biological paternity only in the presence of women, children, younger men and inquisitive white observers. Why Aboriginal elders should conceal the part of their theory of conception consistent with Western biology was not clarified. Nor did Strehlow explain why they denied their physical contribution to procreation when speaking to the uninitiated. What initiated men typically conceal is their contribution to the metaphysical sources of reproduction.

In the same year that Scheffler found in favour of the co-existence of complementary levels, Robert Tonkinson published an account of an episode in his fieldwork that would have consoled Ashley-Montagu.[69] Trained by Ronald and Catherine Berndt at the University of Western Australia, Tonkinson commenced a research project at Jigalong on the fringe of the Gibson Desert in 1963. His initial inquiries on the subject of procreation were addressed to several English-speaking adults, whose answers were similar to those recorded by the Berndts at Ooldea twenty years earlier. However, when he raised the matter with an older and more traditional man who was teaching him the language, he was told in no uncertain terms that semen and menstrual blood were not fit topics for conversation. During a field trip seven years later, Tonkinson was in the middle of a conversation about conception with one of his initial informants and a younger man when his erstwhile language teacher walked in. The old man soon left, and an hour later Tonkinson and his two informants were summoned to appear before a large meeting of senior men away from the general camp. After some accusations and explanations, they were admonished for discussing a dangerous and forbidden topic and warned not to do it again. Tonkinson's mentor told him in front of the gathering that, according to Aboriginal law, the *only* thing relevant to the topic of procreation is spirit-children. Men did not know about such things as semen and menses and did not want to hear the words mentioned. Tonkinson apologized for his solecism and offered to provide a ritual feast by way of atonement. The offer was accepted.

Tonkinson went on to document spirit-child beliefs in admirable detail. Reflecting on the events later, he concluded that his early data on procreation had probably been influenced by contact with

Europeans and that traditional explanations of reproduction were quite unconcerned with physiology. Senior men attributed the proliferation of plant and animal species to spirits left behind by the ancestors; they were firm in their belief that pollination and insemination had nothing to do with it. Although rain-making ceremonies were replete with body metaphors (blood, sweat = rain, penis = snake = lightning, testicles = hail, female loins = lightning), reference to semen was conspicuous by its total absence. All the same he was reluctant to rule out knowledge of the role of semen altogether. One of his informants who had been rebuked at the public meeting expressed the opinion that the traditionalists were lying in order to cover up their embarrassment. But, given their normal lack of prudishness in sexual matters, not to speak of their active opposition to Christian missionaries, what were they upset about? Tonkinson speculated that his inquiries caused discomfort because they juxtaposed competing explanations on a matter of great ontological importance. By posing semen/menses as an alternative to spirit-children, the investigation threatened to undermine a critical link with the life-giving forces of the Dreaming. Jigalong culture, especially since colonization, had a proven capacity for accommodating incompatible beliefs by keeping them in separate compartments. The anthropologist in this case was forcing them into the open and putting them at loggerheads.

Although Tonkinson's hypothesis was not entirely new, it was advanced at a time when anthropology was facing an epistemological crisis of its own. The conceptual apparatus we use to interpret non-Western cultures, it was argued, is itself a cultural product whose claim to be a method of discovering objective and universal truths is not only ethnocentric but imperialistic to boot. Rational discourse is a Western invention posited on the view that *p* and *not-p* cannot simultaneously be true. By adopting and applying the scientific paradigm, anthropology has consistently approached native thought as its own antithesis. Such an attitude is no longer defensible, either intellectually, morally or historically. The lesson of anthropology, confuting its own founding dogma, is that truth is culturally conditioned and hence relative. Anthropologists must henceforth abandon all vestiges of their traditional role as collectors of the superstitions and fetishes of savage races for the benefit of an amused cognoscenti. Instead, all cultures should be approached respectfully as systems of shared meanings, each valid in its own right. The anthropological project is to interpret these systems so as to make them universally intelligible, not to analyse and evaluate them in terms of the categories of Western science.

A few years after the appearance of Tonkinson's paper, Francesca Merlan published an essay in *Man* called 'Australian Conception

Beliefs Revisited'.[70] While not disowning the positivist past, it sought to relocate and extend the debate within a postmodernist framework. In Merlan's view the controversy had been largely fruitless because, unable to free themselves of their own folk-categories, anthropologists had worked with a conceptual distinction between physiology and religion which had no counterpart in the belief systems under investigation. The question whether the two modes of reproduction (physiological and spiritual) were perceived by Aborigines as being in a relationship of contradiction, complementarity or disjunction was thus totally misplaced. Disjunction occurred not between the spiritual and the non-spiritual (as Tonkinson had argued), but between sex and reproduction. Once this was acknowledged, we could begin to make sense of Aboriginal conception ideology on the basis not of its negative relation to Western science but its active role within indigenous social formations.

Although Aborigines usually acknowledged a relationship between copulation and impregnation, they did not regard the latter as the main purpose of the former. Sex was seen both as an end in itself and as an instrument for manipulating social relationships. Marriage for females began when they were ready for sex, which was typically earlier than their readiness for reproduction. In discussions with anthropologists, women tended to identify sexual desire as the reason for marriage rather than the desire for children. Men's interventions, both physical and ritual, were intended to develop and enhance the sexuality of women, which in turn was deployed in the service of men's political and ritual interests (ceremonial wife-exchanges, wife-lending as an act of hospitality to trading partners, granting sexual access to a wife in expiation of an injury to another man, and so on). Although such practices did not in themselves account for the emergence of a belief in spirit conception, ideological disjunction of sex and reproduction undoubtedly created a space in which the doctrine was able to take root and flourish.

In the course of reviewing literature on conception ideology and relationships between the sexes, Merlan mentioned several reports suggesting that child-spirit notions were of greater concern to men than women. I would put it this way: men steeped in Aboriginal traditions prefer to talk about the metaphysical dimension of conception, whereas in appropriate circumstances (e.g. when discussing the matter with a female anthropologist) women are prone to express matter-of-fact observations on physical aspects. Why should this be so? To say that men have pre-empted the spiritual domain begs the question, since Aboriginal religion is conspicuously concerned with fertility and procreation. Perhaps the doctrine of spirit conception was institutionalized under male authority precisely because men's physical role seemed so nebulous. By proclaiming as all-important a spiritual aetiology of human generation, and simultaneously assuming instrumental responsibility for it, men overtook by cultural means the procreative head-start conferred on women by nature.[71]

In some tribes men affirmed their significance in the reproductive process by attributing intra-uterine growth to food supplied by the father directly to the foetus via the mother.[72] Semen itself was regarded as nourishment.[73] Fathers thus 'found' spirit-children through the agency of dreaming, then gave them substance by 'feeding' them; the mothers in these circumstances were mere conduits through which, by the good offices of men, beings from the invisible world materialized as humans.[74] But there may be more to it than collective male pride in a context of epistemological uncertainty. In 1971 Jane Goodale described how the Tiwi appealed to physical resemblance between offspring and mother's sexual partner (husband or lover) as clinching evidence of physical paternity. At the same time they declared that for conception to occur, the woman's husband must 'find' the spirit of his child in a dream. Tiwi doctrine thus entailed that while any individual must be procreated spiritually by his father, he might be procreated physically by some other male. Goodale included in her account the case of a man who saw his unborn son in a dream just before departing for Darwin without his wife.[75] Given the high levels of infidelity prevailing under the traditional marriage system, we may say that Tiwi conception ideology conferred on husbands a guaranteed transcendental role in circumstances where their carnal role was notoriously precarious.[76]

There were undoubtedly variations on this theme. For instance, Warren Shapiro has argued that in north-eastern Arnhem Land spirit-child ideology promoted clan solidarity (specifically, among men related as 'brothers') by affirming the common transcendental affinities of members and masking potentially divisive concern with unique physical relations between genitor and offspring (as aroused, for instance, by perceived physical resemblances and the gossip of women).[77] From this perspective, the doctrine appears less as a female subterfuge for dealing with adulterous pregnancies (as Walter Heape suggested) than as a male mystification insulating brotherhood against the corroding effects of sexual jealousy and cuckoldry anxiety.[78]

For those who like their facts cut-and-dried ('were the Aborigines ignorant of the connection between sex and reproduction?, answer yes or no'), the outcome of a hundred years of research must seem singularly disappointing. Unless we find good grounds for discrediting some of the published evidence, generalization is impossible. The best we can do is set out a collection of particulars in obverse relation and diminishing spatio-temporal reference, e.g., some tribes said there was a connection, others denied it; some individuals said there was a connection, others within the same tribe denied it; some individuals sometimes said there was a connection and sometimes denied it; and so on. Assuming the anthropological record gives at least a rough idea of the reality, the question is why there should have been so much variability from one place to another, from one person to another, and even from one time to another in the same person. A full answer would be difficult and no doubt tedious. Nevertheless, it seems worth trying to identify some of the main factors.

As numerous commentators have remarked, the empirical difficulties in arriving at the 'facts of life' were of no mean order. Only after the invention of the microscope was it possible to confirm that the necessary and sufficient condition for conception was the coalescence of two tiny parcels of genetic material, one produced and located inside a mature female, the other ejaculated into the female by a mature male. It was not, of course, necessary to wait that long in order to infer a relationship between sex and reproduction. But what sort of relationship? The natural occurrence of infertility in both males and females must have made it obvious that sexual intercourse was not sufficient for conception. Inferring its necessity from gross observation might be simple where female celibacy was practised ('females who do not have sexual intercourse do not become pregnant'), but such a state was unknown among Aborigines. The temporal relationship between copulation and pregnancy was haphazard, while the spatial correlation between entry of the penis and exit of the infant, though suggestive, was hardly decisive.

In the absence of compelling evidence, the subject was therefore wide open for conjecture. Although spirit-entry was by far the most popular theory, there were places where it was apparently not taken seriously (viz. in Cape York Peninsula). Sexual intercourse was often thought to facilitate spirit-entry, but credence was also given to the possibility of conception as an autonomous mystical event. Materialist speculations implicating semen and menses gained wide currency (usually in conjunction with animistic assumptions), but in some places they were severely discountenanced by the custodians of sacred lore. In modern times the diffusion of European notions added a new dimension, generating distinctions between the enlightened and the benighted both within tribes and between them.

It is a fair inference from archaeological data that news of discoveries with important adaptive consequences tends to travel quickly over long distances. Probably the best example in prehistoric Australia is the relatively sudden appearance of microliths throughout the continent about 5000 years ago. It is a moot point whether biological knowledge about conception, even of a rudimentary kind, was ever adaptively significant in the prehistoric past. Men did not need to understand the role of semen in order to copulate frequently; nor was male sexual jealousy dependent upon a knowledge of fertilization. The attraction of a mystical theory of conception, as compared with materialist conjectures about semen and menses, was its amenability to serve as an ideology ascribing to men reproductive powers in excess of those evident to ordinary observation. Once harnessed to powerful sectional interests within the traditional Aboriginal polity, it either eliminated rival theories or maintained them in a state of subordination where they languished until the arrival of the first anthropologists.[79]

8

Dangerous mothers-in-law and disfigured sisters

One day last century A.W. Howitt was conversing with an Aboriginal man in Gippsland when he noticed a woman passing at a distance. Wishing to attract her attention, but suffering from a cold, he asked the man to call out to her. The man stared vacantly at the ground and seemed not to hear him. Howitt spoke again, in a sharper voice, but there was still no response. This was too much. 'What do you mean by taking no notice of me?', Howitt expostulated. Thereupon the man called out to his brother-in-law: 'Tell Mary that Mr Howitt wants her.' He then turned to Howitt: 'You know I cannot speak to that old woman', he said reproachfully, 'she is my mother-in-law'.[1]

Some years later, in a now much-celebrated article on anthropological method, Edward Tylor quoted Howitt's anecdote as an example of the 'barbaric etiquette between husbands and their wives' relatives'[2] in accordance with which they could not speak to each other, look at each other, or even use each other's names. This absurd custom, Tylor noted, was by no means peculiar to the natives of Australia. Over the years he had collected information on the laws of marriage and descent in some 350 societies in widely separated parts of the world. Institutionalized avoidance between in-laws was practised in almost one-fifth of them.

Tylor's purpose was to see whether it was possible to throw light on certain customs by establishing statistical relationships with other customs. Consider, for instance, conventions concerning residence after marriage. In societies where a man lives with his wife's family (either permanently or for a period immediately following marriage), the custom of ceremonial avoidance occurs more frequently than we would expect on the basis of chance. Conversely, where the wife lives with her husband's family, it occurs less frequently. We may infer that the formal constraints observed by a husband and his in-laws have something to do with the fact that he lives with them. Tylor ventured the opinion that the custom signifies and underlines the husband's status as an outsider. By not speaking to him or looking at him, the in-laws indicate that they do not recognize him as one of themselves.

Unfortunately, Tylor admitted, the data from Australia seemed anomalous. There, even though the wife leaves her parents to live with the family of her husband, his formal avoidance of her mother not only occurs but is carried to ludicrous extremes. The theory could be saved, however, by supposing that at an earlier stage of social evolution men had in fact lived with their in-laws; for some reason the residence custom then changed but the avoidance custom survived. Accordingly Tylor wrote to Howitt, the acknowledged authority on the Aborigines, and put it to him that further inquiry would disclose hitherto unnoticed evidence of residence with or near the wife's parents. After due consideration Howitt replied: 'I am now satisfied that your surmises are correct', and enclosed gratifying assurances from Mr Aldridge of Maryborough, Queensland.[3]

A shaky start, no doubt, but the ball was at least in play. In 1902 Ernest Crawley, schoolmaster and author of books on tennis and skating, published an extensive review of primitive marriage practices entitled *The Mystic Rose*, in which he noted that few customs in savage society had 'so increased the gaiety of civilized nations as the common taboo between a man and his mother-in-law'.[4] Professor Tylor's application of statistics was an important departure for serious study of the subject, but his theory left much unexplained. Why is it, for instance, that for males the prohibition in its strictest form consistently focusses upon the mother-in-law and not some other relation by marriage? If the avoidance is merely a matter of signifying social differences, why is there such an intensity of feeling in observing it, often amounting to 'horror' at the thought of proximity? Last but not least, in cases where the husband lives with his own people, how can the taboo on the mother-in-law be explained merely as a cultural relic from former times when it is obviously still so active?

In Crawley's view, the custom had the appearance not of a symbolic expression of status difference but of a sex taboo. That would make the behaviour more puzzling than ever: why go to such lengths to prevent a sexual relation that would be unlikely to occur anyway? Crawley reasoned as follows. As a boy approaches manhood, he is steadily weaned from female associations within the family. His sisters, once his companions, are now redefined as sexually dangerous and therefore taboo. After initiation and a period of bachelorhood, he re-enters the feminine sphere in order to marry. As his wife in a sense replaces his sisters, so does her mother become a kind of new mother for him – in English, a 'mother-in-law'. Just as he would avoid all sexual intimacy with his biological mother, so he must likewise act with propriety towards his mother-in-law. Indeed, precisely because she is not his actual mother but an unrelated woman, the avoidance conventions must be reinforced.

There are additional considerations, Crawley suggested, arising from the fond attachment between mother and daughter. Mothers may resent the loss of their daughters at marriage; and in some cultures, they give vent to their feelings through ceremonial aggression. They are subsequently anxious about the daughter's welfare and are prone to exercise some degree of surveillance over the son-in-law's treatment of her. Such attitudes, however understandable they may be, are bound to create rancour. That is why, even in modern society, avoidance of the mother-in-law is a feature of bourgeois manners and a subject of music-hall jokes.

Sigmund Freud was undoubtedly one of the great trail-blazers of the twentieth century. In 1911, having traversed the royal road to the unconscious through the analysis of dreams, he set out on a journey of exploration in the realm of anthropology. The result was a book entitled *Totem and Taboo: Resemblances between the Psychic Lives of Savages and Neurotics*. For reasons readily intelligible to his contemporaries he chose as his main source of information the relevant literature on the natives of Australia, 'whose fauna has also preserved for us so much that is archaic and no longer to be found elsewhere'.[5]

Unlike Tylor, who regarded mother-in-law avoidance as barbaric and absurd, Freud thought the custom had a good deal to commend it. There were obviously factors in the relationship that generated antagonism and made close proximity an undesirable state. As we know now from his biographer, Freud's own experience was a case in point. In a letter to his fiancée, he told her that her mother was 'alien and will always remain so to me. I seek for similarities with you, but find hardly any... I can foresee more than one opportunity of making myself disagreeable to her and I don't intend to avoid them.'[6] He informed his future wife that she must expect to belong entirely to his family and no longer to her own, and that 'the first condition in every marriage should be the right to expel one's in-laws'.[7] The axiom did not deter him from seeking a loan (unsuccessfully) from his future mother-in-law, who told him that: 'At the moment you are like a spoilt child who can't get his own way and cries, in the belief that in that way he can get everything.'[8] She signed the letter 'Your faithful Mother'.

In proposing a general theory on the mother-in-law taboo, Freud took his cue from Crawley. There could be no doubt that some of the strains in the relationship stem from the reluctance of the mother-in-law to part with her daughter, or to modulate her maternal love and influence in accordance with the requirements of the new situation. Conversely, the son-in-law not only guards his marital prerogatives against unwanted intrusion but may even resent the fact that his mother-in-law preceded him in her daughter's affections. Worse still, she disturbs the idealization of love and marriage by presenting him with a preview of his wife when the charms of her youth have disappeared.

Given such negative currents in the relationship, mutual avoidance makes good sense. But why should it take the form of a sex taboo? Here psychoanalysis could provide a new dimension to the analogy between mother and mother-in-law suggested by Crawley. It is not just that a man transfers behavioural constraints from one to the other; as well, he carries across the unconscious sexual feelings against which they are directed. A boy's first love object is his mother, and the sexual feelings she arouses are normally forbidden and repressed. Much later, when he marries, his mother-in-law becomes a structural counterpart of his mother. As such she reactivates his infantile unconscious wishes and herself becomes an incest temptation.

That, according to Freud, partly explains why the taboo on the mother-in-law characteristically seeks to obliterate her sexuality: avoidance shields men from reminders of their primal sexual preference. But there is another angle to it, in some ways even more surprising than the first. Analysis of the hidden psychic feelings of married women has revealed much sexual unhappiness, usually through monotony or loss of interest on the part of their husbands.[9] Ageing mothers seek consolation in the lives of their children, a tendency that may easily result in such a degree of identification with their daughters that they secretly fall in love with their daughters' husbands. The necessity for a conscious repudiation of any such development may in some degree account for the harsh and sadistic components contained in the attitude of the women to their sons-in-law. The institutionalization of sexual separation between mother-in-law and son-in-law, as practised in many savage societies, enables these problems of individual psychology and adaptation to be resolved at the level of public convention.

In what eventually came to be the standard explanation of the mother-in-law taboo in anthropology textbooks, psychoanalysis was conspicuous by its absence. During the 1940s, Radcliffe-Brown published two essays in the journal *Africa* in which he argued that institutionalized avoidance was simply a device for stabilizing fragile links in the social structure.[10] Marriage in simple societies, particularly when it is fruitful, creates or strengthens a conjunction of interests between the families, lineages or clans of the respective partners. Nevertheless, the interests of the two groups are not thereby made identical, and the persisting disjunction between them remains a potential source of tension and conflict. One way to preserve harmony between persons simultaneously conjoined and disjoined is to enjoin upon them a maximum of mutual respect and a minimum of personal contact. This method occurs in its most rigorous form in the conventions of mother-in-law avoidance.

Another way is to promote a relationship not of mutual respect but privileged disrespect. Such relationships occur commonly between in-laws of the same generation, notably between a man and his wife's brothers and sisters, and are expressed through teasing, ridicule and horse-play. Known by anthropologists as 'joking relationships', they manifest a peculiar combination of friendliness and antagonism. Utterances that in an ordinary context would be offensive are made and reciprocated in jest. Joking relationships and avoidance relationships are thus to be understood as opposite sides of the same coin; and, indeed, they may occur together in the same society. Licensed disrespect allows antagonisms to dissipate harmlessly; exaggerated respect contains them in silence.

Radcliffe-Brown pitched his theory at a high level of generality and made only a few references in passing to the Aborigines. To gain a firmer notion of the empirical content of Australian avoidance customs, we may begin with a review published by Elkin in *The Australian Aborigines*.[11] Institutionalized avoidance, Elkin stressed, is not an expression of enmity. It is to be understood as a set of prohibitions, formalities and circumspections observed by individuals in specified relationships, by blood, marriage or both. In many parts of Australia some degree of avoidance is required between brothers and sisters. Among relationships of affinity, the taboo on the mother-in-law occurs everywhere and is by far the most exaggerated in its constraints and observances. It may even take in her parents, though in muted form, and is usually extended in varying degrees to all females who stand to the subject in the relation of a potential mother-in-law. Men

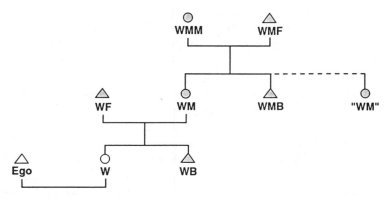

Fig. 5   Affinal relationships requiring avoidance or restraint.

are expected to behave with reserve in the company of their wives' maternal uncles, fathers and brothers.

In the course of his review, Elkin briefly referred to a special language or code used between brothers-in-law. We know now that over wide areas of Australia such modes of communication are also obligatory whenever a man is speaking to someone within hearing distance of his mother-in-law. Typically they consist of some fifty or so substitutes for the most common words in everyday discourse, although in certain cases they have been elaborated to the point where they function for practical purposes as independent languages. English-speaking Aborigines refer to them as 'mother-in-law language', while linguists prefer to designate them simply as 'avoidance styles'.[12]

A notable characteristic of avoidance styles is that they tend to eschew all references to sexuality. As John Haviland has put it for the Cooktown area of north Queensland:

> Strikingly, some words in the EV [everyday] language have *no equivalent* in BIL [brother-in-law] language. Words in this category clearly form a coherent and significant class. They include the EV words for 'bad smell (e.g. human sweat)', 'testicles', 'vagina', 'pubic hair', 'masturbate', 'woman's pubic area', 'have sexual intercourse', 'penis (also means greedy)', 'erect phallus', 'rape', and 'clitoris'.[13]

Men said: 'You can't use those words against your mother-in-law.' Haviland noted, however, that words concerned with excretory functions appear in the avoidance lexicon and are presumably not regarded as embarrassing. We may infer, therefore, that avoidance discourse is specifically orientated away from the idea of sex. The same can be said of avoidance behaviour. Haviland was told that nowadays it is permissible for a man to sleep in the room next to his wife's mother, so long as the door remains shut. If it is opened, she must leave. Men and women in avoidance relationships should never sit in each other's presence with their legs parted.

What explanation do Aboriginal people themselves give for avoidance customs? The most general formulation offered by men is that affines must be treated circumspectly because of shame – not merely the embarrassment that results from any breach of etiquette (though this may be a component), but something deep-seated and difficult to express that seems inherent in the relationships themselves. Here is how one of Haviland's mentors sought to explain it to him: 'Mother-in-law is poison. You know why? You married her child. And her daughter has your children. For that reason, real shame...'[14]

This is remarkably similar to an explanation quoted by Crawley for a man's avoidance of his mother-in-law in an African tribe: 'It is not right that he should see the breasts which suckled his wife.'[15] In some

Aboriginal languages the verb meaning 'to be ashamed' also means 'to be afraid';[16] and when men accidentally encounter their mothers-in-law, they may experience a mixture of shame and fear.[17] Sometimes the fear arises from the perceived danger of pollution. Haviland was told: 'If I were to touch my mother-in-law, *hiii*, shame! Then I might have to wash my hand.'[18] In north-eastern Arnhem Land the word referring to the taboo on the mother-in-law also means pollution associated with corpses.[19] The complex of shame, fear, and pollution has clear parallels in mother-in-law avoidance elsewhere.[20]

When Radcliffe-Brown once asked an Aboriginal man why he had to avoid his mother-in-law, he replied: 'Because she is my best friend in the world; she has given me my wife.'[21] The gift of a wife is made initially in the form of a promise or understanding that in due course a daughter, who may now be merely a baby, or even unborn, will go to the son-in-law as a bride. From the time that undertaking is given, he must send gifts to his mother-in-law, particularly meat from the hunt. The contractual basis of the relationship is stated vividly in the following didactic narrative recorded by Annette Hamilton in north-west South Australia:

> The rainbow, often seen during summer thunderstorms, represents a man sitting in his mother-in-law's camp. The faint left-hand band of colour is the man himself, the middle band is his mother-in-law, and the right-hand band is his wife. The man is unable to consummate the marriage because his mother-in-law is sitting between him and his wife. Only after the appearance of a stronger rainbow, in which the order of colour in the bands is changed, does the man realise that he must compensate the mother-in-law for her daughter. The disappearance of the pale band of colour represents the departure of the man to go hunting in order to obtain meat for his mother-in-law. The gradual fading of the rainbow means that the man has made his gift and has been allowed to take his wife to his own camp.[22]

The interpositioned mother-in-law as an impediment to consummation is the theme of another myth, recorded by Lloyd Warner in north-eastern Arnhem Land.[23] Here the ulterior motive is rather different:

> Three men on a sea journey were forced by bad weather to take shelter on a small island. They encountered an old woman, who gave her daughter in marriage to one of them and persuaded her two sisters to do likewise for his two companions.
>
> That night the first old woman sneaked up to her son-in-law's camp just as he was about to have sexual intercourse with his new wife. She pushed her daughter aside and lay down in the middle. 'I am cold', she complained, and stayed where she was until morning. Her two sisters did the same thing.
>
> The next day the three men took the old women on a turtle-hunting expedition and threw them overboard in deep water. They paddled

quickly back to shore and made straight for where their wives were waiting for them. They went into the trees at the edge of the camp and had almost reached a climax when who should arrive but the three mothers-in-law. They had stretched their legs to the bottom of the sea and walked back to the land. The old women again inserted themselves between husband and wife, saying to the men: 'If you want somebody, take us. These daughters of ours are too young'.

This was not true, and the girls protested: 'Mothers, why don't you let your sons-in-law alone? You've given us to them. Why don't you let them have sexual intercourse with us?'

The men became angry. 'Why did you give us your daughters if you behave like this?', they asked. They then attacked the old women with clubs and left them lying on the ground, apparently dead. They made a camp in the jungle and tried once more to consummate their marriages. Again, however, they were interrupted by their mothers-in-law, whose powers of recovery were apparently as prodigious as their insensitivity. 'Son-in-law', each said as she pushed her way in, 'get on top of me'.

This was too much. The three men decided to set sail for home. On seeing their preparations, the three mothers-in-law relented. 'You can take our daughters now', they said. 'No', the men replied, 'you can keep them. We'll go back and marry our own women so we can do as we please. We won't have any fooling with our mothers-in-law. No man likes to copulate with an old woman'. They returned to their own country and stayed there.

Freud, we recall, spoke of a tendency on the part of the mother-in-law to imagine herself in her daughter's place. He also referred to harsh and sadistic elements in her attitude to the son-in-law, which the following myth from south-eastern Arnhem Land carries to unusual excess. It was recorded by Ronald Berndt.

An ancestral woman called Mumuna enticed several men to her camp by making a smoky fire, and, after giving them a meal, encouraged them to have sexual intercourse with her daughters. While the guests slept soundly from hospitality, she murdered them by dropping large boulders on their chests.

The next morning she asked her daughters to go and collect food. During their absence she cooked and ate her victims, leaving the heads, hands, and genitals suspended from trees. When the daughters returned she invited them to share in the feast. They retained pleasant memories of the guests, however, especially their genitals, and refused.

The same sequence was repeated a number of times, with increasing numbers of victims, until the thinning ranks of men in the district gave cause for alarm. Eventually a hero called Eaglehawk woke in time to avoid the fate of his predecessors. He killed Mumuna, but was struck dead himself by Lightning, her husband, who returned from a hunting expedition and saw what had happened.[24]

The representation of the mother-in-law as dangerous, particularly in relation to the son-in-law's genitals, seems widespread in Aboriginal mythical thought. Berndt recorded another myth, this time from the Western Desert, in which seductions of potential mothers-in-law are followed by mutilation of the offending organ, temporary loss of the genitals, and death:

> (a) Ancestral women called Ganabuda were travelling across the country in a group. A Lizard Man named Spiky Head seduced a woman related to him as a potential mother-in-law. He had a penis capable of proceeding underground and rising to the surface under the object of his desire. The Ganabuda women attacked his testicles with sharpened digging sticks, cut off his penis, and killed him.
> (b) The Ganabuda women encountered Crow Man, who proceeded to have sexual intercourse with a young potential mother-in-law, as well as a classificatory mother's mother. His mega-penis inflicted severe injury upon them, and they died. The Ganabuda women then killed the Crow Man.
> (c) An ancestral man named Dangidjara had intercourse with a potential mother-in-law. He then went hunting and brought meat back to her. Eventually she gave birth to a son. Dangidjara continued his journey. One day ants bit his genitals, which detached themselves from his body and ran away. He pleaded with them to return, but they refused. Eventually he retrieved them.[25]

Some years ago the wife of the Prime Minister of Australia was presented with an Aboriginal painting depicting an old man who developed 'a grossly enlarged penis as a result of having sex with his mother-in-law'.[26] It is not clear whether this interpretation came from the painter himself. Berndt's opinion is that an enlarged penis is a precondition rather than a consequence: only a man with abnormal genitalia could commit such an abnormal act.[27] Another possibility is that, through the symbolism of tumescence and castration, the myths are expressing temptations and associated anxieties. A collection of songs from Western Australia published by von Brandenstein and Thomas includes a couplet called 'Wicked Song':[28]

> Who comes to me from the windbreak?
> You, mother-in-law, to my windbreak?

The authors comment that in view of the strong traditional taboo on the mother-in-law, the wickedness is obvious; nevertheless, for that very reason it is relished.[29]

From further north in the same culture area, Phyllis Kaberry describes how women perform love-magic rituals with a view to seducing their tribal sons-in-law.[30] Among the Aranda of central Australia mother-in-law avoidance appears to have been unusually strict. Yet, according to Spencer and Gillen, on special occasions the relationship was inverted. In the context of large ceremonial gatherings, a man might instruct his wife and son-in-law to go into the bush together to fetch native cotton for decorations. After their return, the woman was accessible to men at the ceremonial ground. Spencer and Gillen remark: 'In the case of the women who attend the corrobboree, it is supposed to be the duty of every man at different times to send his wife to the ground, and the most striking feature in regard to it is that the first man who has access to her is the very one to whom, under normal conditions, she is most strictly tabu – that is, her *Mura* [son-in-law].'[31]

If we attempt to construct a pen-portrait of the mother-in-law of a man from these fragments, a truly enigmatic phantom emerges. She is a benefactress, his dearest friend because she gave him his wife. In return he must hunt for her and give her meat, yet he must not go near her, look at her, speak to her, or utter her name. She arouses in him feelings of profound shame, as well as fear, and her sexuality must be expunged from his consciousness. She is poison, a source of danger, polluting like a corpse. Yet myths tell of mother-in-law rape and son-in-law seduction, and rituals license forbidden conjunctions.

How old is she? In the collective consciousness of the Western world, the mother-in-law is a woman of mature years. Warner's tale of frustrated consummation suggests a similar stereotype among the Aborigines. Yet in fact the mother-in-law taboo operates upon females of all ages, from girls through to old women. Typically, boys approaching adolescence are taught to behave with reserve and circumspection towards all females from whom, in accordance with marriage rules, they could expect to receive a wife. Some of these may be girls of their own age, or younger. The taboo intensifies once an actual commitment has been made and reaches its fully fledged form as the promised bride approaches puberty. It may be relaxed some-what when the mother-in-law grows old.

In his section on mother-in-law avoidance in *The Australian Aborigines*, Elkin remarked that the custom 'prevents the possibility of any competition between a girl and her mother for the affection of the same man – a danger which might be very real where so often the wife is much younger than the husband and the husband and mother-in-law are of the same age'.[32] The implications of this suggestion were taken up a few years later by Frederick Rose and A.T.H. Jolly in an essay published in *The Annals of Eugenics*.[33] The authors noted that, in accordance with bestowal practices prevailing over wide areas of Australia, a man is not only often as old as his mother-in-law, or older, but may expect to receive younger sisters of his bride as additions to his harem. Were he to have sexual relations with a potential or actual mother-in-law, he might therefore beget his own wife. The taboo seeks to prevent this possibility and thus may have been instituted in order to avoid harmful biological consequences of in-breeding between genetic father and daughter.

The theory attributes to Aborigines a keener sensitivity to the risks of homozygosity than they probably possessed. If we put genetics to one side, however, the point made by Elkin remains to be considered. As noted earlier, when Tylor reviewed the information available on residence rules, the consensus of opinion was that in Australia a man and his wife's parents typically lived in separate local groups, making it difficult to understand why so rigorous a taboo on the mother-in-law should be necessary. In retrospect we can see that the communication from Howitt's informant in Queensland, though largely ignored at the the time, pointed to a widely distributed pattern of 'groom service';[34] according to Nicolas Peterson, it was normal in many tribes for a man upon marrying to take up residence in the band of his wife's father.[35] Given the contractual obligations of a son-in-law, it was obviously convenient to have him near at hand. At the same time, proximity increased the risk of a sexual entanglement of the kind envisaged by Elkin. To put people's minds at rest, especially no doubt that of his wife's father, the son-in-law signalled day-in and day-out through his ritualized and over-stated avoidance behaviour that there was no cause for worry: 'I am here to give my mother-in-law gifts of meat, nothing else.'

I believe this is as far as the existing evidence will take us. There is no use denying that after a hundred years of observation and argument, the mother-in-law taboo retains its sphinx-like countenance. Let us therefore pass on to another riddle, this time concerning an unusual elaboration of the etiquette of avoidance between brothers and sisters.

During his fieldwork in north-eastern Arnhem Land, Lloyd Warner witnessed a number of incidents in which, more or less without warning, men attacked their sisters with spears. The circumstances were puzzling. Typically the attacks were made during domestic quarrels in which the brothers were not involved. For instance, one evening a man returned home and found that his wife had not prepared his supper. Tempers flared, and the husband shouted abuse, using an obscenity meaning 'incestuous'. The wife's brother heard the quarrel and became angry. Arming himself with spears, he ran towards his brother-in-law's camp and attacked his sister. He then sought out other sisters and threw spears at them as well.

It was possible, of course, that the brother entered the dispute in order to punish his sister for her negligence as a wife. But why in that case should he extend the punishment to her sisters? Furthermore,

Warner recalled another episode which began when a young woman swore at her mother for trying to stop her from having an illicit love affair. Her maternal uncle heard the obscenity and threw spears, not at his niece, but at his sister, even though he knew she was blameless and had remonstrated with her daughter for good reason.

When Warner sought enlightenment on these fraternal interventions, his informants replied in terms of a custom known as the *mirriri*, which they glossed in English as 'ear-thing'. If a man hears obscenities directed at his sister, he has to show his feelings by attacking her, and other sisters as well. It was hard to explain why. One informant said, 'It is silly, but when I hear those words at my sister I must do something. I throw spears at her.' Another said, 'It is just the same as if I had been hit on the head with a club when I hear that'; and another, 'My heart jumps and stops, jumps and stops...'

In 1931, shortly after returning from the field, Warner published an interpretation of the *mirriri* in the *American Anthropologist*, which he reproduced a few years later in his book *A Black Civilization*.[36] It obviously owed much to his association with Radcliffe-Brown,[37] who at this time was actively articulating his ideas on structure and function in primitive society. Following Durkheim and the French sociologists, he argued that the scientific study of society was best conducted on the assumption that the object of study is an organic whole made up of functionally interrelated parts. Social institutions, defined as standardized modes of behaviour, constitute the means by which the social structure maintains and reproduces itself. The function of an institution, according to Radcliffe-Brown, is the contribution it makes to the continued existence of the social structure of which it is a part.[38]

In the early sections of *A Black Civilization*, Warner described the social organization of north-eastern Arnhem Land as a system of territorial clans held together by links of marriage. Each clan owned an area of land, and its members were males and females related to each other by patrilineal descent. Marriage between members of the same clan was forbidden. When a woman married, she joined her husband's band but retained full membership in the clan of her birth.

According to Warner, the decision concerning to whom a girl should be promised in marriage was made by her father and brothers. Jointly they guaranteed that she would remain with her husband and undertook to punish her if she misbehaved. The necessity of keeping a woman with her husband in order to protect the kinship structure was a cardinal value of Murngin culture. No brother or father would interfere with a husband bent on disciplining his wife, unless it was to help him. Of course, there were limits. If a woman were killed for no good reason, her father and brothers might feel impelled to take action. Normally, however, the clansmen of a brutal husband pressed him to desist in the interests of maintaining good relationships between the clans.

For any man, the betrothal and marriage of a sister created a potential for conflict between kinship love and affinal obligation. A sister was among a man's closest relatives. She was his childhood companion, and emotional ties to her were very strong. They belonged to the same family and clan, they shared ownership of the same land, and they were affiliated with the same totems. Yet custom decreed that a brother should refer to his sister as *wakinu*, meaning 'without relatives', 'rubbish', 'of no account'. Warner interpreted this usage as a symbolic denial of kinship love for the benefit of the sister's husband and his clan. By using such an expression, the brother was in effect saying, 'She is not ours any more, she is of no value to us. We do not want her back. She is yours absolutely.'

Throwing spears at a sister after her husband had reviled her was an even more dramatic symbol of rejection. At precisely the moment when she needed the support of kinsmen, her brother threatened her with injury or death. His gesture signified that his formal obligation to his brother-in-law took precedence over his natural love for his sister. In structural terms, the *mirriri* shored up the contractual bond between two sets of in-laws in the face of emotional forces capable of destroying it if allowed to go unchecked. Warner assumed that a brother would be profoundly upset on hearing his sister's honour defiled. His inclination would be to avenge her by attacking the person who had insulted her. But to act on such an impulse would be to risk initiating a major conflict between the clans concerned, with serious repercussions for other marriage contracts, including perhaps the brother's relationship with his own wife's people. On the other hand, doing nothing in the face of provocation was difficult. Therefore, to give vent to his anger without endangering the social structure of his community, the brother treated his sister not as the victim but as the culprit. As well as letting off steam, he signalled to his brother-in-law his displeasure with the way he was treating his wife: 'This time I am attacking her. Desist from insulting her, or next time it will be you.' Warner regarded the *mirriri* as a safety-valve whose adoption by the Murngin indicated great brilliance in social engineering.

The remaining question was why a brother should throw spears at all his sisters, rather than just the one sworn at. Warner suggested that, as all sisters were structurally equivalent, attacking a plurality magnified the symbolic significance of the intervention. Also, the feelings aroused by the *mirriri* were intense and needed a high level of physical activity to discharge them. Because attacking numerous sisters was emotionally more satisfying than attacking merely one, it enhanced the 'safety-valve' function of the institution.

Some twenty years after the publication of *A Black Civilization*, I encountered a similar phenomenon among neighbours of the people Warner had studied. The Gidjingali knew the word *mirriri* but themselves used an expression meaning 'he has been speared through the ear' (cf. Warner's gloss of *mirriri* as 'ear-thing'). This was the answer they gave me when I asked why a brother would attack his sister on hearing someone swear at her.

I had with me a copy of Warner's book and studied the section on the *mirriri* closely. The analysis, although plausible, left a number of facts unexplained. I was struck first of all by the case of the man who attacked his sister when she quarrelled with her daughter, which Warner quite rightly appealed to as evidence that *mirriri* attacks could not be explained as punishment for bad behaviour. But if the *mirriri* was a device for preserving good relationships between in-laws, why would a man throw spears at his sister when she was abused by her own flesh and blood? Warner later admitted that a man would attack his sister not only when her husband swore at her, but when anyone else did. His theory, however, accounted only for instances where the swearer was the husband.

Then there was the problem of the father. In his section on the *mirriri* in *A Black Civilization*, Warner maintained that, with regard to affinal obligations, the feelings and responsibilities of a woman's father and her brother were much the same. She was a close relative and clanswoman of both, she had been the object of their affections since childhood, and they both felt an obligation to protect her interests and welfare. At the same time, they acknowledged a joint responsibility to ensure that she honoured the marriage contract with her husband. Why, then, was it only the brother who addressed her as *wakinu* ('without relations', etc.)? More importantly, why was it only the brother, and not the father as well, who felt obliged to throw spears at her? If the *mirriri* was devised as a safety valve for the former, why was it not also required by the latter?

Early in *A Black Civilization*, some fifty pages before the structural analysis of the *mirriri*, Warner gave an account of some of the constraints evident in the relationship between males and their sisters. Apparently he had been told that, should a man accidentally come upon his sister while she was having sexual intercourse with her husband, he would feel bound to attack her. This statement puzzled me considerably. If reliable, it would certainly give a new meaning to *coitus interruptus*. But it would also constitute a difficulty for Warner's theory on the *mirriri*. If men threw spears at their sisters to express consternation on hearing sounds of marital discord, why should they react in exactly the same way when presented with the proofs of harmony?

Finally, I was puzzled by the discrepancy between Warner's theory and the answers he received from his informants. The latter seemed at a loss to explain the *mirriri*, unable to go beyond graphic descriptions of the brother's psychosomatic state. If Warner were correct in surmising that the *mirriri* was a mechanism for protecting the social structure, why could not his friends have said so? We might have expected a statement like: 'When a man hears his sister's husband say bad words to his sister, he becomes angry and would like to throw spears at him. But he does not want to start a big fight with his in-laws. So he throws spears at his sister instead. That way, there is no trouble, and it makes him feel better.'

I had not been at Maningrida long before I realized that the relationship between men and their sisters had to be treated with care. When I began collecting genealogies, male informants told me they could not tell me the names of their sisters. I should ask someone else. Women, on the other hand, were able to give me their brothers' names without embarrassment. One evening, in the course of documenting Gidjingali bestowal arrangements, I asked my mentor Gurrmanamana about events leading to the marriage of one of his classificatory sisters, though without mentioning her by name. He shied away from the subject and instead told me how I had recently embarrassed one of his affines when I asked him whether his conspicuously pregnant sister had given birth to her baby. I took the point of etiquette: a woman's reproductive functions were not a fit subject of discussion with her brother. Even photographs could cause problems. On one occasion I visited Gidjingali patients in the leprosarium in Darwin and later showed some snapshots to their relatives back at Maningrida. I was enjoying the pleasure this seemed to be giving everyone when a man sharply turned his face away from a photograph and thrust it back at me as though I had shown him something obscene. Someone quietly told me that his sister was in the picture.

Constraints upon a boy's relationship with his sister began to be imposed from about the age of six. At this stage his father would tell him he should no longer sleep near his sisters, nor allow them to see him urinating or defaecating. Instead of using the normal kinship term for sister (*jarla*), he should address them as *rirrigmin*, meaning 'diseased' (e.g. disfigured by leprosy or yaws). Males were conditioned to respond to their sisters with embarrassment and sexual shame. Close proximity was avoided and sexual intercourse between them strictly forbidden. Nevertheless, it was widely believed that sibling incest occurred.

Although none of my teachers in anthropology was enthusiastic about psychoanalysis, and some were actively opposed to it, I found myself pursuing a cautious and no doubt perverse interest in it. Could it provide a better understanding of the *mirriri* than Warner's 'structural-functionalism'? According to Freud, 'the basis of taboo is a forbidden action for which there exists a strong inclination in the unconscious'.[39] In the present case, we might infer that brothers harboured repressed desires for their sisters, formed through close association during childhood, before the imposition of avoidance rules. The incest prohibition constituted a barrier to the expression of these wishes, and shame represented the work of the superego in transforming them into feelings of discomfort. With regard to the *mirriri*, we could deduce that when the sister's sexual organs or sexual relationships were forced upon the brother's consciousness through hearing obscenities directed at her, or by seeing her in the sexual act itself, his repressed incestuous longings gained the upper hand, and he attacked her in a jealous rage.

An awkward empirical difficulty for such a theory was that in the six cases of *mirriri* attacks for which I had detailed information, five of the assailants had not had a close childhood association with the women they attacked. Two of the women were true sisters of their attackers, while the other four were classificatory sisters in other clans.[40] One of the true sisters was about eight years younger than the brother who attacked her, the other about ten years older. Two classificatory sisters were some twenty and thirty years younger than the brother, another a contemporary, and in a case that occurred long before my arrival I was unable to determine the age relationship. In short, if the basis of the *mirriri* was repressed incestuous feelings for the particular sister attacked, there would be a problem in explaining how they came into being.

Although *mirriri* attacks were full of menace, they rarely resulted in serious injury. On one occasion a man speared his sister in the leg and was reprimanded by relatives for having gone too far. I began to think that the attacks were not so much expressions of latent wishes as public affirmations of moral rectitude. In the course of my inquiries I had been told that there were two types of men: 'clean men', who feel shame in relation to women classified as their sisters, and 'dirty men', who commit incest with them. A *mirriri* attack was a sign that a man is 'clean'. On this basis I argued in the journal *Oceania* that when a brother heard obscene references to the sexuality of any woman classed as a sister, he might attack her in order to show his revulsion. The important aspect of *mirriri* behaviour was the brother's public demonstration of outrage. The identity of the person uttering the obscene words was irrelevant. What counted was their content and the fact that the brother had heard them.[41]

It has been said that academic writings are like messages in bottles cast into the sea from desert islands: one never knows who will chance to read them or, indeed, whether they will ever be read by anyone.[42] I was pleasantly surprised, therefore, when the editor of *Oceania* rang me one day in 1966 to say that a comment on my *mirriri* article had come in from Paris. He would send it over to me. Perhaps I might write a reply that could be published in the same issue.

The comment, entitled 'Incest and Redemption in Arnhem Land', was by Raoul Makarius. Although Makarius agreed that Warner's theory on the *mirriri* was unsatisfactory, my own was little better. The clue to the problem was to be found in Durkheim's article on the origin of the incest taboo, published in 1897 in the first volume of the *L'Année Sociologique*. Durkheim had argued that the corporate identity of each totemic clan was based on a notion of common ancestry and being of one blood: 'the totemic being is immanent in the clan; it is incarnated in each member, and it is in the blood that it resides'.[43] It followed that bloodshed was an emanation of the deity, and various prescriptions and interdictions had been evolved to deal with it, depending on the circumstances. The periodic loss of blood from the sexual organs of women was regarded with religious awe of unusual intensity. The fear of incest, and consequently the incest taboo, originated in the dangers attributed to contact with the menstrual blood of a clanswoman.

Durkheim's thesis on the relationship between blood and incest was, according to Makarius, of abiding and incontestable importance. His argument that the sanctity of blood was a derivative of totemic religion, however, was now outmoded. In an essay entitled 'On the Origin of Exogamy and the Fear of Incest', Laura and Raoul Makarius had shown that, among peoples who depended for their existence on killing wild animals, blood was the central symbol of danger and death.[44] Primitive mentality, which confused presage with cause, treated any flow of blood as a cause of future bloodshed. To guard against injury and death, the hunter had to avoid all contact with the menstrual blood of a kinswoman, which in Durkheim's sense was also his own blood. Conversely, incest within the clan endangered all its members. The only antidote, once it was known to have occurred, was to shed clan blood voluntarily in expiation.

Unbeknownst to me when I wrote my article for *Oceania*, L. and R. Makarius had devoted a paragraph to the *mirriri* as an example of a custom which 'appeared as senseless to those who practised it as to the observer who recorded it',[45] and which could be explained only within the framework of their own theory. In essence the authors suggested that the object of a *mirriri* attack was to spill the sister's blood in order to forestall the consequences set in train by the mere allusion to incest within the clan. In his submission to *Oceania*, R. Makarius recapitulated this interpretation, with some amplification. He also posed this question for Warner: if the brother turned on his sisters simply to vent his anger on someone, why did he use spears rather than the emotionally more satisfying method of beating them with his bare fists?[46]

Redemptive blood-letting was certainly a new angle. Nevertheless, the Makarius theory was not without problems. Like Warner's structural hypothesis, it failed to explain why the attacks were made only by brothers. If the object was to let female blood in order to nullify allegations of clan incest, why did fathers not spear their daughters on hearing obscenities directed at them? Or, more generally, why did not men spear *any* woman of their own clan in such circumstances? The attacks on classificatory sisters outside the brother's own clan were also a difficulty. Last but not least, men sometimes attacked their sisters with sticks, and no one suggested that the main purpose of the *mirriri* was to draw blood.

Makarius made one point, however, that forced me to rethink my own position. If, as I had suggested, the *mirriri* was a public display of good citizenship and moral purity, why would a man feel constrained to attack his sister upon chancing to see her in the sexual act with her husband? Perhaps we could see this as a case where the sister was punished for an act of carelessness resulting in a breach (albeit accidental) of the avoidance taboo. The more I thought about it, however, the more convinced I became that we were paying insufficient attention to what our informants were trying to tell us about the brother's pain. My Gidjingali friends responded to questions about the *mirriri* by articulating a stock phrase, 'I have been speared through the ear', while simultaneously groaning and acting as though this had literally happened. What could be the cause of this suffering? Presumably it was the fact that from childhood a man had been socialized to regard his sister's sexuality as shameful even to think about, and now without warning it was thrust into his ears in the form of obscenities, or before his eyes in the form of the sexual act itself. I wrote a note to the editor of *Oceania* in which I modified my earlier view on the *mirriri* by suggesting that when a man attacked his sister he did so because she was the 'real cause' of his pain. The behaviour was not so much irrational as regressive.[47]

A few years later Kenneth Maddock presented a paper on the *mirriri* at Sydney University. By that time the theories of Claude Lévi-Strauss were attracting much interest in Australia, and Maddock was foremost among those keen to apply and extend them in Aboriginal studies. Inspired by Lévi-Strauss's suggestions and examples in his essay on 'Structural Analysis in Linguistics and Anthropology',[48] he argued that previous interpretations of the brother's behaviour had erred in isolating it from the system of relationships to which it properly belonged. The *mirriri* was to be understood not in terms of motives or states of mind imputed to the actors but by showing its consistency

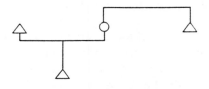

MB/ZS : B/Z :: F/S : H/W

Fig. 6   Lévi-Strauss's formula for the avunculate.

with other elements in a total pattern. Maddock's paper appeared in *Oceania* in 1970, entitled 'A Structural Interpretation of the *Mirriri*'.

In his essay on linguistics and anthropology, Lévi-Strauss had demonstrated how anthropological problems could be illuminated by the methods of modern phonemics, which analysed the sound systems of languages in terms of contrasting features or paired oppositions (e.g. 'voiced' versus 'unvoiced' consonants). Radcliffe-Brown had already taken an intuitive step in this direction when he showed that in numerous cultures the emotive cast of the relationship between maternal uncle and nephew was inversely correlated with that between father and son (if the former was informal and friendly, the latter was formal and reserved, and vice versa). Unfortunately he had not understood, according to Lévi-Strauss, that he was dealing with a larger system of four relationships, of which he had examined merely two. The other two were brother/sister and husband/wife. Once this is appreciated, we can go on to show that if an individual's relationships with his maternal uncle and his sister are both negatively charged (e.g. formality, antagonism, avoidance), his relationships with his father and his wife are positively charged (e.g. informality, affection, companionship). If the first two are positive, the second two are negative; and if one pair is positive and negative, so is the other.

We do not need to enter into a substantive discussion of this example. It formed the model on which Maddock based his approach to the *mirriri*,[49] and I present it here merely to make his interpretation more readily intelligible. The unit of abstraction in which Maddock located the *mirriri* for analytical purposes included, in addition to the brother/sister relationship, the relationships between brothers, between brothers-in-law and between spouses. Two cousin relationships were also included, but as the outcome of the analysis was not significantly affected by them, I omit them for the sake of simplicity.

In Arnhem Land the relationship between brothers contrasted strongly with the relationship between brothers and sisters. Relationships with sisters, as we have seen, were taboo-ridden, embarrassed

B/B : B/Z :: H/W : WB/ZH

\+   -   +   -

Fig. 7   Maddock's formula for the mirriri.

and constrained. Brothers, however, were often in each other's company, the relationship was familiar and often warm, older brothers were protective on behalf of younger brothers, and mutual solidarity in times of trouble could almost always be taken for granted. Relationships with wives, and indeed with women classified as potential wives, were normally free and easy. Relationships between wife's brother/sister's husband were reserved and polite, and for a period after circumcision youths observed silence in the presence of an older brother-in-law. In terms of positive and negative values, the *mirriri* structure as identified by Maddock was as shown in Fig. 7.

With this structure exposed to view, it was now apparent why men felt obliged to throw spears at their sisters. If a man came to his sister's aid when she was in trouble, he would be treating her as if she were his brother. Attacking her was consistent with his general relationship with her, supporting her would run counter to it. Thus the *mirriri* attack dramatized and simultaneously endorsed the binary opposition between siblings of the same sex and siblings of opposite sex. Moreover, and perhaps more importantly, it served to highlight the opposition between the marriageable and the unmarriageable (i.e. between 'W' and 'Z'). Rules of etiquette reinforcing this distinction in everyday life were essential in kinship systems of the Australian type. The *mirriri* was a case where etiquette took the stronger form of expressive ritualization.

For me, Maddock's innovative contribution was important less for its application of Lévi-Strauss than for its location of the *mirriri* within the framework of rules of etiquette (what he referred to as the 'ritualization of daily life'). I could accept the assertion that the brother's attack was, in some sense, consistent with the general taboo on the sister, or even with the so-called *mirriri* structure as a whole, but what was lacking was any evidence that consistency was the driving force. Even if it were, we would still need to explain why a man was required to attack his sister rather than her husband (i.e. his brother-in-law), since that would also be consistent with the alleged global structure (though perhaps 'less consistent'). On the other hand, it would make good sense to say not only that the brother's attack was required by etiquette but, more importantly, that it was provoked by a breach of etiquette. Everyone knew that a woman's sexuality must on no account be mentioned, even discreetly, in the presence of her brother. Yet here was someone blatantly disregarding the convention by shouting obscenities at her. To reaffirm the convention, the brother could no doubt attack the ill-mannered person who had disregarded his sensibilities. But the same result could be achieved by attacking the object of the taboo, namely the sister herself. The *mirriri* represented a cultural choice through which the brother dramatically announced: 'I want everyone to know that I have been the victim of a serious breach of etiquette. The swearing at my sister must stop, otherwise I shall be forced to kill her.'

In the mid-1960s Annette Hamilton studied childrearing at Maningrida, among the people I had worked with a few years earlier. In 1971 she published an article on 'The Equivalence of Siblings' which, as well as containing several interesting observations on the *mirriri*, cast doubt on the positive value assigned by Maddock to the relationship between brothers. It was true that brothers supported each other and affirmed their structural unity in the context of ritual. Nevertheless, their interests did not always coincide, especially in regard to the acquisition of wives. Because marriage rights were defined in genealogical terms, brothers were often potentially in conflict for the same women. Unmarried men were liable to seek liaisons with the wives of older brothers, and older brothers were not always liable to respond in a spirit of fraternal solidarity. Hence, 'the brother–brother relationship, ideally the closest that a man has, contains elements of both positive and negative value'.[50]

At first sight, the brother–sister relationship seemed unequivocally negative. Women even believed that a child who was succeeded in birth by a sibling of opposite sex would grow weak and sickly. Nevertheless a man and his sister called the latter's offspring by the same kinship terms.[51] The children were considered to be of the same flesh as their mother and her brother, and certain usages might be interpreted to suggest that a man and his sister were thought of as having jointly produced her children in a fleshly (though not spiritual) sense. Hamilton suggested that in order to dissociate this belief in the most unambiguous way from any implication of sexual reproduction (and hence brother–sister incest), the cultures of Arnhem Land had imposed the most severe constraints on the relationship between opposite-sex siblings, culminating in spear attacks by men on their sisters when reminded publicly of their sexual functions.

Some years later, while discussing theoretical problems in gender relationships, Gillian Cowlishaw drew attention to the intimidatory effect of the *mirriri* on females.[52] She noted that, in the Aboriginal community she had studied in southern Arnhem Land, girls came to realize from an early age that they were at risk from unpredictable fraternal violence. Their brothers shouted furiously at them if they came too close, or threatened them with weapons if they accidentally breached avoidance taboos while urinating or defaecating. Only as they grew older did they acquire a knowledge of the precipitating causes. They were then able to sense danger and take appropriate evasive action.

In 1985 Victoria Burbank interpreted *mirriri* as a form of ritualized aggression.[53] Originating in the work of zoologists such as Konrad Lorenz, the concept as applied to humans referred to aggressive behaviour governed by rules that reduced the likelihood of injury.[54] A related notion was displaced aggression, as when people vented their anger on weaker individuals after being provoked by more powerful ones. During her fieldwork at Numbulwar, on the east coast of Arnhem Land, Burbank observed numerous incidents in which grievance against persons was expressed in blind fury against inanimate objects (garbage containers, tape recorders, buildings, and so on). Sometimes the attacks occurred after disciplinary actions by white authorities, sometimes after vexatious actions by close relatives, and sometimes after perceived neglect or irresponsibility on the part of some undifferentiated social collectivity. It was reasonable to infer that these aggressive displays were substitutes for attacks on the persons whose actions (or inaction) caused the anger.

Burbank then went on to relate her observations to the *mirriri*. At Numbulwar the word referred specifically to the intense shame caused by any violation of etiquette involving a sister's sexuality. Instead of attacking the person guilty of the violation, the brother attacked the sister. In this context, according to Burbank, there was a sense in which she could be likened to an object: she would not hit back, and there would be no fight. Cultural constraints on the brother ensured that she would not be seriously injured, so that overall the ritualization reduced physical damage to people. The sister was the culturally and psychologically appropriate target for the aggrieved brother's outrage, since from childhood he had been taught that she was 'rubbish'.

In the final part of her essay on the equivalence of siblings, Annette Hamilton tentatively suggested the following isomorphism from the viewpoint of a male subject:

$$WM : Z :: W : ZC$$

Her reasoning was that a man's mother-in-law and his sister both produced children for his benefit, respectively, his wife, and his nieces and nephews.[55] He avoided the first pair (WM and Z), and controlled and cared for the second pair (W and ZC). The possibility of common factors is no doubt an important one to explore in future deliberations on cross-sex avoidance relations. Following Maddock, we might begin by arguing that the public behaviours typical of avoidance of mothers-in-law and sisters are ceremonial forms signifying on the part of sons-in-law and brothers a conscientious concurrence in the cultural defini-tion of their sexual ineligibility. To explain why, from the panoply of prohibited categories in Aboriginal society, only the mother-in-law and the sister have been selected for this special treatment, we might then suggest on the basis of Hamilton's formula that it is because they are the two to whom a man is notoriously indebted. We thus start with the concept of a signal and the most general circumstances underlying its deployment and purpose. Beyond that, the task is presumably to explore and interpret the signal's idiosyncratic forms, elaborations, convolutions and inversions. Whatever guidelines we use in this poorly lit underworld, we should try not to lose sight of the fact that the semiotic functions of sexual taboos do not necessarily explain their aetiology. Nor can they prevent them from exciting the very tendencies they are supposed to outlaw.

9

Initiation: the case of the cheeky yam

In 1912 Melbourne University released Baldwin Spencer from his duties as Professor of Biology to enable him to take up a one-year appointment as Chief Protector of Aborigines in the Northern Territory. In March, after two months of concentrated administrative work in Darwin, Spencer accepted an invitation from a buffalo hunter named Joe Cooper to spend a few weeks at his base on Melville Island.[1] By good fortune a ceremony started shortly after he arrived; and, despite torrential rain, he observed, recorded and photographed with unremitting zeal throughout the three days of its duration. The ceremony was evidently an initiation of some kind, with a lad of fourteen or fifteen as the central figure.[2] But no operations, such as circumcision or tooth evulsion, were performed. Moreover, several girls were also being inducted into the ceremony. By the standards of most of the mainland tribes with which Spencer was familiar, initiation into manhood without bodily mutilation and in the company of female novices would not count as initiation at all. Even more puzzling was the fact that the initiatory aspects were bound up with, and to some extent overshadowed by, an elaborate treatment of a particular variety of bush yam known locally as *kolamma*.

Early in the morning of the first day, before Spencer was abroad, a large party of men went into the bush and dug up enough *kolamma* yams to fill several bark baskets. On their way back to the main camp, they placed the yams in a waterhole and then decorated themselves with pipeclay and birdsdown. The senior men also coated their beards with sticky sap from a milkwood tree, making the hair stand out like a ruff. About mid-afternoon a dancing ground was cleared, around which men and women built a temporary encampment. After a series of individual performances by singers, the initiand[3] was brought into the clearing by his future wife's brother and presented to his father, who paraded him before the assembled community. Towards dusk everyone repaired to the waterhole where the yams had been immersed. After inspecting them, several old men seized the initiand and plunged into the pool with him, dragging him backwards and

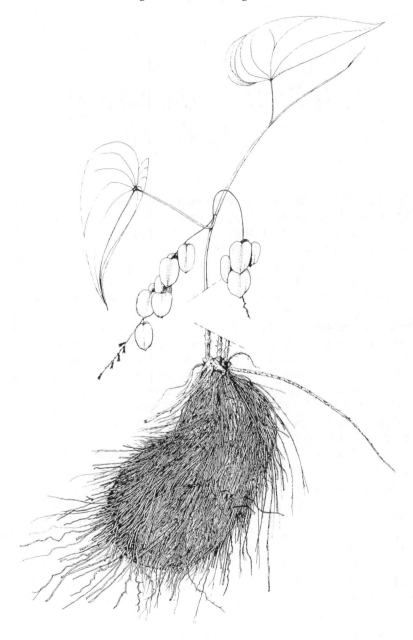

Pl. 13   Round yam. Dioscorea bulbifera, also known as 'Hairy Yam' and 'Cheeky Yam', is called kulama (kolamma) by the people of Melville Island.

forwards under the water by the head and feet. They then turned their attention to three younger lads designated as novices and due to be initiated at the next ceremony.[4] After holding their heads under the water inside yam baskets, they brought them to the surface, rubbed yams vigorously into their chins and bit their chins until they bled. Mangrove mud was applied to the lacerations, and the whole group returned to the camp for an evening of singing and dancing.

Spencer rose at six the next morning and found men piling wood within a circular framework in the middle of the ceremonial ground. On top they placed a thick layer of antbed. Dancing commenced, and after an hour or so the men went to the waterhole and returned with the yams, carried by the initiand and the novices. The wood was then lit by the four youths, aided by a female initiand aged about eleven. Once the fire was alight, the father of the girl took her by the hand and led her several times around the dancing ground. Shortly afterwards, several men surrounded the male initiand and pulled out all his pubic hairs, as well as those around his lips.

As the fire died down, men beat it flat, placed the yams on the embers, and covered them with sheets of bark and damp earth. Onlookers applauded the completion of the oven by striking themselves fiercely on the buttocks. At this stage the four youths retired inside their bark shelters. When the yams were cooked, the female initiand and three other girls were called to the fire and instructed to help skinning and slicing them. The rootlets were carefully excised and put to one side. While this operation proceeded, the men sang the words 'Yams, you are our fathers'. The father of the female initiand took some of the yam slices and rubbed them in his daughter's hair. The four girls retired from the ceremonial ground, whereupon all the men rubbed cooked yam flesh into their beards.

Shortly afterwards those present began painting each other's faces and bodies with elaborate designs. A bark hut was built beside the remains of the fire and the four youths told to go inside. Two men paced ominously around it, singing a song about a spear attack. A crocodile dance and a shark dance followed in succession. Then came, in Spencer's words, 'a curious part of the ceremony, quite unlike anything that is known in connection with initiation on the mainland'.[5] The father of the female initiand, after painting her with ochres and decorating her hair, led her to the bark hut and put her inside with the four youths. After more threatening singing and dancing ('the shark has a big mouth...'), the men made a mock spear attack on the hut. The occupants were 'killed' and the hut dismantled. At this point the girl and the three male novices left the ceremonial ground. The men divided into two teams, seniors and juniors, the latter being joined by the initiand. After a brief tug-of-war, they mingled together in a single, excited mass of bodies. Once disentangled, the participants returned to the yam oven and stood while an elder led the initiand around the remains of the fire. Other elders picked up embers and threw them away in all directions

In the late afternoon the men set off in single file to the waterhole, bearing with them the cooked yams. Once there, they put the yams into the water, together with the excised rootlets. Then, to Spencer's astonishment, men began plucking out their own whiskers, starting at the ear on each side and working down to the middle of the chin. Though the hair was pulled out in bunches, no blood appeared and no signs of pain were evinced. The removed whiskers were carefully placed in the baskets alongside the yams. With this remarkable depilation completed, and everyone being somewhat tired out, the day's work came to an end.

Early on the third morning the female initiand and one of the male novices were taken by several senior men along the track leading to the waterhole and concealed under branches at the base of a tree. The rest of the community set out in the same direction not long afterwards and, on discovering the pair in hiding, simulated great surprise and formed a circle around them. The boy danced first; then, after the girl's father presented her with an ochred ball of feather-down, she held it in her mouth and danced in the company of her father and his three brothers. The party moved on to the waterhole, where men recovered the cooked yams from the baskets, leaving the rootlets and human whiskers undisturbed. Everyone then returned to the main camp and, starting at the same time, ate the yams. This brought the ceremony to an end.

Spencer's record of what he had seen was, in both senses, phenomenal. On the morning of 13 March, two days after the ceremony ended, he sat under Cooper's verandah with a group of elders and questioned them as to meanings. Communication problems were considerable and results meagre. Nevertheless, it seemed that the ceremony was performed with a view to obtaining two related outcomes: a proliferation of all varieties of yams, and a proliferation of human hair, especially whiskers. This was a congenial exegesis, since Spencer was by now famous for his discovery of 'increase rites' in central Australia.[6] It was true that the *kolamma* yam was not a favourite dietary item; in fact, it required special treatment to make it edible, and even then was very hot on the mucous membranes. Perhaps for that reason it was regarded as mystically superior to more palatable species and hence the appropriate representative of the genus for the operation of magic. At the same time its unusual 'hairiness' could be transmitted directly, through ritualized operations, to desired parts of the human anatomy. The men of Melville Island were obviously proud of their beards, and

Pl. 14   Procession of Tiwi men. This photograph, taken by Baldwin Spencer in 1912, shows men of Melville Island proceeding in single file through the forest during the Yam ceremony.

Spencer conceded that they were more impressive than practically any he had seen on the northern mainland.

Spencer visited Melville Island again in November. By then the initiand had completed his initiation, having spent much of the intervening period living by himself in the bush. He was painted from head to foot with red ochre and wore a special horseshoe-shaped necklace, a replica of which his mother was also expected to wear. At the end of April he came to his mother's camp, took off his ornaments, and washed himself in salt water. After receiving new decorations, he resumed his solitary life until September. Returning to his mother's camp once again, he sat fully decked out in his adornments while she called up all the senior women. Once they arrived, he took half his ornaments off; then, when the senior men assembled, he removed the other half. The elders formed a circle around the initiate and his mother and cut themselves in sorrow. The youth was now a man. While they mourned, the symbols of his initiation were placed on a platform in a tree, where in ordinary circumstances they would never have been touched again. In this case, through the good offices of Cooper's Aboriginal wife Alice and the kind permission of the elders, they were reprieved from the normal processes of decay and placed in the National Museum in Melbourne.

In 1954 Charles Pearcy Mountford led a small scientific expedition to Melville Island under the sponsorship of the National Geographic Society of America. Mountford was a telephone mechanic from Ade- laide who had gained a reputation as an ethnologist and photographer. Assisting him were W.E. Harney, a Territorian bushman with wide experience among Aborigines, and Jane Goodale, a graduate student in ethnology at the University of Pennsylvania. One of Mountford's stated objectives was to observe and record a performance of the yam ceremony.[7] Hardly anything had been added to Spencer's description in the intervening years, and mission influences had effectively put an end to it on neighbouring Bathurst Island. The expedition counted itself fortunate, therefore, when a fortnight after arriving in mid-April a *Kulama*[8] ceremony took place within walking distance of its campsite. Mountford, Harney and Goodale watched throughout the three-day duration, and both Mountford and Goodale later published descrip- tions.[9] By this time the people of Bathurst and Melville Islands were known collectively in anthropological literature as the Tiwi, a word in their language meaning 'human being'.[10]

The ceremony commenced on the evening of 30 April, when a clearing was made and singers sang late into the night. Early next morning a small group of men gathered at the clearing, washed themselves, sprayed water from their mouths in all directions, cleaned out their ears, and applied white clay to various parts of their bodies. They then set out in search of yams, bearing digging-sticks specially made for the occasion. When *kulama* vines were found about half a mile away, they patted the ground and softly called 'Wake, wake.' The yams were then carefully extracted, placed in a basket, and later laid out under a tree near the camping area. After resting for most of the afternoon, the men formed a ring about 20 feet in diameter and placed firewood in the centre. They then collected the yams and immersed them in a billabong close by. After splashing themselves with water, they returned to the ring and sang for several hours.

The next morning antbed was placed on the firewood and the fire was then lit. Men painted themselves with ochre and sang songs stating that they had become women. One man facetiously sang: 'I am my sister Dolly, and I am combing my hair'. About ten o'clock the men collected the yams from the water. When the fire had burnt down, they placed them carefully on the hot antbed and covered them with paperbark and sand.

Early in the afternoon, as the cooked yams were removed from the oven, men applied them to various parts of their bodies and those of their children. At three o'clock they started slicing the yams and placing them in the basket, mashing a few in their palms and rubbing the flesh into their hair, whiskers and skin. The rest of the afternoon was spent painting up. At sunset the basket of yams was placed in the centre of the ring. Dancers pretended to fight over its possession, then together carried it off to the billabong with loud shouts. A grass bed was made for the yams in shallow water, where they were immersed and left for the night. The men returned to the ring and continued to sing into the night.

At dawn on the last day the men returned to the billabong and woke the yams with soft calls. They then carried them back to the camp, where they were distributed and eaten. Fully initiated men ate first in order to 'tame' the yams for the uninitiated. The antbed from the oven was broken up and placed around the ring. This brought the ceremony to an end, and within a short time the area was deserted.

Now there were undoubtedly broad similarities of form and se- quence between what Spencer saw in 1912 and what Mountford, Harney and Goodale saw in 1954. The remarkable difference, however, was that in the 1954 ceremony no one was initiated. When Goodale asked why, she was told that the *Kulama* ceremony must be performed annually, regardless whether there were candidates for initiation or not. Her informants confirmed Spencer's observation that females as well as males were initiated, and that initiation took place in stages. Indeed, it seemed that an individual had to pass through six separate stages, each entailing participation in a *Kulama* ceremony, in order to achieve the status of a full adult member of society. The lack of candidates in any grade during the 1954 ceremony was not explained. Even more puzzling, against the background of Spencer's report, was the insistence of Goodale's informants that initiation normally did not begin until the age of about thirty. All the men she spoke to said they were married before they entered the initial grade.

At this stage Goodale began to wonder whether the *Kulama* cere- mony was an initiation rite, or whether it was simply a rite into which people were initiated. Normally in Aboriginal Australia initiation into adulthood begins at puberty, or even before; and puberty rites have as their central objective the symbolic transformation of boys and girls into men and women. How could the *Kulama* ceremony be classified as an initiation rite if it could be performed meaningfully without candidates for initiation; and if, moreover, candidature began at the age of thirty? It was possible that the initiatory components, when present, merely constituted the apparatus for reproducing the ritual from one generation to the next. In that case the explanatory task would be to determine the main purpose for which the ritual had been evolved.

One possibility, in the light of Spencer's exegesis, was that it was primarily an increase ceremony. Goodale found this difficult to accept. From personal experience, she was in a position to say that the consumption of *kulama* was a distinctly unpleasant experience. She had no reason to doubt her informants when they told her the only time it was eaten was at the annual *Kulama* ceremony. As the Tiwi did not perform increase ceremonies for their staples, why should they institute one specially for a plant of no dietary significance? Spencer had suggested that it might have been chosen as a symbol for yams in general, but evidence for such an hypothesis was entirely lacking.

During the 1954 ceremony, Goodale heard the word *tarni* uttered frequently, particularly in response to her inquiries as to the meaning of various parts of the ritual. For instance, at the beginning of the ceremony when the men painted themselves with white clay, they held their paint-covered hands towards the sun, 'so that *tarni* will not kill them'.[11] Before digging the yams, they patted the ground, saying softly 'Wake, wake.' If they neglected this courtesy, the yams would inflict serious illness upon them.[12] When one of the diggers accidentally damaged a yam as he was extracting it from the ground, he rushed off with it through the bush, then returned and placed it in the basket. 'He ran to escape *tarni*', Goodale was told.[13] *Tarni*, it seemed, was some kind of sickness, and *kulama* yams were capable of inflicting it. Once soaked in water and cooked, however, they became potential sources of strength and good health. On removing them from the oven, men applied them to their arms, legs, heads and chests, and to the heads of their children. Later they rubbed the mash into their hair and beards. During the latter operation they sang a jocular song which, to Goodale's puzzlement, they declined to translate, probably because it concerned sexual potency and therefore might have embarrassed the visitors.

On the second morning of the ceremony, after the fire had been lit and the men were painting themselves with ochre, Goodale listened to a discussion about how 'the white people brought other tribesmen into this land who sang magic songs of poison, which caused the Tiwi tribe to die'.[14] The alien tribesmen in question were mainlanders from Port Essington who had acted as a bodyguard for Joe Cooper some fifty years earlier. Just before the turn of the century, during his first buffalo-shooting expedition to Melville Island, Cooper was speared in the neck by a Tiwi warrior. With the help of his Port Essington wife he escaped by canoe, abducting four Tiwi adults at gunpoint. In due course he returned with Alice, a large and well-armed detachment of her countrymen, and the four Tiwi. A *modus vivendi* was worked out, but relationships soured when several Tiwi women deserted their husbands in favour of mainlanders. This was probably a few years after Spencer's visit; and, when fighting escalated into full-scale combat, the government intervened and ordered Cooper and his henchmen off the island.[15]

Not long before Cooper's expulsion, a devastating epidemic broke out among the Tiwi. The death toll reached almost 200 out of a total population of about 1000 people. Although a medical officer, Dr H.K. Fry, was sent to investigate, the nature of the disease remains a mystery. The provisional diagnosis of measles turned out to be most unlikely, as only two of the victims were infants.[16] Apparently Fry arrived too late to see actual cases. The Tiwi themselves attributed the sickness to black magic worked on them by Cooper's mainlanders. During his visit Fry observed part of a *Kulama* ceremony, in the course of which a man sang of magic 'planted' by the mainlanders on the northern beaches at the beginning of the wet season. The sun heated the magic, which the wind then blew everywhere. It acted by crawling up the leg of a victim like a snake, through the belly, and up to the heart, whereupon the patient ceased eating and died.[17] Fry conceded that his investigation 'supported the native diagnosis of magic'.[18]

When Goodale read Fry's recollections, published nearly forty years after the event, it occurred to her that the discussion she heard during the 1954 *Kulama* ceremony about mainland magic and Tiwi genocide probably referred to the epidemic of 1913. If so, it was possible that the cultural memory of this terrible event was encoded in the word *tarni*; and, moreover, that the *Kulama* rite, whatever its traditional function, was performed as an antidote and prophylaxis against future out-breaks.[19] The question was, why choose *kulama* for such a purpose? The clue, speculated Goodale, was to be found in the yam's own poisonous nature. In its untreated state it is inedible; and even after the toxin has been removed by soaking in water, the taste remains unpleasant. Nevertheless, it is well known to cultural ecologists that in various parts of the world the toxic cycad nut is resorted to as a famine food, and the same may have been true of the *kulama* yam among the Tiwi. Long before the epidemic of 1913, the *Kulama* ceremony may have evolved as a means of transmitting the technique of detoxification from one generation of Tiwi to the next. By some curious thought process, the poison of *tarni* was identified with the poison of *kulama*. The *Kulama* ceremony, already in existence as a public health measure in relation to the latter, was accordingly adapted for the purpose of protection against the former.

Goodale first advanced her theory in 1970, in a collection of essays on cultural change among the Aborigines. In the same year the journal *Anthropological Forum* published an article entitled 'Adaptation or Disintegration? Changes in the Kulama Initiation and Increase Ritual of Melville and Bathurst Islands', by Maria Brandl. Mrs Brandl was a graduate student at the University of Western Australia who had recently completed field research among the Tiwi and who in 1969 had witnessed several *Kulama* ceremonies not far from where Goodale had camped fifteen years earlier. No doubt because of similarities in interpretation as well as subject matter, the editor of the journal added a note stating that Goodale's 1970 article had come to hand only after Brandl's paper was already at the galley proof stage.

As indicated by her title, Brandl accepted Spencer's representation of *Kulama* as both an initiation rite and an increase rite. To her mind the question raised by such a conjunction, which Spencer had barely considered, was as follows: 'What is the unifying element in the *kulama* that enables the islanders to combine the two seemingly distinct sets of operations involved in initiation and increase of yams?'[20] Independently of Goodale, Brandl had sensed that the key to the connection was located somewhere in the ritual's preoccupation with sickness and health. But whereas Goodale turned to culture history and ecology for inspiration, Brandl sought an answer in the theory of sacrifice.

A decade before Brandl studied religious practices on Melville Island, W.E.H. Stanner published a provocative and highly influential article in *Oceania*, entitled 'The Lineaments of Sacrifice'. His subject matter was a ceremony he had witnessed in 1935 at Port Keats in the Northern Territory. As its manifest purpose was to induct a number of young men into the mystery of the bull-roarer, Stanner acknowledged that it belonged to the anthropological category of initiation rites. Yet looked at from another perspective, it could as justifiably be classified as a sacrificial rite. Sacrifice, in Stanner's view, comprised four essential elements: (a) the consecration of something of value; (b) the offering of the consecrated object to a spiritual being; (c) the return of the sacrifice to the offerers in a transformed state; (d) the sharing of benefits among those who made the sacrifice. In the bull-roarer rite at Port Keats, the youths were taken to a sacred ground where they were led to believe that the Mother Creator was about to swallow and regurgitate them. They were anointed with human blood and made ready for the goddess's approach, heralded by the sound of the bull-roarers. Suddenly initiated men leapt into view, swinging the sacred objects above their heads. Though the candidates had not literally been killed and reborn, the experience had changed them into men of mystical understanding. The good that flowed from this ritual transformation was a benefit to the whole community.[21]

Brandl argued that Stanner's model of sacrifice was readily applicable to the *Kulama*. While in this case the obvious objects of sacrifice were yams, there was a degree of identification between them and the candidates, and therefore a sense in which both were being sacrificed. Consecration of both yams and youths took the form of cleansing through immersion. The offering of the yams followed their transformation from a raw to a cooked state in an oven; at roughly this stage of the ritual the candidates were placed in a hut and 'killed'. The yams, now leached, cooked, and without their whiskers, were brought from the sacred domain back into the secular world, where their benefits as food and medicine were shared by all. The candidates likewise returned with added maturity in their progression towards full adult-hood.

To whom, however, was the sacrifice offered? In keeping with a notable absence of evidence on the matter, Brandl spoke merely of a 'potent force concerned with growth and health/sickness'; and of 'an ambiguous, potent and dangerous force which will work for human purposes only under stringent conditions'.[22] The *Kulama* ceremony, she maintained, was held with the objective of releasing this force in order to control and benefit from it. It was an initiation rite, an increase rite and a sacrificial rite all in one.

Brandl focussed her analysis almost entirely on the data provided by Spencer. By 1969, performances of the *Kulama* were reduced to collecting the yams, leaching them in drums of water, cooking them in an antbed oven, and rubbing the flesh into the faces and joints of the participants. Although ten ceremonies occurred during the year, only forty-two men out of a total adult male population of 324 took part, most of them of mature age. No candidates for initiation were in evidence, and members of the Christian community stayed away. In most cases the yams were left uneaten. The reasons given to Brandl for performing the ceremony were to make bush foods grow, to keep away sickness from the settlement, and to stop the rain. People felt that unless *Kulama* was performed regularly, catastrophes would occur.

Undoubtedly the best-known anthropological work on the native inhabitants of Bathurst and Melville Islands is *The Tiwi of North Australia* by C.W.M. Hart and Arnold Pilling. First published in 1960, it has been through three editions (with Jane Goodale added as a co-author in the third) and for many years has served as a main teaching reference on the Australian Aborigines for American college students. Hart, the senior author, was among Radcliffe-Brown's first graduates at Sydney University. In 1928, after a brief apprenticeship in the field with Lloyd Warner, he arrived on Bathurst Island, where he lived for the next two years among northern groups as yet little affected by missionary and other white intrusions. Unfortunately, although he was obviously familiar with the *Kulama* ceremony, he died without pub-lishing a description of it. By way of compensation, his writings contain information on Tiwi initiation lacking in all other accounts and enabling us to locate the *Kulama* ceremony in a more familiar mainland perspective.

At the Brisbane ANZAAS meeting in 1930, Hart presented a paper on personal names among the Tiwi, in the course of which he set out the vernacular terms for seven grades of initiation.[23] The first grade for males began at about 15 years of age, and the seventh grade was completed by about 26.[24] Females began at 10 and finished at 21. The period spent in each grade ranged from six months to four years. We may conclude from the lists that the male initiand in the *Kulama* observed by Spencer was passing through third grade, while the three male novices were in first grade. The female initiand was in fourth grade, and the three other girls were either in first grade or fifth grade.[25] Spencer may have underestimated the ages of the candidates by a year or so.[26]

Hart's preliminary statements on the Tiwi[27] were followed by almost a quarter of a century of silence. In 1954 he gave a paper entitled 'Prepubertal and Postpubertal Education' at a conference in San Francisco on 'Anthropology and Education'. One of his main points, presented with characteristic panache, was that in non-literate societies males before puberty acquired their knowledge entirely from intimates, while after puberty their formal education was under the control of strangers. Take the case of the Tiwi. Once boys reached fourteen or fifteen, they were ceremonially removed from their families by heavily armed men from outside their natal communities. The lad's mother howled in protest and tried to hide him, while his father, who had authorized the visitation, resisted the invaders with spears. To no avail. The boy was pitilessly wrenched from the bosom of his family and taken into seclusion. For the next decade he was subjected to restrictions, taboos, deprivations and hardships under the authority of mature men from neighbouring bands who had already married his sisters, or who hoped to do so in the future.

We may presume that the seizure of the boy marked his entry into the first grade of initiation.[28] In his Brisbane paper, Hart stated that for males 'the normal initiation ceremonies are carried out continuously from the age of seventeen'.[29] The meaning of this statement became clearer in 1960:

> Breaking in on the long years of austerity spent either in seclusion in the bush or in *pukimani* [taboo] at home, were periodic collective ceremonies when the youth was ritually advanced from one stage of initiation to the next. These were public ceremonies, witnessed by large crowds, and the more important of such transition ceremonies took place in January and February when the *kolema* yams were ripe.[30]

In the first edition of *The Tiwi of North Australia*, Hart gave the impression that the yams provided nutritional support for the *Kulama* ceremony, rather than a symbolic purpose.[31] In the third edition, published after his death, the editors added a footnote suggesting that *kulama* was too scarce and too toxic to be used as a staple food, even for the duration of a ceremony.[32] Hart evidently thought that the initiatory purpose of the *Kulama* ceremony was paramount, and whether he was aware of other objectives is impossible to know. In his paper on 'Prepubertal and Postpubertal Education' he dwelt at length on the traumatic aspects of Tiwi initiation, and elsewhere maintained (though without amplification) that the crucial grade for males was when their pubic hair was forcibly pulled out.[33] He also highlighted the father's complicity in the ritual separation of the lad from his mother; and, for the benefit of those with Freudian tastes, compared Tiwi procedures with those of the Kiwai Papuans, where the initiand was required to step on his mother's stomach, thereby signifying that he was now 'finished with the place he came from'.

For his own part, Hart was content with the sociological framework provided by Arnold van Gennep in his classic work *The Rites of Passage*[34]. Notwithstanding regional differences in content, Aboriginal initiation conformed to a common tripartite structure of (1) separation from the associations of childhood; (2) a state of indeterminacy; and (3) incorporation into the status of male adulthood. But there was a further consideration, at least in the case of the Tiwi. Here gerontocratic polygyny[35] was unusually well developed and normally entailed the postponement of first marriages for men until at least the age of thirty. Just as they were becoming not only sexually mature but also competent hunters, youths were removed from domestic production units for extended periods and placed in seclusion for the purpose of religious education. Perhaps this was an intellectual luxury facilitated by a rich tropical environment. A more cynical view, to which Hart himself subscribed, would be that in forcing junior males to undergo a prolonged period of discipline and social isolation, the Tiwi initiatory system protected the marital prerogatives of the senior males who presided over it.[36]

The professed objectives of initiation were, of course, quite different, and no one has expressed them more elegantly for Aboriginal Australia than Stanner in the opening sentences of his description of the Murinbata bull-roarer rite:

> A few years after circumcision when youths are – in the eyes of mature men – egotistical and refractory because they do not yet understand the restraints of adult life, and do not listen to the prudent counsel of age, they are asked to submit themselves to the disciplines of *Punj* [the bull-roarer rite] and to learn its secrets. No force is used as at circumcision and pre-pubertal initiation. The youths are offered a discipline which is at the same time a privilege and a means of acquiring status. But

177

acceptance of the discipline is a virtual necessity, for there is a back-ground of mystical as well as human threat.[37]

On the second day of the rite, as witnessed by Stanner at Port Keats, the novices were taken to a concealed place in the bush, where they were told to remove their pubic covering and ornaments. From now on, until the end of the ceremony, they must go naked. As well, their personal names must not be used; they would be addressed and referred to as 'flesh of wild dogs'. Stanner interpreted this to mean that the lads had been transformed into wild beasts for the purpose of sacrificing them to the Mother Creator.[38]

The interpretation of the bull-roarer rite as sacrificial has had a mixed reception.[39] My own opinion, echoing Hart in the case of the *Kulama* ceremony, is that it is best approached as a rite of passage with a structure and purpose of the kind delineated by van Gennep.[40] With regard to the metaphorical transformation of novices into 'flesh of wild dogs', the unresolved problem in Stanner's account is why dingoes should have been conceived figuratively as sacrificial animals, since they were not sacrificed in fact, and indeed were rarely if ever eaten by humans.[41] A more likely explanation is that they offered an apt metaphor for novices in a state of transition from boyhood to manhood. In the whelping season, Aboriginal hunters often took dingo pups from their mothers in order to tame them.[42] Wild dingoes were not hunted for food and were allowed to scavenge around camps. The species was thus marginal, neither an integral part of Aboriginal society nor yet entirely outside it. Novices likewise were marginal, often spending lengthy periods on the outskirts of the general community. They lived in a state of limbo: expelled from boyhood, but not yet fully qualified for manhood.

Whereas the Murinbata designated youths as wild dogs during their initiation, the Tiwi associated them with a species of fiery, unpalatable yam. It seems not unreasonable to suggest that, while the food-technology component of the *Kulama* ritual tamed wild yams for human consumption, the initiatory component 'tamed' the wildness in youths and made them ready for incorporation into the body politic. In many parts of northern Australia toxic yams are described in English as 'cheeky'; in keeping with this idiom we could say that when they are detoxified by immersion in water the 'cheekiness' is leached out of them. By simultaneously immersing youths, Tiwi elders were probably seeking a similar outcome.

Cleansing the lads of unruliness made them ready to receive the positive essence of the *kulama* yam. Its hairiness, in conjunction perhaps with its gonadic shape, apparently constituted for native medical thinkers presumptive evidence of a property capable of promoting desirable sexual characteristics and, more generally, good physical condition. We recall, however, that when male elders applied the yams to the chins of adolescent boys they subjected them immediately afterwards to a painful episode of chin-biting. It would seem that the gift of virility went hand-in-hand with aggression from the same source; and it is a fact that, for young men, departures from celibacy necessarily entailed adultery[43] and therefore the risk of physical retribution by an injured husband, who acted with the endorsement and protection of collective gerontocratic authority.[44] A similar point could be made about circumcision on the mainland: senior males ritually conferred manhood, stated in the idiom of castration, on the understanding that it should not be exercised against their own sexual interests.

It is perhaps on this basis that we can grasp the significance of the phrase 'yams, you are our fathers', sung repeatedly by the men during the ceremony of 1912. The Tiwi knew that the *kulama* yam was toxic, but they also believed it to be prophylactic. In the context of initiation, these properties may have suggested a metaphor for collective male authority, which is both punitive and protective. Spencer was told that if a boy later disobeyed what he was told to do by the old men when he was being initiated, he would fall ill and die.[45]

The erosion of gerontocracy among the Tiwi and its replacement by institutionalized white authority began in 1911, with the establishment of a Roman Catholic mission on Bathurst Island. The founder, Fr Gsell of Alsace, made his first converts among adolescent boys: 'The breach in the native defences, if breach there was, had to be found amongst the adolescents; and it had to be found in the teeth of the bogey of initiation.'[46] At first only boys lived at the mission; but with the arrival of nuns, girls came as well. In 1921 a crisis developed when a Tiwi elder came to the mission to claim a girl named Martina who had been promised to him in marriage. She went under protest and five days later sought refuge at the mission with a spear wound in her leg. A confrontation between the missionaries and armed tribesmen was resolved when the husband accepted trade goods worth about two pounds sterling in exchange for Martina, on the condition that she should never be given to any other man. A few years later Fr Gsell solemnized her union with one of his Christian converts. Over the next two decades the bestowers of 150 girls sold their rights to him. Monogamy became the norm, the age of marriage for men came down dramatically, and puberty rites fell into desuetude.

In describing the salvation of Martina in his book *The Bishop with 150 Wives*, Fr Gsell referred repeatedly to her first husband as 'the hairy anonymous old man'. The disparagement no doubt expressed his hostility towards the conjunction of hirsuteness, age and sexual privilege that characterized Tiwi gerontocracy; at any rate, this was the central locus of power in Tiwi society that he systematically and successfully undermined during his long tenure of office. The decline of male elders under the mission regime was matched by an elevation of women; and this, in conjunction with dissolution of the nomadic patrilineal hunting bands, created conditions in which matrilineal social groupings acquired a new importance. Hart's collaborator Pilling, an American anthropologist who studied the Tiwi shortly after World War 2, went so far as to claim that there had been a 'change from patriliny to matriliny'.[47] However that may be, it is noteworthy that Harney, in a report published in 1943, described *kulama* as 'a small hot yam that embodies the spirit of the "old woman" and guardian of the horde'.[48] In 1954 Goodale found a strong shift towards femaleness in the symbolism of the ceremony: men pretended to be women ('I am my sister Dolly'), the oven in which the yams were cooked was referred to as 'mother', the fire was called 'mother-in-law', and the yams after cooking were spoken of by the men as 'our daughters'.[49] The transition from patriarchal identifications to female associations among the Tiwi, following the weakening of traditional male authority, is reminiscent of Stanner's conjecture that in the Daly River region men abandoned the cult of the All-Father after the conquest of their society by Europeans and turned instead to veneration of the 'Old Woman' (All-Mother).[50]

In the light of these historical forces, it is not surprising that by 1954 initiatory elements in the *Kulama* ceremony had been subordinated to a concern with health and well-being. Mountford gained the impression that initiation had virtually ceased. Senior men talked about inducting men now in their thirties, but procrastinated whenever an opportunity arose.[51] Brandl fifteen years later likewise saw no initiation, though she was informed that men and women were still graduating through the *Kulama*. The first three stages were normally omitted, and induction into the fourth grade began after the age of thirty.We may see this as a compromise between accepting white opposition to initiation and a desire nevertheless to keep alive an important facet of Tiwi tradition. In 1974 the linguist C.R. Osborne published a text on the mythological origins of the *Kulama* ceremony which ended with the following asseveration:

> We will never give it up, our old custom. Kurlama is too dear to us, too dear. We shall never give it up. You white people, too, you white people as well, have your own old customs...We shall keep on dancing – always – we shall keep on dancing...Do you understand now? No one can say to us 'Hey! Leave off! Give up your dancing!'. Definitely not. No one. No one will ever make us stop.[52]

The relationship between *Kulama* and female initiation remains problematic. In 1960 Hart stated flatly that 'for females there were no initiation ceremonies', apparently having forgotten that thirty years earlier he had listed female initiation-grade names.[53] Probably he meant that girls were not captured, placed under various taboos and forced to spend lengthy periods in seclusion. Goodale regarded *Kulama* as a rite of passage principally for men. The important puberty rite for a female took place at the time of her first menses, which normally occurred after she had begun living with her husband. After a brief period of isolation, she was taken to a bush camp where her father placed a barbed spear between her legs and then formally presented it to the man who had been chosen as her future son-in-law.[54]

On Bathurst and Melville Islands, as on the Australian mainland, suicide in traditional society seems to have been unusual if not unknown. In recent years, however, there has been an outbreak of self-destruction and self-mutilation among Tiwi young men. According to Gary Robinson,[55] a contributing factor is prolonged psychological dependence on maternal kin, well beyond adolescence, and a conflict-laden enmeshment in the vicissitudes of the parental family. Traditionally, as we have seen, this would have been impossible. At puberty, a lad was ritually removed from his family surroundings and placed under the tutelage of outsiders. More importantly, clearly defined status objectives were implanted in his mind, and by the time he had attained them by passing through a series of initiatory grades, he was ready to marry and start his own family. Masculine values were reinforced through regular engagement in male corporate activities, particularly hunting, fighting and ceremonial; while idealization of the father, who by now was unlikely to be alive, provided an individualized role model for the firm delineation of personal identity.

The Tiwi say that when a boy's pubic hair begins to grow, dogs bark at him in camp and crocodiles and bulls chase him in the bush. In the old days the source of provocation was forcibly plucked out. As a son's burgeoning sexuality was potentially a destabilizing force in his father's harem, the preservation of paternal and filial goodwill depended on separation through the institution of initiation, followed by the son's growing absorption in the corporate affairs of men (which included the cultivation of patronage necessary for the promise of a wife from outside his own band). All these traditional structures have now collapsed, and nothing viable has been put in their place. The transition from childhood dependence to adult autonomy, once mediated by external authority, is now beset by incoherence and uncertainty of aims. The family itself is the remaining authority, and children often lack the motivation to solve their problems by making a clean break with it. Ambivalence inherent in the father–son relationship remains unresolved and a source of instability, fluctuating between violence and mutual aid. Young men have nightmares about death, and suffer chronically from melancholy, depression and rage.

In 1986 three Tiwi brothers travelled to the mainland in order to establish contact with a descendant of one of Joe Cooper's buffalo-shooters, related to them as a classificatory father. They had fantasies about being initiated and in the process acquiring power to win fights, get women, and in general overcome their anomy. The pilgrimage proved futile. Within a short period following their return to Melville Island, one brother had narrowly survived a suicide attempt after grasping an electrical power line. Another, just before his thirtieth birthday, broke into a store and hanged himself while awaiting police questioning.

> My father, you were a king and you died.
> I want to be like you, my father.
> Be rich and have lots of money.
> Have a flag, all blue, white, and red.
> Have a warship with me and live in a big house.
> This song is for you – the dead man.
>
> Kulama song recorded by Jane Goodale in 1954,
> the year of the visit to Australia of the new sovereign,
> Queen Elizabeth II, and her consort Prince Philip, in
> the royal yacht *Britannia*.

10

Epilogue

The conditions of a century ago that conferred on the Australian Aborigines their privileged position in anthropological discourse no longer exist. The Empire has dissolved, Social Darwinism is out of fashion, and the search for social origins has long been abandoned as futile and misconceived. Even the notion of elementary structures has fallen from vogue. Moreover, as the unique adaptations of the original inhabitants were progressively modified or destroyed, research necessarily became more and more preoccupied with dislocations, predicaments and miseries of a kind common to indigenous peoples throughout the post-colonial 'fourth world'. While it is true that hunter-gatherer studies have managed to preserve a modest contemporary niche in the discipline, Aborigines are accorded no preeminence and in any case attract more attention as leaders in the struggle for a better future than as models of an ancient past.

It is difficult to forecast what the future holds for the preceding arguments. Land rights and the position of women contain an unexpended political charge and seem certain to generate further disputation. In March 1995 the High Court rejected an appeal by the Western Australian Government against the Native Title Act, thus shifting further argument from the court into the political arena. In the matter of Aboriginal women's rights, the keenest debates at the moment seem to be (a) whether, in the interests of black solidarity against white racism, discussion of violence perpetrated on Aboriginal women by Aboriginal men should be muted or suppressed; and (b) whether white female anthropologists have any business talking about such matters anyway.[1] In a more general sense Aboriginal politics seem destined to form a permanent and significant element in Australian public life as the new millennium approaches, and no doubt continuities and contrasts with traditional practices will continue to be discussed.

Tony Swain's challenging book on Aboriginal religion has already injected new life into the 'High Gods' issue.[2] Group marriage, conception beliefs, avoidance relationships and initiation may attract scholarly interest and rethinking from time to time, though new evidence will be increasingly hard to come by. It is also safe to assume that regional variation will receive due emphasis in future debates, making it more problematic than ever to use Aborigines categorically as a case history in speculative inquiry.

Readers familiar with the history of social anthropology will have noted that a number of famous arguments are missing. In my initial prospectus I outlined a chapter entitled 'Totemism: The Death of a Concept', but after drafting 'High Gods' I realised its inclusion would entail too much repetition. Happily, I became aware soon afterwards that Adam Kuper had already dealt with the issue admirably in his book *The Invention of Primitive Society* (1988). My prospectus also included plans for an essay entitled 'What Happened to the Murngin?', the reference being to a debate on north-east Arnhem Land kinship that engaged some of the best minds of yesteryear, but in the event my good intentions were undermined by the fear that no one nowadays would read it.[3] In a further omission in the field of kinship, my chapter on the 'group marriage' issue stopped short of discussing alliance theory and I could only agree with an anonymous report on the manuscript which said that 'group marriage could entail discussion of almost all aspects of anthropological approaches to the study of marriage'. Nevertheless, as John Barnes once said to me, every essay has the potential to become a prolegomenon to the history of the universe, and rightly or wrongly I decided not to extend the argument beyond Radcliffe-Brown's polemic against Morgan. It should be noted, however, that the former's interpretation of kin classification itself later became a subject of controversy.[4]

The longest argument about Aborigines, involving by far the greatest number of participants, arose from the perennial question, 'What is to be done about them?'. Readers may justifiably wonder why, having introduced it through reference to the Aborigines' Protection Society in my 'Prologue' and having pursued it somewhat in 'Real Estates and Phantom Hordes', I subsequently let it drop out of sight. Partly, I suppose, the answer is that the institutional cleavage between philanthropy and learning initiated in 1843 by Richard King widened throughout the whole period in which anthropological issues concerning the Australian Aborigines began to take shape. The rallying cry of the Victorian anthropologist was the advancement of his science rather than the advancement of its subject matter; reputation was achieved by unveiling the new truths of the doctrine of evolution, while God's truth, compassion and the saving of souls were left to the missionaries.

Another reason is that questions of policy introduce criteria for the evaluation and resolution of debates that are for the most part not relevant to the species of argument discussed in the preceding chapters. We do not advance the empirical question whether Aborigines practised 'group marriage' by discussing whether 'group marriage' is a desirable policy. Of course, academic debates may have moral and political implications and from time to time get caught up in political and moral debates outside the academy, as in the case of Aboriginal land rights, but often they remain merely academic.

Finally, there is the matter of competence. In my draft prospectus I included a chapter on the origins and prehistory of the Aborigines but in the event dropped the proposal through lack of confidence in my ability to do it justice. I gained my qualifications as an anthropologist by working in the field of traditional Aboriginal social life. Some of my colleagues specialized in social change and race relations and in the course of their research became more competent than I in topics relevant to policy issues. Furthermore, over the last quarter of a century increasing numbers of scholars trained in history, law, economics and political science have turned their attention to relationships between Aborigines and the white majority. Many matters that once belonged to the province of do-it-yourself anthropologists are now safely in the hands of experts.

The emphasis I have placed on the interpretation of traditional social life for the above reasons should not be understood to mean that I am indifferent to the dislocations it suffered in the wake of invasion or unconcerned about the fate of those whose cultural heritage has disappeared or survives under threat. Through the experience of intensive fieldwork, which became a fully fledged and integral part of the anthropological endeavour following the example of Boas, Malinowski and others, twentieth-century anthropologists have increasingly sought to heal the breach between philanthropy and science that was tolerated, if not enshrined, by their nineteenth-century British forebears. An unsentimental view would be that they have done so in order to serve their own interests. But mutuality is not to be despised, especially when it becomes (as it so often has) the foundation of respect, amity and compassion.[5] In a sense the anthropologist in contemporary Australian political life has resumed the role of the missionary of the Aborigines' Protection Society resented by editors of the *Sydney Herald* a hundred and fifty years ago. It is also true that nowadays the editors themselves are likely to be converts.

A further mercy is that the very question, 'What is to be done about them?', can no longer be asked on the assumption that the objects of its concern are passively available for solutions devised by the agents of their predicament. The last thirty years have seen the emergence of political activism among Aborigines all over Australia and a determination to take their fate as far as possible into their own hands. Although the terms and limits of this new-found independence are still under negotiation, and are likely to remain so for some time, there is now little doubt that representatives of the Aboriginal people will continue to seek reparation for wounds suffered in the past and that representatives of the white majority will continue to respond in a mood of reconciliation and atonement.

Anthropology is not exempt from the processes set in motion by resurgent pride and desires for autonomy, particularly as Aborigines have become aware of the role assigned to them in the early days of the subject and find it offensive.[6] Some black activists have expressed the view that Aboriginal studies should be carried on only by Aborigines. In confessional mode, perhaps, some white anthropologists have repudiated not only their own tainted origins but in various degrees the principles of detachment and objectivity that have been regarded as hallmarks of the scientific tradition. Most of us, I think, hope that the subject will be taken forward into the twenty-first century by white and black scholars working in collaboration.[7] Most of us also hope, perhaps piously, for a workable mix of 'science and sympathy'[8] in which neither one component nor the other is too seriously compromised. The extent to which it will be seen as possible or desirable in the immediate future to approach Aboriginal culture in a disinterested way as an object of inquiry is not easy to predict.[9] For what it is worth, my own view is that in contemporary Australia the dialectical quest for truth about the indigenous culture, by open argument and counter-argument, is no less important than about the culture of the invaders and oppressors. Both investigations, I believe, are best carried on by scholars whose primary loyalty is not to one heritage or the other but to the principle that nothing is sacrosanct except the spirit of free inquiry itself. The custodians of that particular flame are without race, as are their enemies.[10]

Notes

1 Prologue

1 Blackstone was the leading authority on English law and author of *Commentaries on the Laws of England*, 4 vols.,1765–9. See Note 6 below.
2 See George Stocking's article 'What's in a Name? The Origins of the Royal Anthropological Institute (1837–71)' (Stocking 1971b). Although Stocking did not mention Sharp, his article set me on a trail that led to him. Professor Stocking's article, together with an earlier essay by John Barnes ('Anthropology in Britain Before and After Darwin', 1960), provided the inspiration for this entire introductory chapter, and I express my gratitude accordingly.
3 Biographical materials on Sharp come mainly from Hoare 1820; see also Coupland 1964. *Black England: Life before Emancipation* by Gretchen Gerzina (John Murray, London) appeared late in 1995, after the present work had gone to press.
4 Hoare 1820:23.
5 Beaglehole 1962:II, 88.
6 Hoare 1820:90. Hoare records an earlier case in which counsel representing a runaway slave quoted in court a passage from Blackstone previously transcribed by Sharp: 'And this spirit of liberty is so deeply implanted in our constitution, and rooted even in our very soil, that a Slave, or a Negro, the moment he lands in England, falls under the protection of the laws, and with regard to all national rights, becomes *eo instanti* a freeman.' Opposing counsel in reply triumphantly produced a copy of Blackstone's *Commentaries* in which the critical sentence read: 'A Negro, the moment he lands in England, falls under the protection of the laws, and so far becomes a freeman; though the master's right to his services may possibly still continue.' Sharp, badly shaken, checked his sources and found that Blackstone had added the qualification in a subsequent edition. Apparently the revision was made after Blackstone had been consulted by Sharp and then apprised himself of the Lord Chief Justice's opinion as it appeared to be at the time. See Hoare 1820:91, footnote.
7 Coupland 1964:59.
8 Coupland 1964:93.
9 For an introduction to the debate on self-interest versus altruism in the abolition movement, see Bender 1992.
10 *Second Annual Report of the Aborigines' Protection Society*, May 1839, p. 8. It should be noted that capitalization of the word 'Aborigines', adopted in

official and anthropological publications in the second half of the twentieth century as a courtesy, was standard practice in all publications of the Aborigines' Protection Society. The term, of course, was not confined to the indigenous peoples of Australia.

11 *Ibid.*

12 *Extracts from the Papers and Proceedings of the Aborigines' Protection Society,* Article 3, June 1839.

13 In 1832 Hodgkin described a disease of the lymph glands that later bore his name. He also came to be known as 'the father and founder of the Aborigines' Protection Society' ('The APS: Chapters in its History', *Transactions of the Aborigines' Protection Society,* 1896–1900, p. 24).

14 Prichard was brought up in a Quaker family but moved towards the Evangelicals in adulthood; Hodgkin, by contrast, continued to wear the black Quaker dress until his death (Stocking 1971b:369).

15 For a detailed account of the origin and subsequent history of this publication, see Stocking 1993.

16 Keith 1917:14.

17 Prichard 1847:302.

18 Council Minute Book of the Ethnological Society, 7 June 1860 (Royal Anthropological Institute Archives).

19 Broca was a surgeon and anatomist who identified the speech centre of the human brain, now known as 'Broca's area' (see Schiller 1979). According to Schiller, the Anthropological Society of Paris, formed in 1859, was the first learned society to designate itself as 'Anthropological' (Schiller 1979:135). However, it seems that an Anthropological Society of London was established in 1837. It was devoted mainly to phrenology (a crude precursor of Broca's own speciality) and later merged into the Christian Phrenological Society. According to one contemporary observer (Davis 1868), the existence of this first Anthropological Society of London (which had no connection with the second) may have influenced King in choosing 'Ethnological' rather than 'Anthropological'. However that may be, it should be noted that the former term (from *ethnos*, meaning 'nation') accorded very well with Prichard's conceptualization of the subject matter.

20 Hunt 1864:viii.

21 Hunt 1864:viii.

22 Burton 1865:317.

23 Pritchard 1865.

24 Sellon 1865.

25 Lund 1865:cxxi–cxxii.

26 Prichard 1973 [1813].

27 *Journal of the Anthropological Society* (1864), xlv.

28 Hunt 1854. The apparent success of Thomas Hunt's method (which bears some similarities to the Alexander technique) provoked the editor of *The Lancet* into attacking him for practising without a medical degree. Hunt urged his son to obtain such a qualification, but he acquired a Ph.D. instead. Thus, while the medical doctors of the Ethnological Society addressed themselves to philology, the doctor of philosophy who founded the Anthropological Society concentrated on anatomy.

29 Knox 1850.
30 Hunt 1863:472.
31 Hunt 1868:438.
32 Hunt 1869:cvii.
33 *Journal of the Royal Anthropological Institute* 37 (1907), 421.

2 Real estates and phantom hordes

1 Maine's critique was set out in a course of lectures given at the Inns of Court during the 1850s, and possibly earlier at Cambridge. The lectures formed the basis of his book *Ancient Law*, published in 1861 (Burrow 1963:140).
2 Blackstone 1876 [1765–69]:II, ch. 1; Maine 1876 [1861]:251–2. The most celebrated source of the doctrine that labour conferred property rights was Locke's second treatise on government, published in 1690.
3 Blackstone 1876:II, p. 6.
4 Blackstone 1876:I, 81. Blackstone qualifies his assertion with the words: 'or at least upon that of nations'. For an analysis of the relationship between the laws of nature and the laws of nations, see Maine 1876.
5 '... the movement of the progressive societies has hitherto been a movement *from Status to Contract*' (Maine 1876:170).
6 'In applying to the discovery of new countries the same principles which the Romans had applied to the finding of a jewel, the Publicists [writers on international law] forced into their service a doctrine altogether unequal to the task expected from it' (Maine 1876:250).
7 Beaglehole 1955: cclxxxiii.
8 Beaglehole 1955:306.
9 Watson 1914:1–8.
10 Collins 1804:10.
11 Tench 1961:ch. 10; Currey 1957.
12 Collins 1804:385.
13 Collins 1804:385.
14 *Extracts from the Papers and Proceedings of the Aborigines Protection Society*, I (1839), pp.140–2; Grey 1841:II, 232–5.
15 Eyre 1845:II, 296–7.
16 Eyre 1845:II, 158–9. Twenty years later, as Governor of Jamaica, Eyre put down a slave rebellion by declaring a period of martial law in the course of which over 400 people were executed and 600 flogged. Members of the Ethnological Society, whose Quaker forebears helped to cultivate precisely the liberal sentiments expressed by Eyre in regard to the treatment of Aborigines, felt obliged to condemn his ruthlessness in Jamaica. High ideals are not always compatible with high office (see Geoffrey Dutton, *The Hero as Murderer*).
17 Howitt 1967a [1880]:182.
18 Howitt and Fison 1883.
19 See, for example, Fison and Howitt 1880:332–4.
20 Morgan 1877:Part 4 ('Growth of the Idea of Property').

21 Howitt and Fison 1885:143.
22 McLennan 1970 [1865]:93; see Chapter 3 ('Group Marriage') for further details.
23 Howitt 1904:89. Darwin also used the term 'horde', though not specifically with reference to Australian Aborigines (Darwin 1871:II, 370).
24 For example, 'each tribe was composed of local divisions, which we have found it convenient to call *Hordes* where descent is through the mother, and *Clans* where the line of descent is through the father' (Howitt and Fison 1900:46).
25 Howitt and Fison 1885: 143–5.
26 Howitt and Fison 1885:145.
27 Radcliffe-Brown 1913:144–60.
28 Radcliffe-Brown 1918:222–4.
29 Radcliffe-Brown 1931:28–9.
30 Radcliffe-Brown 1952 [1935a]:34.
31 Kaberry 1939:136, 176.
32 Radcliffe-Brown 1956:365.
33 Piddington 1932:351.
34 Stanner 1933:403; 1936:187.
35 Sharp 1934:31–2.
36 Warner 1937:389.
37 Elkin 1950:17–18.
38 Elkin 1953:417.
39 Radcliffe-Brown 1954:106.
40 Meggitt 1962: ch. 5. This book, entitled *Desert People*, was initially presented in 1955 as an M.A. thesis.
41 Meggitt 1962:288.
42 Meggitt 1962:214.
43 Meggitt 1962:51.
44 Hiatt 1962.
45 Stanner 1965; Hiatt 1966a.
46 Birdsell 1970; cf. Falkenberg 1981:68–9.
47 Wells 1982:80, appendix 2 (which contains the wording of the petition).
48 *Report from the Select Committee on Grievances of Yirrkala Aborigines, Arnhem Land Reserve*, 1963, p. 9.
49 Blackburn 1971.
50 It is possible they believed such a model would serve the interests of the plaintiffs better than the looser framework described by Meggitt, myself and others. I have a letter from Stanner that would bear such an interpretation. See also Hiatt 1982a; Maddock 1983:54.
51 Blackburn 1971:169–71; for an extended commentary, see Gumbert 1981, 1984.
52 Blackstone 1876, I, 81.
53 Woodward 1974:162.
54 Hiatt 1965:53–60.
55 Maddock 1983:ch.5; Hiatt 1984.
56 Hamilton 1979:78.

57 Myers 1976, 1986.
58 Von Sturmer 1978. If we can extrapolate from Cape York to Botany Bay, von Sturmer's observations might suggest that Bennelong was a traditional 'big man' before his aggrandisement under the patronage of Governor Phillip; cf. Malinowski (1913:137), who speculated that early reports of individual ownership were in fact statements about territories made in the first person by local-group headmen.
59 The largest of three islands known collectively as the Murray Islands.
60 Brennan 1993:27.
61 Toohey 1993:140.
62 Brennan 1993:36.
63 Maine 1876:45.
64 See, for example, Durack 1992. Justice Dawson in his minority judgment expressed the view that 'if traditional land rights ... are to be afforded to the inhabitants of the Murray Islands, the responsibility, both legal and moral, lies with the legislature and not with the courts' (1993:136).
65 Gibbs 1993:xiii.
66 Lavarch 1994:iv.

3 Group marriage

1 I have drawn biographical details mainly from Resek 1960.
2 Morgan 1851:86.
3 Quoted in Resek 1960:79.
4 Resek 1960:96–7.
5 Resek 1960:125; Rivière 1970.
6 McLennan 1886:276.
7 Darwin 1871:II, 359.
8 Morgan 1964 [1877]:430–42.
9 Morgan 1872:419.
10 The linking relatives in the case of *cross*-cousins are of opposite sex. Thus father and father's sister link Ego to his or her FZS and FZD, while mother and mother's brother link him or her to MBS and MBD. The linking relatives in the case of *parallel*-cousins are of the same sex, viz. father and father's brother, mother and mother's sister. In classificatory systems of the Iroquois type, parallel-cousins are classified as 'brothers' or 'sisters'.
11 Morgan 1872:419.
12 Walker 1971:224.
13 Stern 1930:271.
14 In a letter to Morgan written on 6 January 1880, Fison wrote: 'We find it necessary to withdraw our Mss. from the Smithsonian. Prof. Baird's promise of publication one and a half to two years after acceptance of the work is fatal to its prospects ... E.B. Tylor is a sharp spur to us. It is known that he is collecting material for a work on the natives and he seems to consider that he has a heaven sent right to the use of other people's brains and labours. That letter sketched the whole framework of my memoir and told him several things which I should not have cared to tell him until they

were out of his reach by being well on their way to the publisher. Our sole reason for withdrawal is absolute necessity for speedy publication. The Rev. Geo. Taplin (or rather the S. Australian government for him) has already published a most absurd book on the Aborigines, in which he coolly appropriates things which Howitt and I wrote to him, copying whole paragraphs from our letters without even a hint of acknowledgment. Another man Curr is in the field and he is in possession of several of our facts. Moreover, our printed circulars long ago set him on the track. He wrote to Howitt claiming our territory. As Howitt said in his letter to me thereupon: "If we don't make haste we shall be accused of ploughing with the Taplin and Curr heifers".' (Stern 1930:424–5).

15 Polygyny refers to a state in which a man has more than one wife.
16 Fison and Howitt 1880:73.
17 In 1884 Frederick Engels (1902 [1884]:51, 53–4) stated that: 'The most essential contribution to our knowledge of group marriage we owe to the English missionary, Lorimer Fison, who studied this form of the family for years on its classical ground, Australia ... group marriage is represented in Australia by class marriage, i.e. mass marriage of a whole class of men frequently scattered over the whole breadth of the continent to an equally widespread class of women.' The connection between Morgan and Marx and Engels, and its relevance to arguments about gender relations in Australia, is discussed in Chapter 4.
18 Howitt's first major statement on the Dieri was made in an article entitled 'The Dieri and Other Kindred Tribes of Central Australia', 1891. Subsequently he received further data, especially from Rev. Otto Siebert, and published a revised account in *The Native Tribes of South-East Australia*, 1904.
19 Howitt 1904:186.
20 Spencer and Gillen (1899:62) describe *piraunguru* as the 'exact equivalent' of *pirrauru*, but this is an over-statement.
21 See chapter 6, 'High Gods' below, p. 100.
22 Malinowski 1913:1; my emphasis.
23 Radcliffe-Brown 1952 [1941].
24 Radcliffe-Brown 1931:13.
25 Radcliffe-Brown 1952 [1941]:64.
26 Radcliffe-Brown 1952 [1941]:84.
27 Radcliffe-Brown 1952 [1941]:67.
28 Radcliffe-Brown 1931:14.
29 For an amplification of this point, see 'People without Politics' below. It should be noted that, although Radcliffe-Brown's 'extensionist' interpretation of classificatory kinship systems subsequently came under criticism from 'alliance' theorists, his critique of Morgan was generally accepted outside the Soviet empire.
30 Radcliffe-Brown 1952 [1941]:59.
31 Malinowski 1913:307.
32 For example: 'The husband will often prostitute his wife to his brothers' (Curr 1886, I, 110); 'and as for near relatives, such as brothers, it may almost

be said that they have their wives in common' (Schurmann, quoted in Malinowski 1913:94); 'Of relatives, brothers in particular, it may be said that they possess their wives jointly' (Wilhelmi, quoted in Malinowski 1913:94). See also Warner 1958:61; Meggitt 1962:50, 132; Hiatt 1965:108–9).

33 See Malinowski 1913:124–31; Barnes 1963: xxix.

34 Malinowski 1913:125.

35 And, we might add, against cuckoldry by unrelated males; see Hiatt, 1985.

36 Quoted in Malinowski 1913:94.

4 The woman question

1 Broca 1868. Broca's article was translated from the original French by James Hunt (see Prologue, above).

2 Pike 1869; Harris 1869; Allan 1869.

3 It is true, of course, that Darwin foreshadowed these arguments and demonstrations in *The Origin of Species*.

4 Darwin 1871:II, 316–29.

5 Darwin 1871:II, 323.

6 Darwin 1871:II, 358.

7 Morgan 1868.

8 As we saw in the preceding chapter, Darwin also raised a logical objection to Morgan's inference on the ground that while promiscuity might explain why an individual designates a number of men as his 'fathers' it could hardly account for the fact that the same individual designates a number of women as his 'mothers'.

9 Morgan 1877:418.

10 Morgan 1877:500.

11 Krader 1972:6.

12 Engels 1902 [1884].

13 Engels 1902 [1884]:39–43.

14 Engels 1902 [1884]:70.

15 Tench 1961 [1789, 1793]; Collins 1804.

16 McLennan 1970 [1865]. See also 'Group Marriage' above, pp. 39–40.

17 Grey 1841:II, ch. xi.

18 A few years later Edward John Eyre (1845:II, 318) corroborated Grey on the matter of 'daughter-exchange' between old men, but added that men also exchanged sisters and nieces. In many parts of Australia 'daughter-exchange' was ruled out because marriage with a 'daughter's daughter' was regarded as incestuous. For an analysis of the relationship between bestowal reciprocity and polygyny, see Hiatt 1967.

19 Grey 1841:II, ch. xi. Eyre (1845:II, 387) corroborated Grey on this point too.

20 Howitt 1880.

21 Howitt 1967b [1880]:354–5.

22 Nieboer 1900:19, quoting the Victorian sheep-farmer E.M. Curr.

23 Malinowski 1913:75–6; see 'Group Marriage' above, pp. 51–2.

24 See 'Real Estates and Phantom Hordes' above, p. 23.

25 Warner 1937:6. In *The Savage Mind* Lévi-Strauss took up this point and connected it with weather conditions (Lévi-Strauss 1966:91–6; see Hiatt 1975).

26 See 'Real Estates and Phantom Hordes' above, p. 23.

27 It should be noted that I am attributing a subversive cast to the ritual more pointedly than Kaberry herself does. I should add that, as well as rebellion against system, the ritual may also express real wishes in regard to the son-in-law (see below, 'Dangerous Mothers-in-law and Disfigured Sisters', pp. 150–1).

28 Berndt 1950:29.

29 Goodale 1962; 1971.

30 Hart and Pilling 1960.

31 Goodale 1971:126.

32 Diane Bell (1983:236–7) quotes the inconsistency between my account and Hamilton's as an example of the way in which male anthropologists have either excluded or ignored Aboriginal women. After referring to the discrepancies between Goodale and her male predecessors among the Tiwi, she goes on: 'Similarly, Annette Hamilton has questioned Les Hiatt who worked in the same area as she did in Arnhem Land. Both Hamilton and Goodale illustrate that the received male truths based on data gathered by men from men, about women's lives, may not be a lived reality for women.' Bell leaves it to her readers to discover for themselves that my male-based report attributed primary power of bestowal to mothers, while Hamilton's female-based report located it mainly in fathers.

33 Hamilton 1970; Hiatt 1965. The authority vested in the maternal uncle needs to be viewed as well in terms of expectations of niece-exchange (see Hiatt 1965:38–44; 1967).

34 Hiatt 1990:120–3.

35 Gale 1970.

36 Peterson 1970. Peterson's observations added an important dimension to the debate on local organization (see 'Real Estates and Phantom Hordes' above).

37 I am sure Peterson would agree.

38 If he was without one of his own to give, he arranged a suitable substitute from his wife's matrilineage (Meggitt 1962:266).

39 Bell 1980:255–8.

40 Bell 1980:260.

41 Bell 1983:59.

42 Cowlishaw 1978.

43 See 'High Gods' below.

44 White 1970; see 'Conception and Misconception' below.

45 Berndt 1965.

46 For example, youths might be lifted out of a trench symbolizing the uterus of the All-Mother (Hiatt 1971); see also Hiatt 1978a for an account of the theft of cosmic power from the Queen of Night in Mozart's 'The Magic Flute'.

47 Maddock 1972:156; see also Maddock 1982:140.
48 Keen 1978.
49 Hiatt 1985, 1986:15–16. See also Bern 1979 (discussed below in 'People without Politics', pp. 96–7).
50 Bell 1983: chs. 3 and 4.
51 Merlan 1988:27.
52 See above, 'Group Marriage', pp. 45, 55.
53 Merlan 1988.
54 As Fred Myers expressed it, women's ritual was privatistic, whereas men's ceremonial life achieved a wider inclusiveness; the former made little difference to daily camp life, whereas the latter affected everyone (Myers 1986:252–3).
55 Maddock 1972:146ff; Cowlishaw 1982:503.
56 See chapter 3, note 17.
57 See, for example, Hiatt 1965.
58 Keen 1978.
59 Whereas the 'law of battle' in Darwin's formulation applies to men competing for women, Victoria Burbank's recent book, *Fighting Women: Anger and Aggression in Aboriginal Australia* documents fights between women over men. Women fought over other issues, but most physical injuries occurred in fights arising from sexual jealousy. The extent to which female aggressiveness and fighting ability have reproduced themselves biologically remains problematic.
60 Alexander 1979:240. The irony lies partly in the fact that Alexander has been a prominent member of a school of thought in evolutionary biology firmly opposed to the notion of group selection (see Wilson 1993).
61 See Cowlishaw 1978:279; 1982:497; see also below, p. 96.

5 People without politics

1 These biographical details are from Woodcock and Avakumovic 1950.
2 Huxley 1888; Kropotkin 1939 [1902]. See also Crook 1994:106–12. The cast of the present chapter owes a lot to the fact that Sheila Maddock drew my attention to *Mutual Aid* some years ago, and I take this opportunity to thank her.
3 Irvine 1956:19. Huxley was a 'monogenist', maintaining against 'polygenists' that humans comprised a single species (see 'Prologue' above, p. 11).
4 Huxley 1888:165–6.
5 Hobbes 1946 [1651]:81–3.
6 Rousseau 1984 [1755]; see also Cranston 1984.
7 Rousseau 1984 [1755]:116.
8 In *The Social Contract*, first published in 1762, Rousseau had little to say about the noble savage. The peace, freedom and equality of men in a state of nature were irretrievable. For men in a state of civilization, the closest approximation to these lost virtues could be achieved (paradoxically) only by common submission to the 'general will'.
9 See 'Group Marriage' above, pp. 42–3.

10 Woodcock and Avakumovic 1950:193–4, 334. At a meeting of the British Association held during the year following the publication of *The Origin of Species*, Bishop Wilberforce asked Huxley before a large and partisan audience whether 'it was through his grandfather or his grandmother that he claimed descent from a monkey'. Huxley coolly replied that he would not be embarrassed to have a monkey for an ancestor; but he would be 'ashamed to be connected with a man who used great gifts to obscure the truth' (Irvine 1956:3–6).

11 Tench 1961 [1793]:289.

12 Tench 1961 [1793]:150.

13 Tench 1961 [1789]:186.

14 Wilkes 1845.

15 Troy 1993.

16 Wilkes 1845:205.

17 Wilkes 1845:205.

18 Wilkes 1845:198–200.

19 Grey 1841:II, 218; see 'The Woman Question' above, p. 62; and 'High Gods' below, pp. 115–18.

20 Eyre 1845:II, 212–13.

21 Eyre 1845:II, 386.

22 Eyre 1845:II, 315–18, 384–8.

23 Taplin 1874:25, 89. In 1939 Ronald Berndt met Albert Karloan, born in 1864 on Taplin's mission and among the last of his tribe to undergo full initiation. Karloan not only confirmed Taplin's account of Narrinyeri government but described formal court proceedings which, if truly indigenous, would (as Berndt acknowledges) have been unique in Aboriginal Australia (Berndt 1993:58–73).

24 Stahle 1880:277.

25 Dawson 1881:v. For a fair-minded evaluation of Dawson's and Stahle's accounts, see Corris 1968:16–19, 35–9.

26 Thomas, in Bride 1898:398–403.

27 Smyth 1878:126.

28 Curr 1886.

29 Howitt 1889.

30 In 1904, in his compendious work on *The Native Tribes of South-East Australia*, Howitt reiterated these points, adding verifying evidence that had come to hand in the meantime.

31 Spencer and Gillen 1899:15.

32 Preface to Wheeler 1910:vi.

33 Wheeler 1910:46.

34 Radcliffe-Brown 1913.

35 Maddock 1992, 1993.

36 Radcliffe-Brown's name change has been the subject of a good deal of comment and speculation. For a summary, as well as an intriguing new speculation, see Maddock 1995.

37 Radcliffe-Brown 1931.

38 Reprinted in Radcliffe-Brown 1952.

39 See 'Group Marriage' above, pp. 53–4.
40 Elkin 1938:27–8, 40.
41 Sharp 1958:2.
42 Meggitt 1964; see also Meggitt 1962.
43 Hiatt 1965.
44 Maddock 1972:44.
45 Kropotkin met Morris in London not long after his release from prison, and they became firm friends.
46 Strehlow 1970:130.
47 Von Sturmer 1978; see 'Real Estates and Phantom Hordes' above, p. 32. See also Sutton 1978, Sutton and Rigsby 1982.
48 Kolig 1981:153.
49 Bern 1974.
50 See Williams 1973, 1987; Keen 1978:ch. 8.
51 Keen 1982.
52 Morphy 1977; Keen 1978.
53 Bern 1979. Bern's argument is obviously relevant to the preceding chapter on 'The Woman Question' (especially to the discussion of the views of Diane Bell, p. 73).
54 Hiatt 1986:8–10; 1985.
55 Myers 1986; see also Myers 1980a, 1980b.
56 Myers 1986:308, note 15.
57 Myers 1986:256.
58 Myers 1986:238.
59 Myers 1986:256.
60 See Hiatt 1976.

6 High gods

1 Tylor 1892a.
2 Tylor 1892b:401.
3 Tylor 1903 [1871]:I, 424.
4 Tylor 1903 [1871]:II, 108.
5 Lang 1887:I, 339–40; II, 8.
6 Lang 1898.
7 Lang 1907:14.
8 Hartland 1898.
9 See 'People without Politics' above, pp. 81–4. Following the publication of Hartland's paper, some even earlier references were unearthed by N.W. Thomas (1905).
10 Lang 1899.
11 Hartland 1899.
12 See 'Group Marriage' above, pp. 45–6; The definitive account of the collaboration between Spencer and Gillen is in Mulvaney and Calaby 1985.
13 Frazer 1936 [1890]:I, 234.
14 Marett and Penniman 1932:24–7.
15 Marett and Penniman 1932:69.

16 Marett and Penniman 1932:75.
17 Spencer and Gillen 1927:356.
18 Lang 1899:132.
19 Durkheim 1915:47.
20 Durkheim 1915:1.
21 Durkheim 1915:206.
22 Durkheim 1915:290.
23 Hartland 1898:300.
24 Durkheim 1915:289.
25 Rose 1951:25.
26 Schmidt 1912:54.
27 Durkheim 1915:289, note 4.
28 Eliade 1973. See also Worms 1950.
29 Radcliffe-Brown 1952 [1929].
30 For an account of the derivation of the term from an American Indian word, see Lévi-Strauss 1963:86.
31 Radcliffe-Brown 1926.
32 Radcliffe-Brown 1930:3,8.
33 Radcliffe-Brown 1952 [1945]:172.
34 Warner 1937:261.
35 A bull-roarer is a flat, elongated piece of wood with a hole in one end through which a cord is attached. When swung, the bull-roarer twists and makes a whirring sound. It is of interest that when Pythagoras was initiated into a Dionysian cult in Crete in 530 BC, he noted the use of a bull-roarer to simulate the voice of the god.
36 Howitt 1884:446.
37 Elkin 1951:xvii.
38 I infer Elkin's ignorance of this from the fact that in 1951 he wrote that the cult of the Old Woman had spread to Port Keats by 1944, and gave as his source a serviceman named Parkes who had been stationed there during the war (Elkin 1951:xx, footnote).
39 Stanner 1963:95.
40 Stanner 1979:85.
41 Berndt 1951:12.
42 Berndt 1951:21.
43 Berndt 1951:31–2.
44 Berndt 1951:16. Various explanations have been offered for the practice of subincision, but the religious one implied in this formulation is probably the best: by symbolically bisexualizing the organ, men draw on the supreme bisexual creative power of the Rainbow Serpent.
45 Lommel's account was in German, and I have relied here on Maddock's summary (Maddock 1978:15–16).
46 See 'People without Politics' above, p. 84.
47 Hiatt 1971. In Sydney during 1992 I asked David Mowaljarli, an Aboriginal authority on the religion of the Kimberley region, whether the old people ever talked about the absence of mouths. He replied that *wonjina* spirits *do* have mouths. No one knows why the representations show

them without mouths. He said the matter is inscrutable and beyond human understanding.

48 For a stimulating alternative interpretation, see Maddock 1978:7.

49 A third common property is shininess and luminosity, which are seen by Aborigines as manifestations of cosmic power (see Morphy 1989).

50 Taylor 1990:342.

51 Shortly before this chapter went to press I saw a new book called *A Place for Strangers: Towards a History of Aboriginal Being* by Tony Swain, in which the author attributes the All-Father of south-eastern Australia to invasion by Christian conquerors, and the All-Mother of northern Australia to influences from Indonesia. The indigenous religion in his view was preoccupied with locality ('parochial totemism', as Maddock has termed it). Significantly, Swain makes no reference either (a) to Durkheim's view that Australian High Gods were tribal gods of initiation, or (b) to the ubiquitous and transcendental character of the Rainbow Serpent. He attributes to unnamed scholars the denigratory assumption that Aborigines were incapable of adjusting their world-views to alien impacts, but his own argument discounts the possibility of an indigenous evolution towards transcendentalism that made such creative adjustments feasible. Although Swain quotes with qualified approval Meggitt's important delineation of the common features of male initiatory cults throughout Australia, he fails to mention Meggitt's considered opinion that they constitute an archaic complex. Against this background of omissions, it is hardly surprising that the book makes no attempt to explain why concepts allegedly acquired from the public religion of Europeans and Indonesians would become central elements in the secret religion of Aboriginal men. No modern Australianist, to the best of my knowledge, denies change as a fact of history, but we do affirm the existence of a pre-contact structure of cult belief and practice strong enough to survive the immediate impact of colonization. The consistency of evidence on this point is more compelling than the circumstantial and contextual case presented in *A Place for Strangers*.

7 Conception and misconception

1 In the *Fortnightly Review*, July–September, under the title 'The Beginnings of Religion and Totemism among the Australia Aborigines' (reprinted in Frazer 1910: I, 139–72). Frazer defined a totem as 'a class of material objects which a savage regards with superstitious respect, believing that there exists between him and every member of the class an intimate and altogether special relation' (1910:I, 3). Typically, the class of objects was a natural species.

2 Frazer 1887.

3 Frazer 1899; see 'High Gods' above, pp. 105–6.

4 Spencer and Gillen 1899.

5 From *The Fortnightly Review*, July–September 1905; reprinted in Frazer 1910:I, 161.

6 Spencer and Gillen 1899:123–5.
7 Spencer and Gillen 1899:265.
8 Frazer 1910:155–8.
9 Lang 1905.
10 For instance, matrilineal inheritance of totems characterized many south-eastern tribes, which on Lang's theory made them more archaic than tribes such as the Aranda with patrilineal inheritance of rituals and headmanship. However, their religious ideas (especially belief in a High God) seemed more advanced than those of the Aranda.
11 Quoted in Lang 1905:191.
12 Malinowski 1937:xxiii.
13 Leach 1967; Spiro 1968; Powell 1968:65–8; Schwimmer 1969:132–3; Needham 1969:457–8; see below, pp. 130–2.
14 The article was Barnes 1973; the *Festschrift* was Shapiro 1990.
15 Hartland 1894; see 'High Gods' above, p. 103.
16 This statement was first made in the *Fortnightly Review*, April–May 1899 (reprinted in Frazer 1910:94).
17 Roth 1903:22.
18 Spencer and Gillen 1899:606.
19 Bates 1913, quoted in Ashley-Montagu 1937b:170.
20 Spencer 1914:263–4.
21 'A people so ignorant of the most elementary of natural processes may well rank at the very bottom of the savage scale' (Frazer 1910:94).
22 Van Gennep 1906:lix–lx; see also Barnes 1974:66.
23 Heape 1913:77–101. Heape quoted an unnamed but well-known feminist as stating that 'the woman who tells the truth and is not a liar about such things is untrue to her sex'.
24 Read was Professor of Philosophy and Comparative Psychology at London University.
25 See Robinson 1969:100.
26 Roheim 1938:351–2.
27 An instance of reluctance to come to terms with the brute facts of procreation was reported recently in the education supplement of *The Guardian*, under the heading 'Where Babies Come From' (25 May 1993). When Belinda, an English mother of two, became pregnant for the third time, she gave her sons a no-nonsense account of sexual intercourse, conception and childbirth. Shortly afterwards the elder, aged seven, surprised his parents in the sexual act and exclaimed: 'Mummy, what on earth are you doing?' In describing the incident to *The Guardian*, the mother noted that her son failed to connect it with their previous conversation and never mentioned it afterwards.
28 Malinowski 1913:179.
29 Malinowski 1916.
30 Malinowski modified his position slightly in a special foreword to the third edition of *The Sexual Life of Savages* (1932:xxi).
31 Ashley-Montagu 1937a:207.
32 Malinowski 1937:xxiv.

33 Data from a fifth region were also reviewed viz. south-eastern Australia, but I have omitted them as being of doubtful value.

34 The anecdote appeared first in 'Birth Control in Primitive Society', *Birth Control Review*, 1931 and then some years later in *A Black Civilization*, pp. 23–4.

35 Ashley-Montagu 1937a:112–13, 201.

36 Malinowski 1937:xxiv.

37 Thomson 1933, 1936.

38 Thomson 1936:392.

39 Ashley-Montagu 1937a:142–60; 1937b.

40 Roheim (1933), quoted in Ashley-Montagu 1937a:97.

41 Ashley-Montagu 1937a:98–9.

42 Pink (1936), quoted in Ashley-Montagu 1937a:105.

43 McConnel (1931), quoted in Ashley-Montagu 1937a:167.

44 Radcliffe-Brown (1912), quoted in Ashley-Montagu 1937a:185.

45 Stanner (1936), quoted in Ashley-Montagu 1937a:127.

46 Stanner (1933), quoted in Ashley-Montagu 1937a:124.

47 Sharp, letter to Ashley-Montagu 16 June 36, quoted in Ashley-Montagu 1937a:163–5.

48 Ashley-Montagu also argued that Aborigines were ignorant of physiological maternity, in the sense that women were regarded as mere vehicles for the transmission of spirits from the mystical to the material domain (1937a:ch. 13). For a critical reaction, see Kaberry 1939:54–60.

49 Kaberry 1939:43.

50 Elkin 1939:xxv; 1938:181–2.

51 Berndt, R. and C. 1945:1–10, 78–88.

52 Berndt, R. and C. 1951:81–3.

53 Meggitt 1962:272–3.

54 Leach 1961:376.

55 Spiro 1966:110. Spiro's paper was first presented at a conference on 'New Approaches in Social Anthropology' at Jesus College, Cambridge in 1963.

56 Leach 1967.

57 Leach 1967:46.

58 Spiro 1968.

59 For the benefit of readers who may associate Ashley-Montagu's name with the English aristocracy, it should be noted that he was born in London in 1905 as the son of Charles and Mary Ehrenberg.

60 Spiro actually traces the view to Ernest Jones (Jones 1924).

61 Dixon 1968:653.

62 Scheffler 1978.

63 Dixon 1989:254.

64 Hiatt 1969:12–13.

65 Dixon 1989:254.

66 See 'Dangerous Mothers-in-Law and Disfigured Sisters' below, p. 162.

67 Strehlow 1947:88, 90–1.

68 Strehlow 1971:596.

69 Tonkinson 1978.

70 Merlan 1986.
71 Hiatt 1971.
72 Merlan 1986; Hiatt 1990.
73 Peterson 1969:27–8. Ian Keen was told by Yolngu men that a spirit-ancestor presents a child as a gift, and semen forms the body, arms and legs (Keen 1990:196). My Gidjingali male informants attributed no procreative function to semen; its purpose was to give women pleasure. When a young Gidjingali man had a testicle removed surgically following acute orchitis during a visit to Sydney in 1979, his uncle told me that semen came from the kidneys. He expressed no concern about possible adverse consequences for his nephew's reproductive ability and added that cattlemen castrated bulls to make them less troublesome (Hiatt 1990).
74 Ashley-Montagu 1937a:313–17.
75 Goodale 1971:136–43.
76 Hart and Pilling 1960.
77 Shapiro 1979:14.
78 In several places I have given evidence of fraternal sexual jealousy and its containment, as well as paternity claims and reactions to cuckoldry (Hiatt 1965:108–9, 23–4; 1985; 1990:123).
79 A final, though perhaps incidental, question is why ignorance of paternity has been so often regarded as a symptom of laughable naivety. Part of the answer might lie in a false assumption that any man who did not know the connection between sex and reproduction would be highly susceptible to cuckoldry. Perhaps a more important consideration is that in Sir James Frazer's day the young in Western society usually acquired this surprising piece of information by word-of-mouth from older children. Those inducted into the secret joined an elite about to enter adulthood, while the uninitiated remained children. For Frazer, the nescience of the Aborigines was clinching evidence that they represented the human race in its infancy.

8 Dangerous mothers-in-law and disfigured sisters

1 Fison and Howitt 1880:203.
2 Tylor 1889:246.
3 Tylor 1889:250.
4 Crawley 1902:399.
5 Freud 1946 [1913]:2.
6 Jones 1953:128–9.
7 Jones 1953:153.
8 Jones 1953:162.
9 It would seem that Freud himself took early retirement from sexual duties. According to his biographer, 'While it is likely that the more passionate side of married life subsided with him earlier than it does with many men – indeed we know this in so many words – it was replaced by an unshakable devotion and a perfect harmony of understanding' (Jones 1953:II, 431).
10 Radcliffe-Brown 1952 [1940], 1952 [1949].

11 Elkin 1938:108–15.
12 Dixon 1980:59.
13 Haviland 1979:373; cf. Heath, Merlan and Rumsey 1982.
14 Haviland 1979:377.
15 Crawley 1902:401.
16 Hiatt 1978b.
17 Meggitt 1962:191.
18 Haviland 1979:377.
19 Hiatt 1984a:187.
20 For example, among the Gisu of East Africa; see Heald 1989:218–19.
21 Radcliffe-Brown 1952 [1940]:92.
22 Hamilton 1979:337. I have condensed and modified the narrative here and in subsequent myths.
23 Warner 1937:562–4.
24 Berndt 1951:148–53. Mumuna is the 'Old Woman' of the Kunapipi cult referred to above, chapter 6, p. 113.
25 Berndt 1970:224–33.
26 *The Australian*, 24 October 1981.
27 Berndt 1970:239.
28 Brandenstein and Thomas 1974:48.
29 Brandenstein and Thomas 1974:89. See also A. and J. Falkenberg (1981:81), who report that clandestine affairs between males and their 'mothers-in-law' were common in the Port Keats area.
30 Kaberry 1939. In 'The Woman Question' above, I suggested that such rituals may express rebellion against the bestowal system, which is by no means incompatible with the possibility that they also express forbidden wishes of the kind postulated by Freud.
31 Spencer and Gillen 1927: 476.
32 Elkin 1938:110.
33 Rose and Jolly 1942. Rose was a Cambridge graduate who later became a professor of anthropology in East Germany, Jolly was a medical practitioner. Their collaboration began in Broome (W.A.).
34 Services of various kinds carried out by a man as part of his obligations to his wife's relatives.
35 Peterson 1970.
36 Warner 1931, 1937.
37 See 'High Gods' above, p. 112; and 'The Woman Question' below, pp. 67, 70.
38 See 'On the Concept of Function in Social Science', based on remarks offered at the American Anthropological Association meeting in 1935; reprinted in Radcliffe-Brown 1952.
39 Freud 1946 [1913]:44.
40 For an account of classificatory kinship, see 'Group Marriage' above.
41 Hiatt 1964.
42 Clifford Geertz, personal communication.
43 Durkheim 1897:52.
44 Makarius 1955–6; reprinted in Makarius 1961.
45 Makarius 1955–6:216.

46 Makarius 1966.
47 Hiatt 1966b.
48 Lévi-Strauss 1963a.
49 Maddock 1970:170.
50 Hamilton 1971:17.
51 See 'Conception and Misconception' above, pp. 134–5.
52 Cowlishaw 1982.
53 Burbank 1985.
54 Fox 1977:145.
55 Hamilton 1971:19. In many areas of Aboriginal Australia, men shared the right to bestow their nieces (ZD) in marriage and to receive benefits in return. A nephew (ZS) was expected to support his maternal uncle in armed conflicts.

9 Initiation: the case of the cheeky yam

1 Spencer 1914, 1928. See also Mulvaney and Calaby 1985:chs.14–15.
2 Spencer described the ceremony in a chapter entitled 'Initiation Ceremonies' (1914:ch. 3).
3 I use the term 'initiand', meaning a person in the process of being initiated, rather than 'initiate', which may be used to mean either an initiated person or a person about to be initiated.
4 Spencer is inconsistent about the number of novices, cf. 1914:93, 102. For convenience, I am using the terms 'initiand' and 'novice' to distinguish two vernacular categories rendered respectively by Spencer as *Watjinyerti* and *Marukumana*.
5 Spencer 1914:106.
6 See chapter 6, pp. 105–6.
7 Lamshed 1972:158.
8 Several other spellings occur in the literature: *kolema* (Hart and Pilling 1979 [1960]), *kurlama* (Osborne 1974).
9 Mountford 1958; Goodale 1970, 1971. Goodale's description of the events is much fuller than Mountford's, and she also offers interpretations.
10 Osborne 1974:5.
11 Goodale 1971:189.
12 Goodale 1971:190.
13 Goodale 1971:190.
14 Goodale 1971:194.
15 I have relied mainly on Spencer 1928:657–8 and Goodale 1971:10–11 for this account (cf. Hill 1951:374; Harney 1957:92–4).
16 Fry 1949, 1950.
17 Fry 1949:80.
18 Fry 1949:80. Fry's statement is cryptic, and it is impossible to know what construction he wished his readers to place on it. It may be noted that the linguist C.R. Osborne glosses *tarni* as 'cramp' (Osborne 1974:135).
19 Goodale 1970:362–3; 1971:224–5.
20 Brandl 1970:470.

21 Stanner 1966:2–21; see also 'High Gods' above, p. 113. Stanner was not the first to see lineaments of sacrifice in Aboriginal religion; cf. Durkheim 1915:Book 3, ch. 2/I ('The Elements of Sacrifice'). Stanner's theoretical model of sacrifice was a modification of Hubert and Mauss's classical essay of 1898.

22 Brandl 1970:471. To my way of thinking, the closest approximation to a sacrificial act in the *Kulama* is when the men pull out their own whiskers and place them next to the hairy yams.

23 Hart 1930b:286. ANZAAS is an abbreviation for the Australian and New Zealand Association for the Advancement of Science.

24 Hart later lowered the starting age to 14 (Hart and Pilling 1979 [1960]:93).

25 Spencer (1914:93) says they were passing through the ceremony for the first time, but he gives their grade as *Mikijeruma*, cf. Hart (1930b:286) who gives *Maru-kumarninga* as first grade for females and *Mikin djiringa* for fifth grade.

26 Spencer was also apparently mistaken about certain equivalences between male and female grades (Spencer 1914:93; cf. Hart 1930b:286).

27 Hart 1930a, 1930b.

28 See Hart and Pilling 1979 [1960]:93–4.

29 Hart 1930b:286.

30 Hart and Pilling 1979 [1960]:94.

31 Hart and Pilling 1979 [1960]:38.

32 Hart, Pilling and Goodale 1988:38, note 5.

33 Hart and Pilling 1979 [1960]:94.

34 Hart 1955:135–6. *The Rites of Passage* was first published in 1909.

35 See 'People without Politics' above.

36 Hart and Pilling 1979 [1960]:95; see 'The Woman Question' above, p. 73.

37 Stanner 1966:6.

38 Stanner 1966:11–12.

39 See Worms 1963; Baal 1971; Maddock 1985; Keen 1986.

40 Hiatt 1989.

41 Meggitt 1962:12.

42 Meggitt 1965:14.

43 Since all sexually mature females were either married or, if widowed, about to be re-married.

44 See Hart and Pilling 1979 [1960]:79–87.

45 Spencer 1914:103.

46 Gsell 1955:75.

47 Hart and Pilling 1979 [1960]:111–12.

48 Harney and Elkin 1943:231.

49 Goodale 1971:221–2.

50 See 'High Gods' above, pp. 113–14.

51 Mountford 1958:122.

52 Osborne 1974:89.

53 Cf. Hart 1930b:286 and Hart and Pilling 1979 [1960]:93.

54 Goodale 1971:xxiii, 47–52; see 'The Woman Question' above, p. 67.

55 Robinson 1990. Eric Venbrux's book, *A Death in the Tiwi Islands* (Cambridge

U.P., 1995), appeared after the present chaper had been typeset. It includes material on both violence and the *kulama* ceremony.

10 Epilogue

1 See Bell and Nelson 1989; Larbalestier 1990; Huggins *et al.* 1991; Bell 1990, 1991a, 1991b; Nelson 1991; Rowlands 1991; Huggins and Saunders 1993; Felton and Flanagan 1993.

2 See Chapter 6, Note 52. Ian Keen has reviewed the book at length in the *Australian Journal of Anthropology* (Keen 1993), and *Oceania* plans to publish a forum on the argument shortly.

3 See Barnes 1967. In my judgment the controversy was resolved by new facts and analyses presented by three north-east Arnhem Land fieldworkers Warren Shapiro, Howard Morphy and Ian Keen (for references, see Keen 1988:105–6).

4 See Kuper 1988:ch. 11; Scheffler 1978.

5 See my discussion of the role of anthropologists in Aboriginal land claim research (Hiatt 1982b).

6 See Dodson 1994.

7 John Barnes advocated such a development over thirty years ago, at the conference convened in conjunction with the establishment of the Australian Institute of Aboriginal Studies (Barnes 1963).

8 Maddock 1989:155.

9 For an introduction to some of the obstacles, see Peter Sutton's essay 'Myth as History, History as Myth' (Sutton 1988); see also Adam Kuper's account of similar trends outside Australia, and his plea for a cosmopolitan as distinct from tribalized anthropology (Kuper 1994).

10 In Greece in the fifth century BC, in the context of pressures for a return to tribalism, 'there rose a new faith in reason, freedom and the brotherhood of all men – the new faith, and, as I believe, the only possible faith, of the open society' (Popper 1945:161).

References

Alexander, R. 1979 *Darwinism and Human Affairs*. Washington: University of Washington.

Allan, J. 1869 On the Real Differences in the Minds of Men and Women. *Journal of the Anthropological Society of London* 7:195–215.

Ashley-Montagu, M. 1937a *Coming Into Being among the Australian Aborigines: A Study of the Procreative Beliefs of the Native Tribes of Australia*. London: Routledge.

1937b Physiological Paternity in Australia. *American Anthropologist* 39:175–83.

Baal, J. van 1971 *Symbols for Communication: An Introduction to the Anthropological Study of Religion*. Assen: Van Gorcum.

Bachofen, J.J. 1967 *Myth, Religion, and Mother Right: Selected Writings of J.J. Bachofen*. London: Routledge and Kegan Paul.

Barnes, J. 1960 Anthropology in Britain Before and After Darwin. *Mankind* 5:369–85.

1963a Social Organization: Limits of Contemporary Studies. In H. Sheils, ed., *Australian Aboriginal Studies*, pp. 197–210. Melbourne: Oxford University Press.

1963b Introduction. In B. Malinowski, ed., *The Family Among the Australian Aborigines*, pp. 11–30. New York: Schocken.

1967 *Inquest on the Murngin*. London: Royal Anthropological Institute Occasional Paper No. 26.

1973 Genitrix:Genitor::Nature:Culture. In J. Goody, ed., *The Character of Kinship*, pp. 61–73. Cambridge: Cambridge University Press.

Beaglehole, J. 1962 *The Endeavour Journal of Joseph Banks 1768–1771*. Sydney: Angus and Robertson.

Beaglehole, J. (ed.) 1955 *The Voyage of the Endeavour 1768–1771*. Cambridge: Cambridge University Press.

Bell, D. 1980 Desert Politics: Choices in the 'Marriage Market'. In M. Etienne and E. Leacock, eds., *Women and Colonization: Anthropological Perspectives*, pp. 239–69. New York: Praeger.

1983 *Daughters of the Dreaming*. Melbourne: McPhee Gribble.

1990 Letter to the Editor. *Anthropological Forum* 6:158–65.

1991a Intra-Racial Rape Revisited: On Forging a Feminist Future beyond Factions and Frightening Politics. *Women's Studies International Forum* 14:385–412.

1991b Letter to the Editors. *Women's Studies International Forum* 14:507–13.

Bell, D. and T.N. Nelson 1989 Speaking About Rape is Everyone's Business. *Women's Studies International Forum* 121:403–16.

Bender, T. (ed.) 1992 *The Anti-Slavery Debate: Capitalism and Abolitionism as a Problem in Historical Interpretation*. Berkeley: University of California Press.

Bern, J. 1974 Blackfella Business, Whitefella Law. Ph.D. Thesis, Macquarie University.

1979 Ideology and Domination: Towards a Reconstruction of Australian Aboriginal Social Formation. *Oceania* 50:118–32.

Berndt, C. 1950 *Women's Changing Ceremonies in Northern Australia*. Paris: L'Homme.

1965 Women and the 'Secret Life'. In R. and C. Berndt, eds., *Aboriginal Man in Australia*, pp. 236–82. Sydney: Angus and Robertson.

Berndt, R. 1951 *Kunapipi: A Study of an Australian Aboriginal Religious Cult*. Melbourne: Cheshire.

1952 *Djanggawul: An Aboriginal Religious Cult of North-Eastern Arnhem Land*. London: Routledge and Kegan Paul.

1970 Traditional Morality as Expressed through the Medium of an Australian Aboriginal Religion. In R. Berndt, ed., *Australian Aboriginal Anthropology*, pp. 216–47. Nedlands: Australian Institute of Aboriginal Studies.

Berndt, R. and C. 1945 *A Preliminary Report of Fieldwork in the Ooldea Region, Western South Australia*. Sydney: Oceania Publications.

1951 *Sexual Behaviour in Western Arnhem Land*. New York: Viking Fund Publications.

1993 *A World That Was*. Melbourne: Melbourne University Press.

Birdsell, J. 1970 Group Composition among the Australian Aborigines: A Critique of the Evidence from Fieldwork Conducted since 1930. *Current Anthropology* 11:115–42.

Blackburn, Justice. 1971 Milirrpum and Others v. Nabalco Pty Ltd and the Commonwealth of Australia. In J. Malor, ed., *Federal Law Reports*, xvii, pp. 141–293. Sydney: Law Book Co.

Blackstone, W. 1876 *Commentaries on the Laws of England*. London: Murray.

Brandenstein, C. von and A. Thomas 1974 *Taruru: Aboriginal Song Poetry from the Pilbara*. Adelaide: Rigby.

Brandl, M. 1970 Adaptation or Disintegration? Changes in the Kulama Initiation and Increase Ritual of Melville and Bathurst Islands, Northern Territory of Australia. *Anthropological Forum* 2(4):464–79.

Brennan, Justice. 1993 Mabo v. Queensland. In R. Bartlett, ed., *The Mabo Decision*, pp. 7–56. Sydney: Butterworths.

Bride, T. 1898 *Letters from Victorian Pioneers*. Melbourne: Heinemann.

Broca, P. 1868 Anthropology. *The Anthropological Review* 6:35–52.

Burbank, V. 1985 The Mirriri as Ritualized Aggression. *Oceania* 56:47–55.

1994 *Fighting Women: Anger and Aggression in Aboriginal Australia*. Berkeley: University of California Press.

Burrow, J.W. 1963 Evolution and Anthropology in the 1860's: The Anthropological Society of London, 1863–71. *Victorian Studies* 137–54.

Burton, R. 1865 Notes on Certain Matters connected with the Dahoman. In *Memoirs of the Anthropological Society of London*, I, pp. 308–21. London: Trubner.

Collins, D. 1804 *An Account of the English Colony in New South Wales*. London: Cadell and Davies.

Corris, P. 1968 *Aborigines and Europeans in Western Victoria*. Canberra: Australian Institute of Aboriginal Studies (Occasional Papers in Aboriginal Studies: Ethnohistory Series).

Coupland, R. 1964 *The British Anti-Slavery Movement*. London: Cass.

Cowlishaw, G. 1978 Infanticide in Aboriginal Australia. *Oceania* 48:262–83.

1982 Socialization and Subordination among Australian Aborigines. *Man* 17:492–507.

Cranston, M. 1984 Introduction. In J.-J. Rousseau, ed., *A Discourse on Inequality*, pp. 9–54. Harmondsworth: Penguin.

Crawley, E. 1902 *The Mystic Rose: A Study of Primitive Marriage*. London: MacMillan.

Crook, P. 1994 *Darwinism, War and History: The Debate over the Biology of War from 'The Origin of Species' to the First World War*. Cambridge: Cambridge University Press.

Curr, E. 1886 *The Australian Race: Its Origin, Languages, Customs, Place of Landing in Australia and the Routes by which it Spread itself over the Continent*. Melbourne: Government Printer.

Currey, C. 1957 An Argument for the Observance of Australia Day on the Seventh of February and an Account of the Ceremony at Sydney Cove, February 7, 1788. *Journal of the Royal Australian Historical Society* 43:153–74.

Darwin, C. 1859 *The Origin of Species*. London: John Murray.

1871 *The Descent of Man and Selection in Relation to Sex*. London: John Murray.

Davis, J. 1868 Anthropology and Ethnology. *Anthropological Review* 6:394–9.

Dawson, J. 1881 *Australian Aborigines: The Languages and Customs of Several Tribes of Aborigines in the Western District of Victoria*. Melbourne: Robertson.

Dawson, Justice. 1993 Mabo v. Queensland. In R. Bartlett, ed., *The Mabo Decision*, pp. 91–136. Sydney: Butterworths.

Dixon, R. 1968 Correspondence, Virgin Birth. *Man* 3:653–4.

1980 *The Languages of Australia*. Cambridge: Cambridge University Press.

1989 The Dyirbal Kinship System. *Oceania* 59:245–68.

Dodson, M. 1994 The End in the Beginning: Re(de)finding Aboriginality. *Australian Aboriginal Studies* 1:2–13.

Durack, P. 1992 The Consequences of the Mabo Case. *Current Issues* (Institute of Public Affairs) 1–9.

Durkheim, E. 1897 La Prohibition de l'inceste et ses origines. *L'Année Sociologique* 1:1–70.

1915 *The Elementary Forms of the Religious Life*. London: Allen and Unwin.

Eliade, M. 1958 *Patterns in Comparative Religion*. New York: New American Library.

1973 *Australian Religions*. Ithaca: Cornell University Press.

Elkin, A.P. 1938 *The Australian Aborigines: How to Understand Them*. Sydney: Angus and Robertson.

1939 Introduction. In P. Kaberry, *Aboriginal Woman*, pp. 17–31. London: Routledge.

1950 The Complexity of Social Organization in Arnhem Land. *Southwestern Journal of Anthropology* 6:1-20.

1951 Introduction. In R. Berndt, *Kunapipi: A Study of an Australian Aboriginal Religious Cult*, pp. xv–xxiv. Melbourne: Cheshire.

1953 Murngin Kinship Re-Examined and Remarks on Some Generalizations. *American Anthropologist* 55:412–19.

Engels, F. 1902 [1884] *The Origin of the Family, Private Property and the State*. Chicago: Kerr.

Eyre, E. 1845 *Journals of Expeditions of Discovery into Central Australia*. London: Boone.

Falkenberg, A. and J. 1981 *The Affinal Relationship System: A New Approach to Kinship and Marriage among the Australian Aborigines at Port Keats*. Oslo: Universitetforlaget.

Felton, F. and L. Flanagan 1993 Institutionalised Feminism: A Tidda's Perspective. *Lilith: A Feminist History Journal* 8:53–9.

Fison, L. and A.W. Howitt 1880 *Kamilaroi and Kurnai: Group-Marriage and Relationship, and Marriage by Elopement*. Melbourne: George Robertson.

Fortes, M. 1969 *Kinship and the Social Order*. London: Routledge.

Fox, R. 1977 The Inherent Rules of Violence. In P. Collette, ed., *Social Rules and Social Behaviour*. Totoriva, NJ: Rowan and Littlefield.

Frazer, J. 1887 *Totemism*. Edinburgh: Adam and Black.

1899 The Origin of Totemism. *Fortnightly Review* 65:647–65, 835–52.

1905 The Beginnings of Religion and Totemism among the Australian Aborigines. *Fortnightly Review* 78:162–72, 452–65.

1910 *Totemism and Exogamy: A Treatise on Certain Early Forms of Superstition and Society*. London: MacMillan.

1936 [1890] *The Golden Bough: A Study in Magic and Religion*. London: Macmillan.

Freud, S. 1946 [1913] *Totem and Taboo*. New York: Random House.

Fry, H.K. 1949 A Bathurst Island Mourning Rite. *Mankind* 4(2):79–80.

1950 A Bathurst Island Initiation Rite. *Mankind* 4(4):167–8.

Gale, F. (ed). 1970 *Woman's Role in Aboriginal Society*. Canberra: Australian Institute of Aboriginal Studies.

Gibbs, H. 1993 Foreword. In M. Stephenson, and S. Ratnapala, eds., *Mabo: A Judicial Revolution*, pp. xiii–xiv. Brisbane: University of Queensland Press.

Goodale, J. 1962 Marriage Contracts among the Tiwi. *Ethnology* 1:452–66.

1970 An Example of Ritual Change among the Tiwi of Melville Island. In A.R. Pilling and R.A. Waterman, eds., *Diprotodon to Detribalisation: Studies of Change Among Australian Aborigines*, pp. 350–66. East Lansing: Michigan State University Press.

1971 *Tiwi Wives: A Study of the Women of Melville Island, North Australia*. Seattle: University of Washington Press.

Grant, R. 1986 *Gods and the One God*. London: SPCK.

Grey, G. 1841 *Journals of Two Expeditions of Discovery in North-West and Western Australia*. London: Boone.

Gsell, F.X. 1955 *'The Bishop With 150 Wives': Fifty Years as a Missionary*. London: Angus and Robertson.

Gumbert, M. 1981 Paradigm Lost: an Analysis of Anthropological Models and Their Effect on Aboriginal Land Rights. *Oceania* 52:103–23.

1984 *Neither Justice nor Reason: A Legal and Anthropological Analysis of Aboriginal Land Rights*. St Lucia: University of Queensland Press.

Hale, H. 1846 *Ethnography and Philology*. Philadelphia: Lea and Blanchard.

Hamilton, A. 1970 The Role of Women in Aboriginal Marriage Arrangements. In F. Gale, ed., *Woman's Role in Aboriginal Society*, pp. 17–20. Canberra: Australian Institute of Aboriginal Studies.

1971 The Equivalence of Siblings. *Anthropological Forum* 3:13–20.

1979 Timeless Transformation. Thesis, University of Sydney.

Harney, W. 1957 *Life among the Aborigines*. London: Hale.

Harney, W. and A.P. Elkin 1943 Melville and Bathurst Islands: A Short Description. *Oceania* 13:228–34.

Harris, G. 1869 On the Distinctions, Mental and Moral, Occasioned by the Difference of Sex. *Journal of the Anthropological Society of London* 7:189–95.

Hart, C.W.M. 1930a The Tiwi of Bathurst and Melville Islands. *Oceania* 1(2): 167–80.

1930b Personal Names among the Tiwi. *Oceania* 1(3):280–90.

1955 Contrasts between Prepubertal and Postpubertal Education. In G. Spindler, ed., *Education and Anthropology*, pp. 127–45. Stanford: Stanford University Press.

Hart, C.W.M. and A. Pilling 1979 [1960] *The Tiwi of North Australia*. New York: Holt, Rinehart and Winston.

Hart, C.W.M., A.R. Pilling and J.Goodale 1988 *The Tiwi of North Australia*. New York: Holt, Rinehart and Winston.

Hartland, E.S. 1894 *The Legend of Perseus: A Study of Tradition in Story, Custom and Belief*. London: Nutt.

1898 The 'High Gods' of Australia. *Folk-Lore* 9:290–329.

1899 Australian Gods: Rejoinder. *Folk-Lore* 10:46–57.

Haviland, J. 1979 Guugu Yimidhirr Brother-in-Law Language. *Language and Society* 8:365–93.

Hays, H. 1958 *From Ape to Angel*. London: Methuen.

Heald, S. 1989 *Controlling Anger: The Sociology of Gisu Violence*. Manchester: Manchester University Press.

Heape, W. 1913 *Sex Antagonism*. London: Constable.

Heath, J., F. Merlan, and A. Rumsey 1982 *The Languages of Kinship in Aboriginal Australia*. Sydney University: Oceania Publications (Linguistic Monograph 24).

Hiatt, L. 1962 Local Organization Among the Australian Aborigines. *Oceania* 32:267–86.

1964 Incest in Arnhem Land. *Oceania* 35:124–8.

1965 *Kinship and Conflict: A Study of an Aboriginal Community in Northern Arnhem Land*. Canberra: Australian National University Press.

1966a The Lost Horde. *Oceania* 37:81–92.

1966b A Spear in the Ear. *Oceania* 37:153–4.

1967 Authority and Reciprocity in Australian Marriage Arrangements. *Mankind* 6:468–75.

1969 Fieldwork Carried Out from May to July, 1967, among the Gidjingali of Northern Arnhem Land. Unpublished Manuscript, Australian Institute of Aboriginal Studies, Document No. 69/846.

1971 Secret Pseudo-Procreation Rites among the Australian Aborigines. In L. Hiatt and C. Jayawardena, eds., *Anthropology in Oceania: Essays Presented to Ian Hogbin*, pp. 77–88. Sydney: Angus and Robertson.

1975 Swallowing and Regurgitating in Australian Myth and Rite. In L. Hiatt, ed., *Australian Aboriginal Mythology*, pp. 143–62. Canberra: Australian Institute of Aboriginal Studies.

1976 *The Role of the National Aboriginal Consultative Committee.* Canberra: Australian Government Printing Service.

1978a Queen of Night, Mother-Right, and Secret Male Cults. In R. Hook, ed., *Fantasy and Symbol*, pp. 247–65. London: Academic Press.

1978b Classification of the Emotions. In L. Hiatt, ed., *Australian Aboriginal Concepts*, pp. 182–7. Canberra: Australian Institute of Aboriginal Studies.

1982a Letter to the Editor. *Oceania* 52:261–5.

1982b The Role of the Institute in Land Claims Research. *AIAS Newsletter* 18:47–53.

1984a Your Mother-in-Law is Poison. *Man* 19:183–98.

1984b Traditional Land Tenure and Contemporary Land Claims. In L. Hiatt, ed., *Aboriginal Landowners*, pp. 11–23. Sydney: Oceania Publications.

1985 Maidens, Males, and Marx: Some Contrasts in the Work of Frederick Rose and Claude Meillassoux. *Oceania* 56:34–46.

1986 *Aboriginal Political Life.* Canberra: Australian Institute of Aboriginal Studies.

1989 Introduction. In W.E.H. Stanner, *On Aboriginal Religion*, pp. 19–39. University of Sydney: Oceania Publications.

1990 Towards a Natural History of Fatherhood. *Australian Journal of Anthropology* 1:110–30.

Hill, E. 1951 *The Territory.* Sydney: Angus and Robertson.

Hoare, P. 1820 *Memoirs of Granville Sharp, Esq.* London: Henry Colburn.

Hobbes, T. 1946 [1651] *Leviathan: Or the Matter, Forme and Power of a Commonwealth Ecclesiastical and Civil.* Oxford: Blackwell.

Howitt, A.W. 1884 On Some Australian Ceremonies of Initiation. *Journal of the Anthropological Institute* 13:432–59.

1889 On the Organization of Australian Tribes. *Transactions of the Royal Society of Victoria* 1:96–137.

1891 The Dieri and Other Kindred Tribes of Central Australia. *Journal of the Anthropological Institute* 20:30–109.

1904 *The Native Tribes of South-East Australia.* London: MacMillan.

1967a [1880] The Kurnai: Their Customs in Peace and War. In L. Fison and A. Howitt, eds., *Kamilaroi and Kurnai*, pp. 177–292. Oosterhout: Anthropological Publications.

1967b [1880] Summary and General Conclusions. In L. Fison and A.W.

Howitt, eds., *Kamilaroi and Kurnai*, pp. 315–56. Oosterhout: Anthropological Publications.

Howitt, A. and L. Fison 1883 From Mother-Right to Father-Right. *Journal of the Anthropological Institute* 12:30–46.

1885 On the Deme and the Horde. *Journal of the Anthropological Institute* 14:142–68.

1900 The Aborigines of Victoria. In B. Spencer, ed., *Handbook of Melbourne*, pp. 44–56. Melbourne: Australian Association for the Advancement of Science.

Hubert, H. and M. Mauss 1964 *Sacrifice: Its Nature and Function*. London: Cohen and West.

Huggins, J. and K. Saunders 1993 Defying the Ethnographic Ventriloquists: Race, Gender and the Legacies of Colonialism. *Lilith: A Feminist History Journal* 8:53–9.

Huggins, J. *et al.* 1991 Letter to the Editors. *Women's Studies International Forum* 14:506.

Hunt, J. 1854 *A Treatise on the Cure of Stammering*. London: Longman.

1863 Kingsley's Water Babies. *Anthropological Review* 1:472–6.

1864 Dedication. In C. Vogt, *Lectures on Man: His Place in Creation, and in the History of the Earth*, translated by J. Hunt, pp.v–x. London: Longman.

1865 On the Negro's Place in Nature. In *Memoirs of the Anthropological Society*, pp. 1–60. London: Trubner.

1868 On the Origin of the Anthropological Review and its Connection with the Anthropological Society. *Anthropological Review* 6:431–42.

1869 Anniversary Address. *Journal of the Anthropological Society* 7:civ–cvii.

Huxley, T. 1888 The Struggle for Existence: A Programme. *Nineteenth Century* 23:161–80.

Irvine, W. 1956 *Apes, Angels and Victorians: A Joint Biography of Darwin and Huxley*. London: Weidenfeld and Nicolson.

Jones, E. 1924 Mother-Right and the Sexual Ignorance of Savages. *International Journal of Psycho-Analysis* 6:109–30.

1953 *Sigmund Freud* II. London: Hogarth Press.

Kaberry, P. 1939 *Aboriginal Woman: Sacred and Profane*. London: Routledge.

Keen, I. 1978 One Ceremony, One Song: An Economy of Religious Knowledge among the Yolngu of North-East Arnhem Land. Ph.D. Thesis, Australian National University, Canberra.

1982 How Some Murngin Men Marry Ten Wives: The Marital Implications of Matrilateral Cross-Cousin Structures. *Man* 17: 620–42.

1986 Stanner on Aboriginal Religion. *Canberra Anthropology* 9: 26–50.

1988 Twenty-Five Years of Aboriginal Kinship Studies. In R. Berndt and R. Tonkinson, eds., *Social Anthropology and Australian Aboriginal Studies: A Contemporary Overview*, pp. 79–123. Canberra: Aboriginal Studies Press.

1990 Images of Reproduction in the Yolngu Madayin Ceremony. *Australian Journal of Anthropology* 1:192–207.

1993 Ubiquitous Ubiety of Dubious Uniformity. *Australian Journal of Anthropology* 4:96–110.

Keith, A. 1917 How Can the Institute Best Serve the Needs of Anthropology? *Journal of the Royal Anthropological Institute* 47:12–30.

Knox, R. 1850 *The Races of Man*. London: Renshaw.

Kolig, E. 1981 *The Silent Revolution: The Effects of Modernization on Australian Aboriginal Religion*. Philadelphia: Institute for Study of Human Issues.

Krader, L. 1972 *The Ethnological Notebooks of Karl Marx*. Assen: Van Gorcum.

Kropotkin, P. 1890 Mutual Aid among Animals. *Nineteenth Century* 28:699–719.

1939 [1902] *Mutual Aid: A Factor of Evolution*. Harmondsworth: Penguin.

Kuper, A. 1988 *The Invention of Primitive Society: Transformations of an Illusion*. London: Routledge.

1994 Culture, Identity, and the Project of a Cosmopolitan Anthropology. *Man* 29:537–54.

Lamshed, M. 1972 *'Monty': The Biography of C.P. Mountford*. Adelaide: Rigby.

Lang, A. 1887 *Myth, Ritual, and Religion*. London: Longmans, Green.

1898 *The Making of Religion*. London: Longmans, Green.

1899a Australian Gods: A Reply. *Folk-Lore* 10:1–46.

1899b Are Savage Gods Borrowed From Missionaries? *Nineteenth Century* 45:132–44.

1899c *Myth, Ritual and Religion*. London: Longmans, Green and Co.

1905a *The Secret of the Totem*. London: Longmans, Green and Co.

1905b Introduction. In K. Langloh Parker, *The Euahlayi Tribe*, pp. ix–xxvii. London: Constable.

1907 Appreciation. In H. Balfour, ed., *Anthropological Essays Presented to Edward Burnett Tylor*, pp. 1–15. Oxford: Clarendon Press.

1908 The Origin of Terms of Human Relationship. *Proceedings of the British Academy* 3:1–20.

1913 God (Primitive and Savage). In J. Hastings, ed., *Encyclopaedia of Religion and Ethics*, pp. 243–7. Edinburgh: Clark.

Larbalestier, J. 1990 The Politics of Representation: Australian Aboriginal Women and Feminism. *Anthropological Forum* 6:143–57.

Lavarch, M. 1994 Foreword. In *Native Title*, pp. iii–v. Canberra: Australian Government Publishing Service.

Leach, E. 1961 Golden Bough or Gilded Twig? *Daedalus*, Spring:371–87.

1967 Virgin Birth. *Proceedings of the Royal Anthropological Institute* for 1966:39–50.

Lévi-Strauss, C. 1963a Structural Analysis in Linguistics and in Anthropology. In *Structural Anthropology*, pp. 31–54. New York: Basic Books.

1963b *Totemism*. Harmondsworth: Penguin.

1966 *The Savage Mind*. London: Weidenfeld and Nicolson.

Locke, J. 1924 [1690] *Two Treatises of Government*. London: Dent.

Lommel, A. 1952 *Die Unambal*. Hamburg: Hamburgisches Museum für Völkerkunde.

Lubbock, J. 1870 *The Origin of Civilization and the Primitive Condition of Man*. London: Longmans, Green and Co.

Lund, E. 1865 On the Occurrence of Syphilis in a Monkey. *Journal of the Anthropological Society of London* 3:cxxi–cxxii.

McLennan, J. 1970 [1865] *Primitive Marriage: An Inquiry into the Origin of the Form of Capture in Marriage Ceremonies*. Chicago: University of Chicago Press.

References

1886 *Studies in Ancient History*. London: MacMillan.

Maddock, K. 1970 A Structural Interpretation of the Mirriri. *Oceania* 40: 165–76.

1972 *The Australian Aborigines: A Portrait of Their Society*. Ringwood: Penguin.

1978 Introduction. In I. Buchler and K. Maddock, eds., *The Rainbow Serpent: A Chromatic Piece*, pp. 1–21. The Hague: Mouton.

1982 *The Australian Aborigines: A Portrait of Their Society*, 2nd edn. Ringwood: Penguin.

1983 *Your Land is Our Land*. Ringwood: Penguin Books.

1985 Sacrifice and Other Models in Australian Aboriginal Ritual. In D. Barwick, J. Beckett and M. Reay, eds., *Metaphors of Interpretation: Essays in Honour of W.E.H. Stanner*, pp. 133–57. Canberra: Australian National University Press.

1989 Involved Anthropologists. In E. Wilmsen, ed., *We Are Here: Politics of Aboriginal Land Tenure*, pp. 155–76. Berkeley: University of California Press.

1992 The Mystery of Kropotkin and Radcliffe-Brown. *Red and Black* 22:28–35.

1993 Why Kropotkin Advised Radcliffe-Brown As He Did. *Red and Black* 23:41–7.

1995 The Importance of being Radcliffe. *Australian Anthropological Society Newsletter* 60:14–20.

Maine, H. 1876 *Ancient Law: Its Connection With the Early History of Society, and its Relation to Modern Ideas*. London: Murray.

Makarius, L. and R. 1955–6 Essai sur l'origine de l'exogamie et de la peur de l'inceste. *L'Année Sociologique* série 3:173–230.

Makarius, R. 1966 Incest and Redemption in Arnhem Land. *Oceania* 37:148–52.

Makarius, R. and L. 1961 *L'Origine de l'exogamie et du totemisme*. Paris: Librairie Gallimard.

Malinowski, B. 1913 *The Family among the Australian Aborigines: A Sociological Study*. London: University of London Press.

1916 Baloma: The Spirits of the Dead in the Trobriand Islands. *Journal of the Royal Anthropological Institute* 46: 353–430.

1932 *The Sexual Life of Savages*, 3rd edn. London: Routledge.

1937 Foreword. In M.F. Ashley-Montagu, ed., *Coming Into Being Among the Australian Aborigines*, pp. 19–35. London: Routledge.

Marett, R.R. 1936 *Tylor*. London: Chapman and Hall.

Marett, R. and T. Penniman 1932 *Spencer's Scientific Correspondence*. Oxford: Clarendon Press.

Meggitt, M. 1962 *Desert People: A Study of the Walbiri Aborigines of Central Australia*. Sydney: Angus and Robertson.

1964 Indigenous Forms of Government among the Australian Aborigines. *Bijdragen* 120:163–78.

1965 The Association between Australian Aborigines and Dingoes. In A. Leeds and A.P. Vayda, eds., *Man, Culture and Animals: The Role of Animals in Human Ecological Adjustments*, pp. 7–26. Washington DC: American Association for the Advancement of Science.

Merlan, F. 1986 Australian Aboriginal Conception Beliefs Revisited. *Man* 21:474–93.

1988 Gender in Aboriginal Social Life: A Review. In R. Berndt and R. Tonkinson, eds., *Social Anthropology and Australian Aboriginal Studies*, pp. 15–76. Canberra : Australian Institute of Aboriginal Studies.

Morgan, L. 1851 *League of the Ho-de-no-sau-nee, Iroquois*. Rochester: Sage.

1868 A Conjectural Solution of the Classificatory System of Relationship. *Proceedings of the American Academy of Arts and Sciences* 7:436–77.

1871 *Systems of Consanguinity and Affinity in the Human Family*. Washington: Smithsonian.

1872 Australian Kinship, from an Original Memorandum of Reverend Lorimer Fison. *Proceedings of the American Academy of Arts and Sciences* 8:412–38.

1964 [1877] *Ancient Society: Researches in the Lines of Human Progress from Savagery through Barbarism to Civilization*. Cambridge, Mass.: Harvard University Press.

Morphy, H. 1977 Too Many Meanings: An Analysis of the Artistic System of the Yolngu of North-East Arnhem Land. Ph.D. Thesis, Australian National University.

1989 From Dull to Brilliant: The Aesthetics of Spiritual Power among the Yolngu. *Man* 24: 21–40.

Mountford, C.P. 1958 *The Tiwi: Their Art, Myth and Ceremony*. London: Phoenix House.

Mulvaney, D.J. and J.H. Calaby 1985 'So Much That Is New': Baldwin Spencer, 1860–1929. Melbourne: University of Melbourne Press.

Myers, F. 1976 'To Have and to Hold': A Study of Persistence and Change in Pintupi Life. Ph.D. Thesis, University of Michigan, Ann Arbor.

1980a The Cultural Basis of Politics in Pintupi Life. *Mankind* 12:197–214.

1980b A Broken Code: Pintupi Political Theory and Contemporary Social Life. *Mankind* 12:311–26.

1986 *Pintupi Country, Pintupi Self: Sentiment, Place, and Politics Among Western Desert Aborigines*. Washington: Smithsonian Institution Press.

Needham, R. 1969 Correspondence, 'Virgin Birth'. *Man* 4:457–8.

Nelson, T.N. 1991 Letter to the Editors. *Women's Studies International Forum* 14:507.

Nieboer, H. 1900 *Slavery as an Industrial System*. The Hague: Martinus Nijhoff.

Osborne, C.R. 1974 *The Tiwi Language*. Canberra: Australian Institute of Aboriginal Studies.

Peterson, N. 1969 Secular and Ritual Links: Two Basic and Opposed Principles of Australian Social Organization as Illustrated by Walbiri Ethnography. *Mankind* 7:27–35.

1970 The Importance of Women in Determining the Composition of Residential Groups. In F. Gale, ed., *Woman's Role in Aboriginal Society*, pp. 9–16. Canberra: Australian Institute of Aboriginal Studies.

Pettazzoni, R. 1954 *Essays on the History of Religions*. Leiden: Brill.

Piddington, R. 1932 Report on Field Work in North-Western Australia. *Oceania* 2:342–58.

Pike, L. 1869 On the Claims of Women to Political Power. *Journal of the Anthropological Society of London* 7:47–61.

Popper, K. 1945 *The Open Society and its Enemies*. London: Routledge.

Powell, H. 1968 Correspondence, 'Virgin Birth'. *Man* 3:651–3.

Prichard, J. 1847 On the Relations of Ethnology to Other Branches of Knowledge. *Journal of the Ethnological Society* 1:301–29.

1973 [1813] *Researches in the Physical History of Man*. Chicago: University of Chicago Press.

Pritchard, W. 1865 On Some Anthropological Matters Connected with South Sea Islanders (the Samoans). In *Memoirs of the Anthropological Society of London*, I, pp. 322–6. London: Trubner.

Radcliffe-Brown, A. 1913 Three Tribes of Western Australia. *Journal of the Royal Anthropological Institute* 43:143–94.

1914 The Relationship System of the Dieri Tribe. *Man* 14:53–6.

1918 Notes on the Social Organization of Australian Tribes. *Journal of the Royal Anthropological Institute* 48:222–253.

1923 Notes on the Social Organization of Australian Tribes. *Journal of the Royal Anthropological Institute* 53:424–447.

1926 The Rainbow-Serpent Myth of Australia. *Journal of the Anthropological Institute of Great Britain and Ireland* 56:19–25.

1930 The Rainbow-Serpent Myth in South-East Australia. *Oceania* 1(3):342–7.

1931 *The Social Organization of Australian Tribes*. Sydney: Oceania Publications.

1952 [1929] The Sociological Theory of Totemism. In *Structure and Function in Primitive Society: Essays and Addresses*, pp. 117–32. London: Cohen and West.

1952 [1933a] Social Sanctions. In *Structure and Function in Primitive Society: Essays and Addresses*, pp. 205–11. London: Cohen and West.

1952 [1933b] Primitive Law. In *Structure and Function in Primitive Society: Essays and Addresses*, pp. 212–19. London: Cohen and West.

1952 [1935a] Patrilineal and Matrilineal Succession. In *Structure and Function in Primitive Society: Essays and Addresses*, pp. 32–48. London: Cohen and West.

1952 [1935b] On the Concept of Function in Social Science. In *Structure and Function in Primitive Society: Essays and Addresses*, pp. 178–87. London: Cohen and West.

1952 [1940] On Joking Relationships. In *Structure and Function in Primitive Society: Essays and Addresses*, pp. 90–104. London: Cohen and West.

1952 [1941] The Study of Kinship Systems. In *Structure and Function in Primitive Society: Essays and Addresses*, pp. 49–89. London: Cohen and West.

1952 [1945] Religion and Society. In *Structure and Function in Primitive Society: Essays and Addresses*, pp. 153–77. London: Cohen and West.

1952 [1949] A Further Note on Joking Relationships. In *Structure and Function in Primitive Society: Essays and Addresses*, pp. 105–16. London: Cohen and West.

1952 *Structure and Function in Primitive Society*. London: Cohen and West.

1954 Australian Local Organization. *American Anthropologist* 56:105–6.

1956 On Australian Local Organization. *American Anthropologist* 58:363–7.

Read, C. 1918 No Paternity. *Journal of the Royal Anthropological Institute* 48:146–54.

Resek, C. 1960 *Lewis Henry Morgan: American Scholar*. Chicago: University of Chicago Press.

Rivers, W.H.R. 1907 On the Origin of the Classificatory System of Relationships. In W.H.R. Rivers *et al.*, ed., *Anthropological Essays Presented to Edward Burnett Tylor*, pp. 309–24. Oxford: Clarendon Press.

Rivière, P. 1970 Introduction. In J.F. McLennan, *Primitive Marriage*, pp. vii–xlvii. Chicago: University of Chicago Press.

Robinson, G. 1990 Separation, Retaliation and Suicide: Mourning and the Conflicts of Young Tiwi Men. *Oceania* 60(3):161–78.

Robinson, P. 1969 *The Sexual Radicals*. London: Temple Smith.

Roheim, G. 1938 The Nescience of the Aranda. *The British Journal of Medical Psychology* 17:343–60.

Rose, F. and A. Jolly 1942 An Interpretation of the Taboo between Mother-in-Law and Son-in-Law. *Man* 42:15–16.

1943 The Place of the Australian Aboriginal in the Evolution of Society. *Annals of Eugenics* 12:44–87.

Rose, H. 1951 *Andrew Lang: His Place in Anthropology*. Edinburgh: Nelson.

Roth, W. 1903 *Superstition, Magic, and Medicine*. North Queensland Ethnography, Bulletin No.5. Brisbane: Government Printer.

Rousseau, J.-J. 1973 [1762] The Social Contract. In *The Social Contract and Discourses*, pp. 163–299. Letchworth: Dent.

1984 [1755] *A Discourse on Inequality*. Harmondsworth: Penguin.

Rowlands, R. 1991 Letter to the Editor. *Anthropological Forum* 6:429–35.

Scheffler, H. 1978 *Australian Kin Classification*. Cambridge: Cambridge University Press.

Schiller, F. 1979 *Paul Broca: Founder of French Anthropology, Explorer of the Brain*. Berkeley: University of California Press.

Schmidt, W. 1908–9 L'Origine de l'idée de dieu. *Anthropos* 3:125–1120; 4:207–1091.

1912–54 *Der Ursprung der Gottesidee: Eine Historisch-Kritische und Positive Studie*. 11 vols. Münster: Aschendorffsche Verlagsbuchshandlung.

1933 *High Gods in North America*. Oxford: Clarendon Press.

Schwimmer, E. 1969 Correspondence, 'Virgin Birth'. *Man* 4:132–3.

Sellon, E. 1865 On the Phallic Worship of India. In *Memoirs of the Anthropological Society of London*, Vol. I, pp. 327–34. London: Trubner.

Shapiro, W. 1979 *Social Organization in Aboriginal Australia*. Canberra: Australian National University Press.

Shapiro, W. (ed.) 1990 *On the Generation and Maintenance of the Person: Essays in Honour of John Barnes*. Sydney: Anthropological Society of New South Wales.

Sharp, L. 1934 Ritual Life and Economics of the Yir-Yoront of Cape York Peninsula. *Oceania* 5:19–42.

1958 People Without Politics. In V. Ray, ed., *Systems of Political Control and Bureaucracy in Human Societies*, pp. 1–8. Seattle: University of Washington Press.

Smyth, R. Brough 1878 *The Aborigines of Victoria*. London: Trubner.

Spencer, B. 1914 *Native Tribes of the Northern Territory of Australia*. London: Macmillan.

1928 *Wanderings in Wild Australia*. London: Macmillan.

Spencer, B. and F. Gillen 1899 *The Native Tribes of Central Australia*. London: Macmillan.

1927 *The Aranda*. London: Macmillan.

Spiro, M. 1966 Religion: Problems of Definition and Explanation. In M. Banton, ed., *Anthropological Approaches to the Study of Religion*, pp. 85–126. London: Tavistock.

1968 Virgin Birth, Parthenogenesis and Physiological Paternity: An Essay in Cultural Interpretation. *Man* 3:242–61.

Stahle, J.H. 1880 The Gournditch-Mara Tribe. In L. Fison and A.W. Howitt, eds., *Kamilaroi and Kurnai*, pp. 274–8. Oosterhout: Anthropological Publications.

Stanner, W. 1933 The Daly River Tribes – A Report on Field Work in North Australia. *Oceania* 3:377–405.

1936 Murinbata Kinship and Totemism. *Oceania* 7:186–216.

1963 *On Aboriginal Religion*. Sydney: Oceania Publications.

1965 Aboriginal Territorial Organization: Estate, Range, Domain and Regime. *Oceania* 36:1–26.

1966 *On Aboriginal Religion*. University of Sydney: Oceania Publications.

1979 *White Man Got No Dreaming: Essays 1938–73*. Canberra: Australian National University Press.

Stern, B.J. (ed.) 1930 Selections from the Letters of Lorimer Fison and A.W. Howitt to Lewis Henry Morgan. *American Anthropologist* 32:257–79; 419-53.

Stocking, G. 1971a Animism in Theory and Practice: E.B. Tylor's Unpublished 'Notes on Spiritualism'. *Man* 6(1):88–104.

1971b What's in a Name? The Origins of the Royal Anthropological Institute (1837–71). *Man* 6:369–90.

1993 Reading the Palimpsest of Inquiry: Notes and Queries and the History of British Social Anthropology. MS 322, Royal Anthropological Institute.

Strehlow, T. 1947 *Aranda Traditions*. Melbourne: Melbourne University Press.

1970 Geography and the Totemic Landscape in Central Australia: A Functional Study. In R.M. Berndt, ed., *Australian Aboriginal Anthropology*, pp. 92–140. Canberra: Australian Institute of Aboriginal Studies.

1971 *Songs of Central Australia*. Sydney: Angus and Robertson.

Sullivan, L. 1987 Supreme Beings. In M. Eliade, ed., *The Encyclopaedia of Religion*, pp. 166–81. New York: Macmillan.

Sutton, P. 1978 Aboriginal Society, Territory and Language at Cape Kerweer, Cape York Peninsula. Ph.D. Thesis, University of Queensland.

1988 Myth as History, History as Myth. In I.Keen, ed., *Being Black: Aboriginal Cultures in 'Settled' Australia*, pp. 251–65. Canberra: Aboriginal Studies Press.

Sutton, P. and B. Rigsby 1982 People With 'Politicks': Management of Land and Personnel on Australia's Cape York Peninsula. In N. Williams and E. Hunn, eds., *Resource Managers: North American and Australian Hunter-Gatherers*, pp. 155–72. Colorado: Westview Press.

Swain, T. 1993 *A Place for Strangers: Towards a History of Australian Aboriginal Being*. Cambridge: Cambridge University Press.

References

Taplin, G. 1874 *The Narrinyeri: An Account of the Tribes of South Australian Aborigines*. Adelaide: Shawyer.

Taylor, L. 1990 The Rainbow Serpent as Visual Metaphor in Western Arnhem Land. *Oceania* 60(4):330–44.

Tench, W. 1961 [1789, 1793] *Sydney's First Four Years: Being a Reprint of A Narrative of the Expedition to Botany Bay and A Complete Account of the Settlement at Port J.* Sydney: Angus and Robertson.

Thomas, N. 1905 Baiame and the Bell-Bird. *Man* 5:49–52.

1906 *Kinship Organisations and Group Marriage in Australia*. Cambridge: Cambridge University Press.

Thomson, D. 1933 The Hero Cult: Initiation and Totemism on Cape York Peninsula. *Journal of the Royal Anthropological Institute* 63:453–537.

1936 Fatherhood in the Wik Monkan Tribe. *American Anthropologist* 38:374–93.

Tonkinson, R. 1978 Semen versus Spirit-Child in a Western Desert Culture. In L. Hiatt, ed., *Australian Aboriginal Concepts*, pp. 81–92. Canberra: Australian Institute of Aboriginal Studies.

Toohey, Justice. 1993 Mabo v. Queensland. In R. Bartlett, ed., *The Mabo Decision*, pp. 136–69. Sydney: Butterworths.

Troy, J. 1993 *King Plates: A History of Aboriginal Gorgets*. Canberra: Aboriginal Studies Press.

Tylor, E. 1889 On a Method of Investigating the Development of Institutions. *Journal of the Anthropological Institute* 18: 245–69.

1892a On the Limits of Savage Religion. *Journal of the Anthropological Institute* 21:283–301.

1892b Anniversary Address. *Journal of the Anthropological Institute* 21:396–411.

1903 [1871] *Primitive Culture*. London: Murray.

Van Gennep, A. 1906 *Mythes et légendes d'Australie: études d'ethnographie et de sociologie*. Paris: Guilmoto.

1960 [1909] *The Rites of Passage*. London: Routledge and Kegan Paul.

Von Sturmer, J. 1978 The Wik Region: Economy, Territoriality and Totemism in Western Cape York Peninsula, North Queensland. Ph.D. Thesis, University of Queensland.

Wake, C.S. 1967 *The Development of Marriage and Kinship*. Chicago: University of Chicago.

Walker, Mary Howitt 1971 *Come Wind, Come Weather: A Biography of Alfred Howitt*. Melbourne: Melbourne University Press.

Warner, W.L. 1931 Birth Control in Primitive Society. *Birth Control Review* 15:105–87.

1937 *A Black Civilization: A Social Study of an Australian Tribe*. New York: Harper.

1958 *A Black Civilization: A Social Study of an Australian Tribe*. Revised edition. New York: Harper.

Watson, F. (ed) 1914 *Historical Records of Australia*, I. Sydney: Government Printer.

Wells, E. 1982 *Reward and Punishment in Arnhem Land 1962–63*. Canberra: Australian Institute of Aboriginal Studies Press.

Westermarck, E. 1891 *The History of Human Marriage.* London: Macmillan.

Wheeler, G.C. 1910 *The Tribe, and Intertribal Relations in Australia.* London: Murray.

White, I. 1970 Aboriginal Woman's Status Resolved: A Paradox. In F. Gale, ed., *Woman's Role in Aboriginal Society,* pp. 21–30. Canberra: Australian Institute of Aboriginal Studies.

White, L. 1957 How Morgan Came to Write *Systems of Consanguinity and Affinity. Papers of the Michigan Academy of Science, Arts, and Letters* 42:257–68.

Wilkes, C. 1845 *Narrative of the United States Exploring Expedition 1838–1842.* Philadelphia: Lea & Blanchard.

Williams, N. 1973 Northern Territory Aborigines under Australian Law. Ph.D. Thesis, University of California, Berkeley.

1987 *Two Laws: Managing Disputes in a Contemporary Aboriginal Community.* Canberra: Australian Institute of Aboriginal Studies.

Wilson, D.S. 1993 The Problem With 'The Ant and the Peacock'. *Human Behavior and Evolution Newsletter* 2(3).

Woodcock, G. and I. Avakumovic 1950 *The Anarchist Prince: A Biographical Study of Peter Kropotkin.* London: Boardman.

Woodward A.E. 1974 *Aboriginal Land Rights Commission, Second Report.* Canberra: Government Printer .

Worms, E. 1950 Djamar the Creator. *Anthropos* 45:641–58.

1963 Religion. In H. Sheils, ed., *Australian Aboriginal Studies,* pp. 231–47. Melbourne: Oxford University Press.

Index